Pride and Panic

Russian Imagination of the West in Post-Soviet Film

Pride and Panic

Russian Imagination of the West in Post-Soviet Film

Yana Hashamova

intellect Bristol, UK / Chicago, USA

First Published in the UK in 2007 by
Intellect Books, PO Box 862, Bristol BS99 1DE, UK

First published in the USA in 2007 by
Intellect Books, The University of Chicago Press, 1427 E. 60th Street, Chicago,
IL 60637, USA

A catalogue record for this book is available from the British Library.

Cover Design: Gabriel Solomons
Copy Editor: Holly Spradling
Typesetting: Mac Style, Nafferton, E. Yorkshire

ISBN 978-1-84150-156-7

Printed and bound in Great Britain by The Cromwell Press.

CONTENTS

NOTE ON TRANSLITERATION

I have used the Library of Congress transliteration system for all Russian names and titles except for citations from secondary sources (e.g., Zassoursky instead of Zasurskii). Where familiar spellings for Russian writers exist – Dostoevsky, Tolstoy, etc. – I have opted for them.

Когда в нас что-нибудь неладно, то мы ищем причин вне нас и скоро находим. "Это француз гадит, это жиды, это Вилгельм…" – это призраки, но зато как они облегчают наше беспокойство.

When something is wrong with us, then we look for the reasons outside us and soon we find them. "It is the French, the Jews, Wilhelm…" – these are ghosts, but how they alleviate our anxieties.

Anton Chekhov

The presence of a noble nature, generous in its wishes, ardent in its charity, changes the lights for us: we begin to see things again in their larger, quieter masses, and to believe that we too can be seen and judged in the wholeness of our character.

George Eliot

ACKNOWLEDGMENTS

The financial support of the Ohio State University and the Center for Slavic and East European Studies at the university, as well as the expert advice and the moral support of many colleagues and friends made this book possible. First and foremost, I must thank Nancy Blake and Helena Goscilo, who read and commented on drafts of the manuscript and from whom I have learned a lot over the years. Special gratitude goes to Alberto Hahn who also read the work and who offered excellent feedback on Melanie Klein's apparatus. Luzmila Camacho read this manuscript twice and was a permanent source of advice, aid, and solace. I am indebted to Dina Iordanova for her assistance and encouragement. Delightful and insightful conversations with Charles Batson and Lori Marso influenced this project. In Russia, I received the immense support of my Russian sister, Anna, who opened doors for me and organized exciting meetings with actors, directors, and film critics.

Special appreciation goes to Jeff Parker, Audra Starcheus, Kara Dixon-Vuic, and Robert Cagle who read various chapters and offered helpful editing suggestions. I am happy for the opportunity to express thanks to colleagues from the departments of Slavic and East European Languages and Literatures, Comparative Studies, Women's Studies, and the Interdisciplinary Film Program at the Ohio State University for their moral support. I would like to acknowledge the professionalism of Intellect, which eased the publishing process.

And last, but certainly not least, this book would never have happened without the love and encouragement of my family (my mother, Maria, Christo, and my late father). Maria, who is a psychotherapist, gave me invaluable insights about the mental life of adolescents and the cultural applications of adolescent psychology. My mother, who knows intimately the workings of cinema, was my best discussant. They believed in me when I was desperate and helped me keep my sanity.

The film stills are borrowed from *Séance*, Russian cinema journal, and I thank Aleksei Gusev, its editor, who authorized their use. Various ideas developed in the book (and early versions of chapters two, three, and five) appeared first as journal articles in *The Communication Review*, *Consumption, Markets & Culture*, *The Russian Review*, and *Slavic and East European Journal*.

Introduction

In exploring Russia's fearful adjustment to the expansion of western capital, this book relies on the political, economic, and cultural contexts of Russia's national cinema as the foundation of its investigation. Russian film is a mass cultural phenomenon, one that in both its creation and its perception exposes the intriguing dynamics of societal psychological conditions. My analysis centers on films that illustrate Russia's cultural and psychological ambivalence towards the rise of the West, and uncovers a set of reactions that I identify as fantasies, anxieties, and defenses. I examine the representation of the (western) other in films by some of the most powerful and influential Russian directors as well as in other relevant projects by lesser-known talents. Employing an unorthodox approach, I study changes in Russia's identity formation and the shifting dynamics of Russian attitudes towards the West, as I compare them to stages of individual development (adolescence and maturity), as well as trace the slippery structure of fantasy as support of reality and ideology. The founding of the Soviet Union divided the world into black and white, 'good' versus 'evil', and 'us' against 'them'. The side of the Iron Curtain from which one perceived the world was irrelevant in this division. The West and the East employed similar mechanisms for constructing the other as an 'evil empire' (Rogin). In the aftermath of the cold war, the West has deemed itself victorious, while Russia has painfully struggled with despondency.

Pride and Panic: Russian Imagination of the West in Post-Soviet Film examines film images, characters, and themes in order to investigate how Russia has reacted and adjusted to the most glaring reminder of this despondency – the expansion of western capital and culture in Russia itself. My analysis focuses generally on Russian films produced after the collapse of the Soviet Union, paying special attention to those made during the last five to six years – a period in which the Russian film industry began to revive and became more market-oriented, fully reflecting social angst. In drawing on film imagery, I address a number of compelling questions: How is the image of the other constructed in recent Russian film? Is it possible to embrace a foreign culture and be simultaneously afraid of it? How does this fear affect the perception of self and other in an ever-changing identity formation? What are the fantasies and defenses that operate when national and cultural identity is in flux?

A key common characteristic unites the films that I have chosen to examine. Each film explicitly enters into a dialogue with the West at the level of characters and/or imagery and provocatively problematizes the resulting relationship. Although some of these films are set in the past (*The Barber of Siberia* (1999) and *Of Freaks and Men* (1998) take place at the turn of the last century, and

Gods' Envy (2000) in the 1980s), they all contribute to new ways of thinking about Russia's present. Their narratives suggest an anachronistic investigation of the ongoing transition from communism to democracy and of Russia's problematic relationship with the West.

I use examples from some contemporary films that have chosen to portray Russia's historical past rather than the present to show how their creation, visual texts, and reception recount questions of both the present and history. Feature films, even though historical, often present unreliable historical data, but in doing so they uncover the political and cultural conditions in which the films are created as well as the mental and psychological dilemma of their creators. In the introduction to *American History/American Film*, John O'Connor and Martin Jackson advance the idea that films that inaccurately present history reveal a lot about the political agenda of their creators and their times: '*Mission to Moscow* may tell us nothing of life in Russia, but it speaks volumes about what the Warner Brothers and, through them, the Roosevelt administration wanted the American people to think about Russia in 1943 when the film was released' (xviii).

Since I am interested in the historical and political circumstances that give birth to films, I have chosen works produced at the turn of the millennium, which are representative examples of a mental and psychological dilemma that structures the artistic energy of their creators. The objective that runs through my discussion of film imagery is to uncover the desire or the unconscious processes behind the symbolic efforts of these films to deal with the anxieties, the shattered illusions, and wounded national pride that have arisen in the face of overpowering western influences.

In *Pride and Panic*, I construct a working definition of the West as an imagined and imaginary world, as a cultural, political, and economic imaginary, which the Russian collective mind situates beyond the Iron Curtain. My approach is cross-disciplinary, building on the interaction of psychoanalysis, cultural studies, and film studies. While the project as a whole is inspired by psychoanalysis – adapting ideas mainly of Sigmund Freud and concepts developed by other psychoanalytic schools – it persistently engages with contemporary critical theory (from Mikhail Bakhtin to Julia Kristeva) in order to expand its argument about the social and political anxieties caused by the (western) other and reflected in Russian film. My analysis is as much textual as it is contextual, for I approach post-Soviet desires and fears as discursive formations caused by political and social realities and available through film representations.

Political and Social Realities

The Russian Revolution of 1917 shook the world, but the exit from communism came no less dramatically at the end of the century. Politically, economically, and culturally the disintegration of the Soviet Union opened new unimagined opportunities but at the same time presented unthinkable challenges. The Soviet people euphorically embraced the opportunity to join the rest of the world, and especially the West, after long years of isolation and ideological antagonism. Soon, however, after having faced the problems of visa control and restrictions or after having stumbled into the real of the idealized free world, they grew uneasy and vigilant about their place in the world. Politically, the West encouraged democratic reforms in Russia and at the same time tried to exercise control over these democratic reforms. Once one of the two biggest political powers in the world, the Soviet Union, after many former Soviet republics declared independence much to Gorbachev's surprise and disbelief, turned into a Russian Federation – a devotee of western advisers.

Economically, Russians expected better living standards and prosperous lifestyles. Yeltsin's administration introduced rapid economic reforms without creating the necessary institutional infrastructure, especially in the social sphere, which caused enormous pain in the socially unprepared population. In their book *Anti-Americanism in Russia*, Eric Shiraev and Vladislav Zubok write: 'From 1992–1995, as a consequence of the economic reforms launched exclusively according to the plans of a few individuals in the Kremlin, the GDP went down 49 percent; real income fell 29 percent; and inflation was up 650 percent' (48). From dreaming opulence, the majority of Russians woke up in nightmarish poverty.

Culturally, the Russian artistic spirit rejoiced in the eliminated censorship, eroded ideological taboos, and dismantling of socialist realism. But soon Russian artists faced other restrictions and demands, above all financial ones, which had been unknown during the Soviet times when the state entirely subsidized the arts and culture. Russian artists had to struggle to adjust to new economic conditions, and they were slowly discovering that the old artistic culture – politically stifling and despised in the past – had its advantages because it secured a comfortable life and membership in a privileged layer of society. While Russian artists were trying to find their new voices and new ways to create and produce culture, western, and especially American, cultural products quickly invaded the Russian cultural scene. The new Russian cultural voice was threatened by the invasion of English-speaking television programs and Hollywood films. And while American pop culture is slowly but firmly becoming dominant all over the world, the pace of change in Russia was staggering.

In 2005, the Baltic States, Czech Republic, Poland, Hungary, and Slovakia (former Soviet Union satellites) were already part of the European Union. The new global political reality and the danger of terrorism have constructed an ambivalent position for Russia's political role. On the one hand, the West, especially the United States, supports Russia as an ally in the war on terror, but, on the other hand, the West, and especially Europe, grows more impatient with Russia's abuse of human rights in Chechnya and Russia's increased state control over its politics, economics, and media.

Such are the most significant political, economic, and cultural factors that underlie Russia's search for its new identity and its new place in the world. These are also the conditions that determine Russia's relations with the West and Russia's ambivalent (often contradictory) reactions to the West. In describing Russia's reactions, the present book also attempts to explain the nature of these conflicting sentiments, passions, and desires.

Cultural Studies and Psychoanalysis
Several remarks about terms and concepts used in this study should be made here. First, globalization has been generally understood as the unparalleled expansion of transnational capital advanced by the collapse of Soviet-style socialism (Kang). But globalization also sets up the structural framework for analyzing what happens in today's world and, therefore, it is used here in more precise (dialectical) terms: it refers to an ideology of the global (capitalist) market dictated by the West, mainly by the United States – the triumphant 'winner' of the cold war and the unchallenged superpower in the world – which determines the regulations not only for free trade but also for moral and cultural values (Kapur).

Second, I employ Arjun Appadurai's theory that imagination, building on technological changes and global flows, has become a collective, social fact (5). Collective experiences of the national and international mass media can create conditions for a group of people to imagine and feel things together. Appadurai borrows from Benedict Anderson's understanding of 'imagined communities', based on print capitalism; but he argues that electronic and media capitalism mediate a production of cultural identity and locality in the transnational era (Appadurai 178–99). By applying Appadurai's idea of collective imagination to the Russian experience at the end of the twentieth century as reflected in films, I critically address his insistence on the transnational operation of mass-mediated sodalities.

Finally, I also draw from certain concepts and ideas of two psychoanalytic schools (object-relations as well as Jacques Lacan) to describe qualities and characteristics of the Russian collective imagination. Although these concepts guide the readings of the films, they are not extensively employed for the exploration of the actual film analyses; rather, they structure and organize the understanding of the films and provide the overall framework.

There are many reasons why psychoanalysis can productively contribute to understanding social phenomena, but the most obvious one is the fact that group behaviour is often very irrational. When society behaves in irrational ways, manifested in aggression, destruction, and violence, the assumption can be made that powerful unconscious instincts are at work. Individual psychology can also contribute to the understanding of social phenomena, for individuals develop from a very early age by relating to others. A limited social circle of parents and relatives soon extends to groups such as neighbors, school classmates, and work companions. Freud, Hanna Segal, David Bell, and Michael Rustin, as well as Lacan and Slavoj Žižek, are a few of the many examples of psychoanalysts and sociologists who attempt to apply insights derived from psychoanalytic work with individuals to observations about social and cultural phenomena.

Melanie Klein insists that a person is shaped less by biological drives and more by relationships, and this understanding is widely applied to studies of social and political issues and to the workings of collective identity formation (1975a). My reason for utilizing ideas of the object-relation (British) school has been dictated by the very nature of my study: analysis of anxieties, fears, and fantasies (reflected in film) born of the changing dynamics of the relations between Russia and the West, which in turn affect Russian national identity formation. I draw on Klein, the founder of the British school, as much as I draw on other scholars who apply her ideas to the studies of culture and society (Bell, Rustin, Segal [1997]).

I employ (in broader terms) the British psychoanalytic tradition's major concepts of 'positions' (mental states), of 'splitting' and 'projection', and the understanding that anxieties can be sustained through art, not only at the individual but also at a group level. These concepts enable me to talk about the state of mind of the Russian people before and after the changes of 1991 and to discuss how film deals with the anxieties produced by crushed dreams and fears of uncertainty. Klein's work made it possible to consider the meaning of human behaviour as it is affected by different mental states and the way these mental states exemplify stages of development: childhood, adolescence, and adulthood.

After watching a substantial number of post-Soviet films, I came away with the impression that all these films testify to turbulent and drastic changes of Russian national identity development. The intensity and severity of such changes reminded me of an individual developmental stage, namely the adolescence period. Adolescence is one of the most radical developmental phases: a transition period and a move toward becoming independent and accepting the world with all of its challenges. Although some may find such a comparison culturally suspect, concepts of adolescent psychology are employed only to shed light on the extreme conditions defining Russian identity formation at the turn of the millennium. It is important to stress that the analysis does not intend to generalize, pass judgment, or draw conclusion about Russian national identity in general (before and after the transition period), but merely to point out the psychological cost of political, economic, and cultural changes in the post-cold war era. The parallels drawn between Russian national identity (as it relates to the West) and adolescent development do not in any way suggest that the West appears in these relations in a position of adulthood (parents, family, etc.). On the contrary, if examined, western fantasies and fears in relation to Russia (and other world powers – China and India, for example) would also show adolescent anxieties and conditions. In other words, after the end of the cold war, the two former world powers (Russia and the West) appear to reveal similar (teenage) mentalities manifested in different fantasies and anxieties. Even though western attitudes toward Russia are sporadically noted in this study, they are not its object of focus.

While the nature of this study presupposes the utilization of Kleinian concepts, I realize that Klein's theory of fantasy is underdeveloped. Since tracing Russian collective fantasies as reflected in film is an important part of this book, the analysis also incorporates Lacan's ideas of fantasy. In other words, I employ ideas that belong to different psychoanalytic branches (Klein and Lacan) and hold nothing sacrosanct, for I believe that even though different schools develop different techniques of clinical psychoanalysis, they all describe/analyze the same phenomena; they all offer tools for approaching mental structures and for unveiling the unconscious. Moreover, true to Freud, both Klein and Lacan share the same understanding about the role of fantasy: it organizes one's reality rather than opposes it. My contention, therefore, is that concepts of the two schools of psychoanalytic thought complement each other in this analysis. In addition to the comparative (and complementary) utilization of concepts belonging to the two psychoanalytic schools, the analysis also points out their most significant divergence from each other.

Lacan views fantasy as organizing the relation to meaning or as the ultimate support of our sense of reality. As such, it is most pronounced and often tested during adolescence. Situated already in some way in relation to the mother, the adolescent begins to seek new (sexual) relations with another human being. The fantasy formula often proves difficult (or ineffective) to deal with the new relation, since the other person (in the case of this discussion, the West) has his/her own fantasy. This clash of the two fantasies discourages the search for new relationships and prompts one to safeguard the fantasy. While Klein considers fantasy a defense mechanism against potentially psychotic behaviour, Lacan believes that fantasy is also a way to get in touch with the real of enjoyment, with the traumatic kernel of the unconscious. And this is the most interesting point of departure between Klein's and Lacan's understanding of fantasy, which is addressed and explicated in the book. Taking it a step further, Žižek connects fantasy to ideology and insists that ideology always relies on some fantasmic background. Specifics about the function of fantasy will become clear in the film analyses.

Kristeva's apparatus, which often effectively combines Lacanian and Kleinian ideas in discussions of cultural and national identities and problematics, also becomes productive as I decipher changes of Russian national identity influenced by the presence of the other. Her work on the notion of the 'stranger' – the foreigner, the outsider, the alien in society – as well as the idea of acknowledging the strangeness within the self as the antidote to xenophobia and racism provide useful tools for a discussion of Russia's most recent outbreak of nationalism and xenophobia (Kristeva 1991).

It is important to stress here that, following Victoria Wohl, I understand psychoanalysis in broader terms as a school of skepticism, which questions and challenges a preconceived understanding of culture and society, of images and stereotypes, and which is unwilling to accept the idea that texts mean only what they immediately reveal. In this way, psychoanalytic ideas guide me in describing unconscious structures that underlie cultural and social phenomena.

Certainly, this study does not pretend to advance psychoanalytic theory, which serves mainly as an organizational principle. Psychoanalytic ideas suggest the grouping of post-Soviet films, which in their overall fantasy construction and manifestation of anxieties reveal similarities. Thus, psychoanalytic theory here operates as a framework (on a very general level), while film analysis engages with relevant contemporary scholarship and criticism.

Russian cultural studies
A number of cultural theorists have addressed the overwhelming political, economic, and cultural changes in Russian society since the reforms of 1991 and 1992 and have offered a variety of responses to the ideological transformations and the identity challenges that resulted from the transition period (Berry and Miller-Pogacar, Condee, Freidin, Goscilo [1996], Kennedy [1994a], Shalin). Other scholars focus more on the recent situation, in which Russia finds itself vis-à-vis the West, arguing that, torn between its own heritage and that of the West, Russia embraces a nostalgic desire to recreate a glorious past (Barker, Graubard). While all of these scholars discuss at length the cultural and social changes caused by the collapse of the Soviet system and democratization, none of them focus on film or explore the unconscious desires that drive these cultural changes (except Salecl [1994, 2000] and Žižek [1993, 1997], whose work covers the Balkans and offers little or no insight into specifically Russian culture).

In contrast to these earlier studies, *Pride and Panic* focuses primarily on how film represents Russia's cultural relationship to the West; more importantly, I pursue the cultural manifestations of the cost of a psychological crisis exacted at the level of both society and the individual. By studying the psychological crisis as observed in film and offering parallels to developmental stages, *Pride and Panic* conveys how individual and collective perceptions of self and the world change and acquire meaning and definition. Films such as *Brother* (1997), *The Barber of Siberia, Brother 2* (2000), *Gods' Envy, War* (2002), *Russian Ark* (2002), and *Cuckoo* (2002) show Russia's attempt to cope with these crises and reveal fantasies, anxieties, and defenses that take the form of a fearful and paradoxically euphoric acceptance of the West, which gradually transforms into a paranoid rejection of everything foreign, a nostalgia for Russia's glorious past, or a reflective and mature perception of self and other.

Daniel Rancour-Laferriere's interdisciplinary work, and more precisely his application of psychoanalysis to Russian ethnic identity and Russian nationalism, is pertinent to hypotheses I advance in my study. His exploration of what Russians perceive as Russian identity, and especially his Kleinian interpretation of the Russian understanding of the other, of nationalism, assimilation, xenophobia, and anti-Semitism, open the door to further research on similar approaches and topics.

By exploring the effects of the western invasion in Russian culture, *Pride and Panic* also enters into a dialogue with works in cultural studies that examine the effects of the end of the cold war and Russian and East European identity formation (Barker, Iordanova [2000, 2003]; Neumann [1996, 1999]; Wolff); more broadly, the book engages scholarship on the cultural, political, and economic consequences of the process of globalization (Appadurai, Jameson and Miyoshi, Ong).

Film Studies

Expressing and attributing social, political, and national anxieties and fears in films can be a complex and often disputed process. Yet my study argues that films express, as well as produce, national anxieties because they reflect and signify myths and stereotypes through conscious or unconscious reproduction of sentiments and attitudes. The creation and reception of mass art such as films bare the capacity to reveal anxieties and at the same time sustain them. These anxieties can be observed either at the level of content, characters, and imagery or at the level of cinematic style and techniques. Scholars have already established that films may reflect and produce political meaning and ideology.

In his much acclaimed work *Hollywood from Vietnam to Reagan*, Robin Wood describes films 'as at once the personal dreams of their makers and the collective dreams of their audiences, the fusion made possible by the shared structures of a common ideology' (78). In this sense, films representing anxieties, desires, and fantasies can be viewed as collective (un)conscious expressions of hidden drives. Fredric Jameson also argues that often films assuage viewers' desires and fulfill their needs by tapping into 'the political unconscious' (1981, 20). Jameson's concept informs this study in the realization that films can reflect fantasies of repressed and buried realities and that they can function as symbolic acts through which individuals and society at large can experience and face conflicting desires and realities. Every film text at its most basic level represents a political fantasy and a psychological manifestation of hopes and fears unveiling actual and imagined relations that determine social and national identity. Following Wood and Jameson, Ray Pratt explores 'how popular films (and selected television programs) consumed by Americans...serve as an important way in which individuals and the wider public identify, name, and satisfy some of their deepest psychological needs and desires, as well as their anxieties and their hopes' (35). In a similar manner, I examine Russian films, which inevitably reflect and dramatize conflicts, anxieties, and desires that covertly characterize Russian culture and society in their traumatic class, gender, and national identity developments.

Some can question the understanding that film mirrors/reflects collective desires, fantasies, and anxieties, arguing that the identification process of the spectator vis-à-vis the film text is much more complex and uneven. I follow the tradition established by Wood, Jameson, and Pratt in two specific ways that enable me to consider 'film as mirror'. First, my film analysis adheres to the inter-subjective process occurring between spectator and the film text known as secondary identification. Primary identification, as described by Christian Metz (relying on the Lacanian concept of the mirror stage), is identification with the gaze of the camera, with an idealized point, positioned outside the subject, from which the film can be viewed. This identification destabilizes the subject and complicates the understanding of film as a reflection of collective desires and fantasies. Secondary identification, however – identification with actors, characters, or stars – maintains the mirroring process: collective desires and fantasies can be recognized in film characters, themes, and images. Second, I am also guided by Anne Friedberg's 'extra-cinematic identification', which expands the identifactory process beyond secondary cinematic identification. She argues that the fascination with a film star is not limited to fascination with only one person but extends to the ideology in which the film star is immersed (Friedberg 42–45). Thus, cinematic representation cannot avoid the process of identification, which often is identification with official ideology and the status quo.

I cannot emphasize enough that it is not the goal of this book to offer a comprehensive picture of Russian cinema after 1991, rather, to analyze Russia's cultural, social, and psychological dynamics of the transition period and tackle Russia's identity of pursuit as reflected in film. Therefore, film analyses (although detailed) are by no means exhaustive. They focus mainly on the Russian relationship with the West and serve as discursive material uncovering Russia's collective fantasies, dreams, and fears. As noted earlier, the book incorporates several disciplines and seeks to bring film studies into dialogue with other disciplines, such as cultural studies, psychoanalysis, and globalization studies. One of my goals is to make the monograph accessible to students of Russian and the liberal arts who do not have prior knowledge of film studies proper.

Russian film studies
Aspects of post-Soviet film have been analyzed in a few collections of essays (Barker, Beumers [1999a]) and in George Faraday's monograph *The Revolt of the Filmmakers*. When I was finishing and revising *Pride and Panic*, Anna Lawton's *Imaging Russia 2000: Film and Facts* came out. As a great reference book, it provides an exhaustive and comprehensive survey of Russian post-Soviet cinema, the national film industry, and everyday life after 1991. Lawton's panoramic view of leading Russian film-makers helped me clarify last-minute uncertainties. The contribution of *Pride and Panic* rests in its concentration on Russian film at the turn of the century and its detailed analysis of selected films (such as *Of Freaks and Men, Brother, Brother 2, War, The Barber of Siberia, Russian Ark;* and *Gods' Envy*), which, even though discussed (often briefly) in the above cited works, are explicated here in more detail and in a different light. Although the present study does not pretend to offer a systematic analysis of post-Soviet Russian cinema and its broader trends, it nonetheless discusses a large number of post-Soviet films and thus provides a panorama of the Russian film scene in the last ten to fifteen years. The major difference between *Pride and Panic* and previous works on post-Soviet cinema lies in its interdisciplinarity, combining psychoanalysis, film studies, and cultural studies in order to shed light on Russian national identity transformations (reacting to western challenges) and on the psychological cost of these changes. It concentrates on Russian national cinema, but it also engages in an indirect dialogue with studies on Central and South Eastern European film, which focus particularly on the effects of democratization on the film industry and artistry (Iordanova 2000, 2003).

This study benefits significantly from Lawton's monograph (1992) and Andrew Horton and Michael Brashinsky's book on Soviet films produced during perestroika. Both works, in different ways, present a comprehensive picture of the Soviet film industry and the sensitive and changing dynamics caused by the transition from Soviet-style socialism to democracy. These books trace the developments, dangers, and triumphs of a cinema industry affected by major structural, financial, and ideological changes. My study remains close to the spirit of these early works; in a way it continues to examine changes, but changes in national and cultural identity as reflected in film.

After the collapse of the Soviet state, Russian cinema explicitly revealed the nation's inherited social and psychological problems and began to reflect emergent changes in Russian society. During the first half of the 1990s, Russian film-makers disregarded past ideological constraints and presented a bleak picture of Russian reality. Films such as Pavel Lungin's *Taxi Blues* (1990) and *Luna Park* (1992), Vladimir Khotinenko's *Makarov* (1993) and *Moslem* (1995), Georgii Daneliia's *Passport* (1990), and Aleksandr Sokurov's *The Second Circle* (1990) portray nationalist obsessions, psychological problems, violence, chaos, poverty, and crime. While films such as these suggest a social structure in disarray, the cinematic production of the late 1990s exhibits tendencies that imply a different social, cultural, and national identity, an identity that is recovering from the chaos and is seeking alternative paths. In the new political, social, and economic conditions at the end of the twentieth and the beginning of the twenty-first century, Russian cinema offers abundant material for cultural analysis by reflecting the anxieties and defenses of the Russian collective imagination.

Structure

I could not avoid the inevitable drawbacks of a study that uses representative examples of films to illustrate the dynamics of Russian national identification and the psychological cost of its development and changes. I explore certain films in detail, and while others may deserve the same attention, they are only mentioned briefly to support my major arguments. Occasionally, I abandon balance in favor of outlining tendencies and constructing a cultural argument. Discussion of cinematic texts, elaborate at times, is always culturalized and contextualized, for I attempt to expose the intriguing dynamics of Russia's social and psychological conditions affected by the expansion of western capital. As a book that attempts to reach a large readership not only in the field of Russian cultural and film studies but also beyond these disciplinary borders, this study may frustrate each in turn. The theoretical concepts and their elaboration may appear concise to some and lengthy to others.

Chapter one explores Russia's dialogical relations with the West, which shape its collective identity. I provide a brief history of Russia's cultural and political engagement with the West and study these relations as the foundation of psychological conditions that drive the collective fantasy and imagination. The films that I consider in this chapter – *On Deribasovskaia the Weather is Fine, or, On Brighton Beach It's Raining Again* (1992) and *Window to Paris* (1993), among others, belong to the first half of the 1990s. They reveal temptations and fears provoked by the first opportunities and challenges to emerge after the collapse of the Berlin Wall and invite a parallel to the identity development of the adolescent that require a search and acceptance of new values and self-definitions. The discussion of Russian fantasy of the West in these films reveals that the fantasy is still potent and manifests itself in passé images and constructions. Employing the western cultural screen, the Russian collective imagination tries to build its new national image, which reflects and rejects, promotes and denounces western values and beliefs.

Aleksei Balabanov's *Brother* disturbingly portrays the darker side of Russian reality – poverty, crime, and violence – and hints at the destructive western presence in Russia. I interpret Balabanov's creation of a Robin Hood type of hero as a fantasy of a victimized mind and of wounded national pride. In chapter two, I argue that while in *Brother* there is still some ambiguity about the nature of the hero and the identity boundaries of the self/other, this ambiguity disappears in *Brother 2* and *War*. Encouraged perhaps by the unexpected success of *Brother*, Balabanov tries to construct an even more crystallized fantasy in relation to the anxieties of the nation: he clearly divides the world into us versus them and transforms his character from a defender to an aggressor. The fantasy structure of Russian viewers shifts in these films from demonized/idealized West to a morally superior Russian (masculine) national identity. In analyzing the theme of aggression towards the other in these films, I employ the concept of national paranoia to shed light on the manifestations of Russian nationalism at the turn of the millennium.

In the next chapter, I argue that positive characteristics ascribed to the past, such as faith, honour, and self-sacrifice, as well as the glories of past Russian culture and orthodoxy, are mobilized to cope with the traumatic present. Nikita Mikhalkov's *The Barber of Siberia* addresses the anxieties produced by western triumphalism, which overwhelmed Russians at the end of the twentieth century.

The director situates the presentation of positive national ideals in an imaginary historical context and idealizes this context to promote faith and optimism in Russia's future. In *Russian Ark*, Sokurov historically problematizes the Russian relationship with the West and evokes the uniqueness of the Russian condition, especially the power of Russian artistic culture, which can help Russians sail into the future. Like the adolescent's struggle for separation and uniqueness that determines his/her entry into adulthood, the Russian collective imagination evokes internal sources to emphasize its exceptionality in the global world. In Lacan's terms, both directors attempt to symbolize the irreducible kernel of Russian national identity but they significantly differ in their approach to it.

Chapter four studies the ardent but failed love affairs between western and Russian characters represented in some of the films already discussed, including *On Deribasovskaia*, *Window to Paris*, and *The Barber of Siberia*, as well as in Vladimir Menshov's *Gods' Envy* and Vera Storozheva's *The Frenchman* (2003). Here, emotions and sexual passions are studied against the background of a social and political context that appears hostile to them. The desire to unite with the West is undermined by social and political difficulties and by insecurities about national identity. A confidence in one's national identity can be determined by the capacity to autonomously relate to the other, much as the transition of the unstable world of the adolescent to the stable world of adulthood is marked by the capacity to establish deep and lasting romantic relationships. The construction of Russian-western romantic and sexual relationships inevitably becomes entangled in gender dynamics and power, which reflect the desire of Russian national identity for masculine dominance in these relationships.

Balabanov's *Of Freaks and Men* has puzzled Russian critics, especially compared to his films *Brother*, *Brother 2*, and *War*. I offer a new reading of *Of Freaks and Men*, which explains how the film – as expression of anxieties – actually functions much like *Brother*, supplying fantasies and defenses. In chapter five, I argue that in *Of Freaks and Men* Russia is constructed and perceived not as a unique victim of the West, but rather as a part of a world crisis, which positions the West as the ultimate corruptive possessor of power, subjugating the rest of the world. Destructive western power affects Russian culture, which in turn victimizes its Asian other. Aleksandr Rogozhkin's films *Peculiarities of the National Hunt in Fall* (1995) and *Cuckoo* also explore the ambivalent position of Russia in today's global world, point to Russia's own responsibility for its condition, encourage a new imagination that draws on the complexity of identity in formation, and propose a more reflective and mature perception of self and other. The discussion in this chapter reveals a transformation of Russia's relation to its fundamental fantasy and, in so doing, points out the main differences between Klein's and Lacan's theories.

In addition to summarizing the major observations and findings of the book, the conclusion offers a brief glimpse at the most recent Russian films, which look beyond the western cultural mirror into Russia's own national spirit, trying to seek identity security in universal human values. Films such as Sokurov's *Father and Son* (2003), Andrei Zviagintsev's *The Return* (2003), and Aleksei Popogrebskii and Boris Khlebnikov's *Koktebel* (2003) explore universal generational conflicts between fathers and sons problematizing the symbolic paternal function. Analyzed against the background of Russia's rich cultural and historical legacy of the role of the father figure in society, the films reflect the desire for a miraculous return of the Father and for authentication of homosocial unions.

1

The Western Other (Foe and Friend): Screening Temptations and Fears

In the not-so-rare moments of the conflation of the two pro- and anti-western discourses in Russia, which exemplify the dialectics of Russia's relations with the West, one locates the dynamics of Russian national identification. The West has long functioned as a cultural screen for Russian fantasized identification.[1] On the one hand, the screen presents an idealized image to the Russian collective imagination as a model for identification. On the other hand, the screen opens a possibility of a disjunction between Russian national identification and its idealized (western) model – a disjunction generated by historical, political, and cultural differences. It is in the space of this process that I begin to look for dramatic conflicts that in turn propel fantasies and fears.

Since the time of Peter the Great, Russian writers and thinkers have engaged in heated debates regarding the nature of Russian political and cultural identity in relation to the West. So-called Westernizers and Slavophiles argued about the authenticity of the Russian mind and spirit: the former advocated western values as a path to Russian modernization, and the latter rejected them so as to establish a unique 'Russianness'. In his study about the development of Russian identity in relation to Europe, Iver Neumann writes: 'The Russian state spent the eighteenth century copying contemporary European models, the nineteenth century representing the Europe of the *anciens régimes*, which the rest of Europe had abandoned, and the twentieth century representing a European socialist model which most of the rest of Europe never chose to implement' (1996, 1).

Russia and the (Western) Other

To trace collective identity formation as it has been conceptualized around the nexus of self/other, one can follow various paradigms. Neumann identifies four different paths used mainly by social theorists: the ethnographic path, the psychological path, the Continental philosophical path, and the 'Eastern excursions' (1999, 1–20). In this study, I rely on ideas of identity formation that have psychological and psychoanalytic foundations, some of them identified by Neumann, as well as some ideas that belong to the path he calls 'Eastern excursions', notions proposed by Bakhtin and later developed by Tzvetan Todorov and Kristeva.

In the early 1920s, Bakhtin maintained that the subject's knowledge of itself or the world is impossible without the other, because meaning occurs in discourse where consciousnesses meet. He attributed to the other epistemological as well as ontological necessity and criticized all nineteenth-

and early-twentieth-century philosophy in which 'epistemologism' – reification of a sovereign self separated from the other's consciousness or, in other words, a single consciousness – prevailed:

> In this sense, epistemological consciousness cannot have another consciousness outside itself, cannot enter into relation with another consciousness, one that is autonomous and distinct from it. Any unity is its own unity; it cannot admit next to itself any other unity that would be different from it and independent from it (the unity of nature, the unity of another consciousness), that is, any sovereign unity that would stand over against it with its own fate, one not determined by epistemological consciousness. (Bakhtin 1990, 89)

According to Bakhtin, the absence of the other in this kind of thinking precludes the knowledge of either the self or the world. Pressed by the political practice of totalitarianism, which denied the possibility of a dialogue, Bakhtin sought to reconfigure the problematics of a community, a society, or a way of thinking that erased the space between self and other. Exposing the nature of a totalitarian system, Hannah Arendt spoke of a totalitarian loneliness that permeated through the core of existence under the totalitarian regime. According to her, one thing that unites fascism and communism, despite their radical ideological differences, is the collectivization of people as a mass, which in turn paradoxically produces social isolation. 'The chief characteristic of the mass man is not brutality and backwardness, but his isolation and lack of normal social relationships' (Arendt 310). She resists totalitarian loneliness because it prevents her from thinking. For her, thinking always requires a dialogue between 'me and myself', but for this dialogue she needs the other (Arendt 301–429). The totalitarian system erased the space between self and other and transformed society into one mass man. Although Bakhtin's dialogism has remained largely a literary-studies concept, it is, I believe, a political concept as well, concerned with how totalitarian totality erased meaning produced precisely in the meeting space between self and other (1981).

In the late 1960s, at the time of structuralism and the emergence of post-structuralism, Bakhtin's understanding of dialogism was embraced and introduced to western readers by two Bulgarians living and working in Paris – Todorov and Kristeva. Todorov's later monograph, *The Conquest of America: The Question of the Other*, is one of the first studies to tackle self/other problematics, especially its application to a historical and cultural discourse. Analyzing Columbus's perception of Indians, Todorov outlines two major attitudes to the other that are in practice to this day. The first approach perceives others as equal human beings having the same rights as the subject thus making them identical and leading to the projection of one's own values on the others and consequently to their assimilation. The second views the other as different, which immediately creates feelings of superiority and inferiority. 'What is denied is the existence of a human substance truly other, something capable of being not merely an imperfect state of oneself' (Todorov 42). Bakhtin's insistence on the recognition of a consciousness separate from the self, which generates the knowledge of the self and the other, underlies Todorov's discoveries.

Kristeva has not only familiarized the West with Bakhtin's ideas but has enhanced them and has developed a strong conceptualized theory based on what she calls 'intertextuality':

> The notion of dialogism, which owed much to Hegel, must not be confused with Hegel's dialectics, based on a triad and thus on struggle and projection (a movement of transcendence), which does

not transgress the Aristotelian tradition founded on substance and causality. Dialogism replaces these concepts by absorbing them within the concept of relation. (1986a, 58–59)

The dialogical principle or the concept of relation, as Kristeva calls it, is the basis of this study's investigation of Russia's identity formation. Later in her work and particularly in her book *Strangers to Ourselves*, Kristeva enriches her understanding of the dialogism between self and other, and maintains that individual and collective identity formation is composed not merely in the dialogue and relations between self and other but in the rare moments when one is other to oneself. Deploying Freud's discovery of the unconscious, Kristeva insists that the unconscious integrates into the 'unity of human beings an *otherness* that is both biological *and* symbolic and becomes an integral part of the *same*. Henceforth the foreigner is neither a race nor a nation... Uncanny, foreignness is within us: we are our own foreigners, we are divided' (1991, 180). When one opposes a foreigner, one actually fights against one's own unconscious. She believes that individuals and nations, which are capable of recognizing the other and of experiencing the feeling of being strangers and foreigners to themselves, foster the potential for healthy and positive development. She imagines 'a mankind whose solidarity is founded on the consciousness of its unconscious – desiring, destructive, fearful, empty, impossible' (Kristeva 1991, 192). Like Bakhtin, Kristeva also knows totalitarian loneliness (formulated by Arendt), and one can safely argue that her insistence on the recognition of otherness within the self is politically motivated.

Similar to Kristeva's engagement with the other is Renata Salecl's discussion of the dynamics of the nation-other relationships. She contends: 'But the Other who outrages "our" sense of the kind of nation ours should be, the Other who steals our enjoyment is always the Other in our own interior' (Salecl 1994, 21). Following the Lacanian tradition, Salecl argues that fantasy stimulates and structures enjoyment. 'Therefore hatred of the Other, in the final analysis, is hatred of one's own enjoyment' (Salecl 1994, 22). In this sense, intolerance and aggression toward the other produce fantasies which organize or bring together members of a community or a nation on the basis of their own enjoyment.

Following such an understanding of the other (as both an outsider needed for a dialogue and production of meaning and as the strangeness within the self or the enjoyment that is unbearable and cannot be acknowledged), one asks several questions in analyzing Russian films: How does the idea of the other permeate Russian national identity as reflected in these films? Do the conditions of the period of transition provide the necessary space for a dialogue between self and other (Russia and the West)? The meeting of two consciousnesses is a necessary but often traumatic experience. What is the psychological cost at the level of both the individual and society of the dialogue (all too often confrontation) between Russia and the West?

To begin to answer these questions, I will briefly touch on historical, political, and cultural examples of Russia's confrontation with the (western) imaginary other. Neumann has studied in detail Russian collective identity formation in relation to the other from the Napoleonic wars and the Decembrist uprising to the present, and he finds evidence of the Russian debate about its relation to Europe as early as the mid-fifteenth century (1996). He interprets as the first sign of the debate the decision by Muscovy (the Russian state) to reject a union with the Roman Church in the name of one unitary Christendom (Neumann 1996, 6–7). The fall of Byzantium and the marriage of Ivan III to Sofia Paleologue, the niece of Byzantium's last emperor, gave birth to the idea that Russia was Byzantium's historical successor and a great power. Moscow as the Third Rome emerged in political and cultural symbolism, which further encouraged a belief in Russia's moral superiority and western decline and inferiority.

Conversely, Peter the Great ignored this belief in Russia's uniqueness and began the process of modernization, which included the introduction of western ideas, beliefs, technologies, and practices. Opposition to Peter's reforms insisted on the West's moral inferiority and corruptive practices and on the fruitlessness and fraudulence of his efforts. Peter the Great, however, effectively marginalized the opposition and circumscribed the official discourse in favor of the West, setting the tone for the entire eighteenth century. The nineteenth century was marked by controversy and heated debate about Russia's relation to the West, waged by two distinct groups within Russia's intelligentsia: Westernizers and Slavophiles.[2]

The argument between Westernizers and Slavophiles continued well into the twentieth century, and, depending upon the political climate Russia exhibited either strong interests in the West or cold and hostile attitudes toward it. What clearly emerges in these polemics was Russia's constant preoccupation with western ideas and models. The dialogical nature of identity formation creates meaning exactly where the two consciousnesses meet. Despite (and because of) the fact that there has always been an opposition to Russia's involvement with the West, Russia's identity has developed against the backdrop of its constant relationship to the West. In this dialogical relation between self and other, one comes to read the other and to know oneself. Neumann asserts: 'In discussing Europe, the Russians have always clearly been discussing themselves, and so the debate is an example of how Russians have talked themselves into existence' (1996, 194).

Europe, in turn, regarded Russia ambivalently over the centuries and constructed it as its own other. Russia's Christianity was seen as something positive, but at the same time Russia's ties with non-Christian cultures troubled Europe (Neumann 1999, 113–43). Russians were often referred to as 'Scythians', 'Tartars', and 'Kalmucks'. Such representation hinted at Russia's 'Asiatic' and 'barbaric' nature. Other accusations and pejorative attitudes targeted Russia's 'questionable' civility and the character of its regime. Throughout the nineteenth century, however, Russia was recognized as a great power and an equal player in European politics.[3]

Karl Marx, for instance, epitomized this ambivalent European attitude toward Russia. In the 1850s, he reminded Europe of Russia's territorial gains since Peter the Great and warned that unless Russia was stopped, it would engulf and barbarize the whole continent.[4] At that time Marx firmly denied the possibility of a revolution in Russia because of her backward economic conditions. Marx's argument was entirely motivated by his hatred of tsarism and his theory of revolution. Later on in the 1860s, however, Marx changed his views and considered the possibility that a revolution could begin in the East and spread westward.[5] He reevaluated drastically his early belief in the natural phases of evolution and the natural historical process on the basis of the Russian question.

Despite Russia's perceived backwardness and underdeveloped capitalist structure, the Russian Revolution took place, and the Soviet government eliminated private property and established a new, modern form of collectivism. The Soviet period opened a new door in Russia's relation to the West, in which the Soviets rapidly adopted an aggressive anti-western posture in every sphere. The attempt to preserve Russian identity and economic independence from the 'pollution' of western ideas and capital was passionately revived during the Soviet period in the form of economic isolation and ideological censorship. Over the years, the prohibition on relations with the West took various forms and emerged with different degrees of persistence in the Soviet Union and in the other countries under socialist systems. There were times of severe persecution and punishment, and times of lessened control over relations with the West.[6]

Political and Cultural Demonology

After the October Revolution, Vladimir Lenin set the tone for Soviet-American relations, which in the first two decades after the Revolution developed in various directions:

> Bourgeois civilization has borne all its luxurious fruits. America has taken first place among the free and educated nations in the level of development of the productive forces of the collective United Human endeavor, in the utilization of machinery and of all the wonders of modern engineering. At the same time, America has become one of the foremost countries in regard to the depth of the abyss which lies between the handful of arrogant multimillionaires who wallow in filth and luxury, and the millions of working people who constantly live on the verge of pauperism. (62–63)

On the one hand, Lenin praises American technological advancement and the development of creative and productive resources and, on the other, condemns poverty and the very nature of bourgeois civilization, which opens an abyss between the amorally rich and the besieged poor. This view determined the Soviet attitude toward America, the West, and the capitalist political and economic system in general.

In the 1920s the American work ethic and enthusiasm gained popularity, and the Soviet people were encouraged to learn to work in the American way. American businessmen and workers participated in the construction of the Gorky automobile factory, while Soviet workers went to the States to study methods of modern technology (Zassoursky 15–16). These intensified relations were expressed in I'lia Ilf and Evgenii Petrov's popular book *One-Storey America* and Vladimir Maiakovskii's poem "Brooklyn Bridge". At the same time, Soviet ideology more vehemently criticized the amoral nature of capitalism, its values and aesthetics.[7]

In a sense, this ambivalent Russian tendency to corroborate and simultaneously contest cultural and political products of American capitalism is best enshrined in two films from the 1920s and 1930s: Lev Kuleshov's *Extraordinary Adventures of Mr. West in the Land of the Bolsheviks* (1924) and Grigorii Aleksandrov's *Circus* (1936). In *Mr. West*, viewers detect Kuleshov's curiosity and playful envy of the diverse and powerful Hollywood mythology, and at the same time they identify with the director's belief in his moral superiority, fostered by his belonging to a new progressive revolutionary society.

In a spirit similar to Kuleshov's admiration for the Hollywood apparatus, Aleksandrov created *Circus* by generously borrowing from the genre of the Hollywood musical, which he brought back to Russia after a visit to Hollywood. *Circus* advocates internationalism through the story of an American circus performer, Marion Dixon, who, after a scandal involving her black baby, was forced to leave the US. She ends up in the Soviet Union working for a Russian circus. Western values and aesthetics are attacked on multiple levels. First, Marion is dramatically presented as a victim of American racism.

Second, the Russian circus number that replaces Marion's is far more grandiose and spectacular, no doubt reinforcing a sense of Russian cultural and social superiority. The film naturally proffers a happy and ideologically correct ending, in which spectators – representatives of various nationalities in the Soviet Union – embrace the baby and sing him a lullaby, each in his/her own language, thus celebrating the Soviet policy of equality, internationalism, and collectivism. Not surprisingly, Aleksandrov added a second ending, in which through double exposure, viewers observe Marion, Martynov – her partner both in the circus and in life – and their colleagues happily marching under images of Lenin and Stalin and singing Isaak Dunaevskii's song "I don't know another country where so freely a man can breathe..." After the film's release it became one of the most popular songs in the Soviet Union. The film celebrated Soviet internationalism and at the same time exposed the hypocrisy and racism of American society, which were considered byproducts of the capitalist system. Describing the anti-American fervor in several films from the 1930s, Birgit Beumers writes:

> Thus, several films contain parodic allusions to foreign lands no longer accessible to the masses: in the Soviet Union Marion Dixon is freed from the capitalist exploitation of Kneischitz by the blond, blue-eyed Soviet engineer Martynov; her son Jimmy is liberated from racial discrimination in the United States by the great Soviet collective as embodied in the ethnically mixed circus audience. (2003a, 449)

In order to avoid the 'corrupt' nature of capitalism and the abyss separating its wealthy and poor, the Soviet Union changed the very foundation of its economic system and consequently the very basis of society. Following Marx and Friedrich Engels, the Soviet leadership considered private property the culprit behind all negative and aggressive human manifestations. They set a goal to abolish the institution of private property, first in the Soviet Union and then in the world. After the Bolsheviks nationalized private industries, banks, and communication infrastructures and proclaimed their victory over the old capitalist system, they anticipated that human nature and behaviour would change accordingly. They quickly discovered, however, that economics and politics were not enough to transform human instincts and habits. In his play, *The Bedbug* (1929), Maiakovskii voiced his disillusionment with stubbornly corruptive human nature, easily seduced by the shallow advantages of private property and better living standards.

In *Civilization and Its Discontents*, Freud addressed manifestations of human nature that run against the nonviolent development of societies and civilization. He reacted with surprise and bewilderment when pondering one of the most powerful moral imperatives of Christianity: 'Thou shalt love thy neighbor as thyself.' He believed instead that the existence of aggression (one of the innate human drives) in all human beings is a factor that disturbs our relations with our neighbors, and so the appeal to love one's neighbor as oneself fails. Elaborating on the psychological grounds of communism and the Russian communist leaders' aspiration to eliminate the aggression that to them was rooted in the institution of private property, Freud pointed out:

> The communists believe that they have found the path to deliverance from our evils... If private property were abolished, all wealth held in common, and everyone allowed to share in the enjoyment of it, ill-will and hostility would disappear among men... I cannot enquire into whether the abolition of private property is expedient or advantageous. But I am able to recognize that the psychological premises on which the system is based are an untenable illusion... Aggressiveness was not created by property. (1961, 70–71)

There are advantages, Freud insisted, when a community allows this aggressive instinct an outlet in the form of hostility to outsiders, foreigners, and intruders. It is always possible to bind together a large number of people by love as long as there are outsiders left out to become a target of the aggressive instinct. Freud expanded this idea by saying that aggressiveness needs to direct its impulses onto the other. Cohesion between members of a community becomes easier when aggression finds an outlet. About the new communist state and its construction of an outsider, Freud remarked: '[A]nd it is intelligible that the attempt to establish a new, communist civilization in Russia should find its psychological support in the persecution of the bourgeois. One only wonders with concern what the Soviets will do after they have wiped out their bourgeois' (1961, 73). The Soviets did precisely what Freud described here: they continued to construct the other, within the country and outside.

It is natural, Klein insists, for the ego to experience anxieties, employ defenses, form primitive object-relations in fantasy and reality, and project negativity onto an object as well as to direct aggression against the other (Klein 1975b). In her view, from birth there is a conflict between loving and destructive impulses. The rudimentary ego develops defense mechanisms as it deflects death instincts. This deflection, which functions as projection, constructs a hateful object. The life instinct splits off and creates a good object, again by projection. Bad experiences attach themselves and are also attributed to the 'bad object' and good experiences to the good one (Klein 1975b, 1–24). Groups very often deal with their ambivalence through this mechanism of splitting. The group idealizes itself as a unit held together by a collective love for an ideal, while it directs its aggression toward other groups. Usually a group is self-idealizing, grandiose, and paranoid, and allows itself to sanction aggression and other destructive actions that in normal circumstances would be controlled in the individual.

Applying Kleinian concepts to the analysis of the Russian other and the enemies of Russia, Rancour-Laferriere traces in detail the psychological mechanisms of the ways Russia imagines its foes (113–210). 'Those on the far right such as the extreme Slavophiles, some of the Eurasianists, and today's right wing idealize Russia herself while feeling persecuted by the West, by Jews, and others' (187). Stalin's purges, for example, caused by political anxieties in Russia, created and victimized the 'enemy within'. Persecutory anxieties lead to internal cleansing and imperial ambition and expansion.

Lacan's theory of fantasy (elaborated and applied to cultural studies by Žižek and Salecl) offers a different interpretation of the need of Soviet ideology (or Russian nationalists today) to demonize the West. According to Lacan, the outward projection of aggression (the death drive), the formation of the other, is attributed to the functioning aggression at the level of the imaginary. He contends that the existence of hostility and violence, the threat to civilization, comes not from the destructive drive but from the failure of its symbolic mediation. Lacan introduces the three orders of the imaginary, the symbolic, and the real to discuss stages in human development as well as levels of existence. The symbolic (unlike the imaginary, which is based on sense evidence and relations) exists as a network of social, cultural, and historical signs. The symbolic is also referred to as the Other (or the Law), which in the life of an individual may be represented by social, religious, political, or cultural norms and structures. To the first two registers, the imaginary and the symbolic, Lacan adds the real.[8] The real is that about which one cannot speak; it is everything that escapes symbolization. Contrary to popular belief the Law (or, in this case, Soviet ideology) is there not to repress, but to sustain desire and fantasy. Fantasy situates one's position in relation to the desire of the Law (Lacan 1977).

Taking this structure a step further, Žižek writes: 'The fantasy which underlies the public ideological text as its unacknowledged obscene support simultaneously serves as a screen against the direct intrusions of the Real' (1997, 64–5). In other words, an ideological discourse always constructs (and allows) a certain level of fantasy that supports it and organizes its ideological economy. An ideological discourse provides for a fantasy that, in turn, keeps individuals satisfied with their social reality. In the Soviet Union, and especially during the cold war, the totalitarian discourse directly and openly demonized the West, hoping to distract attention from inefficient social reality by constructing a blatantly artificial and negative picture of the other and by nurturing a positive view of Soviet life. Soviet individuals took solace in the fantasy of a future ideal communist society or of a denounced alternative social, political and economic system (even if and when they did not trust Soviet ideology). At the same time, however, the gap between the political discourse and everyday life was so colossal, that it engendered an opposite fantasy – amorphous and powerful – of western paradise. While the social reality is dark and hopeless, fantasy suggests a lavish and gleaming world (either 'the bright future of communism' or western heaven). Explicating the inconsistency of fantasy in relation to ideology, Žižek writes: 'Ideology is not primarily the imaginary solution of real antagonisms…; rather, it consists in their symbolic solution: the elementary ideological gesture is the imposition of the signifier which starts to function as a kind of empty container for the multitude of mutually exclusive meanings' (1997, 74–5). Or as he says (changing the lexical registers of his utterance): 'in ideology, one can have one's cake and eat it' (Žižek 1997, 75). Thus, one can subscribe to the demonology of the West (as an empty signifier) and at the same time nurture the fantasy of a western paradise.

After World War II, Soviet relations with the West soon reached the stage of the cold war. Soviet ideology attacked western wealth and economic development. It divided the world into black and white, West and East, debauchery and decency. It categorically prohibited relations with the West. For many years the Iron Curtain symbolized the absurd and artificial division between Western and Eastern (socialist) minds, ideals, culture, and information. However, the Iron Curtain was more than a dividing line. It was the boundary beyond which the socialist people were not allowed to see. They were left only to fantasize about a forbidden Garden of Eden ripe with sinful temptation. Thus, the West was simultaneously demonized and desired.

The West began to recover from the war, whereas the Soviet Union, though a victor in the war, could not improve living standards. Mikhail Epstein, describing Soviet economic development, points out: 'How we labored from the twenties to the fifties before becoming lazy in the sixties! Day and night, to bloody blisters and an early grave, we burned to work, as they used to say about zealous laborers. But this didn't make us wealthy, even so' (164). Under these circumstances Soviet ideology demonized western opulence – large, showy cars, elegant suits, and shimmering windows – because it was perceived as signifying the immorality of an unjust society and because almost every Soviet citizen living in a communal apartment, trying for years to save for a car, dreamed of these western hallmarks.

Such cold war feelings ebbed and flowed, and in general during the whole period of the cold war, mostly negative images of the West prevailed in the Soviet media. With relentless persistence,

Russian periodicals pointed out capitalist unemployment, poverty, and exploitation. In 1963, V. Goncharov wrote from Paris for *New Time*:

> The famous Parisian beggarly homeless, who don't care the least about their appearance, wrapped themselves in pieces of fabric, towels, and all they had at hand. And there is yet another sign of early winter: Parisian dogs, and there are a lot of them in the streets, whom their compassionate wealthy owners have dressed in warm little sheepskin coats. (25)[9]

Such writings, echoing Lenin's opinion about American capitalism, try to address the desperate gap between wealth and poverty, and to imply that affluence can be achieved only at the expense of scarcity. One can recall here a socialist slogan, 'From everybody according to his/her abilities, to everybody according to his/her needs', which loudly voiced the advantages of socialism. In the seventh issue of *New Time*, I. Lapitskii wrote about the regions of depression in the United States where unemployment 'has catastrophically increased, evidently demonstrating the incapability of American capitalism to take care of this serious problem' (20).

After World War II, the more Soviet ideology demonized the West, the more fictional and imaginary this demonization became. The image of America, for instance, was transformed from a wartime ally to an imaginary enemy. Most film directors (unlike Aleksandrov) had not visited the United States and knew little of it, but this did not prevent the emergence of films, products of ideological fantasy, such as *Silver Dust* (1953), *Farewell, America!* (unfinished), *Russian Souvenir* (1960), *Game with No Rules* (1965), *Neutral Waters* (1969), *The Silence of Dr. Ivens* (1974), and *Solo Voyage* (1985). In the first two films, America appears on the screen entirely imagined, ideologically and politically inscribed in the narrative and cinematography, which make it appear artificial, stiff, and hyper-theatricalized. Even in the films of the Thaw period, anti-American propaganda appropriates tendencies of Stalinist aesthetics. Iaropolk Lapshin's *Game with No Rules* resembles a Stalinist film, and only the ending connects it to the post-Stalinist period. Americans in the film seek to discover Soviet secrets and shamelessly cooperate with the Nazis; they interrogate young Soviet people (members of the youth communist party) using Nazi methods and forcibly detain Soviet citizens in their occupied territory. At the end of the film, as a result of a chess game won by the Soviets, the Americans free the Russians and they run along the road, all in tears of joy and happiness. The camera poetically spins and follows the liberated Russians with a crane shot – a part of the Thaw aesthetics. Yet the emotional use of the camera at the end of the film – a sign of the cultural and political relaxation of the Thaw period – does not alter the anti-American sentiments in the film.

In later films, Soviet anti-Americanism appears more elegantly masked under a strong patriotic message. In *Neutral Waters* (dir. Vladimir Berenstein), the Soviet people are presented as capable of great heroic deeds: a Russian sailor is ready to drown and never reveal secret documents to Americans who discover him in the ocean. This time Americans are portrayed more neutrally as human, different from the monsters of previous anti-American films. However, Russian patriotism inevitably remains the main political trope of the film.[10] When ideology weakens and the gap between political discourse and reality narrows (as it happened in the 1970s in the Soviet Union), fantasy becomes more latent and amorphous. In films it can be detected camouflaged in a patriotic veil rather than in an open rejection of the West.

The political discourse (manifested in media and film), that demonized the West, even though often laughably obvious and direct, paradoxically achieved its goal: it kept individuals from protesting and rebelling. The films glorified and idealized Soviet society and, in turn, triggered an alternative fantasy of western paradise. Individuals withdrew into this secret fantasy and found enjoyment in privately dreaming, which kept the status quo of the system. Salecl argues: 'The ideal subject of socialism was the one who did not believe in the system, who maintained a certain distance from it. But criticizing the regime privately and telling dirty jokes about the Party amounted to nothing heroic' (1994, 48). Similarly, the fantasy of the prosperous West kept most Soviet subjects privately dreaming and quietly living.

The mechanism of othering (or the construction of fantasy as a screen, sustaining ideology) has not been a trademark only of the Soviet Union. The West too, produced its own evil empire in the face of communism and showed similar symptoms of paranoia. It should be noted here that every ideology uses the same mechanism of denouncing the other. The West and the East employed similar mechanisms for constructing the other as an evil empire. In his provocative work, *Ronald Reagan: The Movie*, Michael Rogin convincingly shows the methods behind American political demonology and the mechanism of constructing the other as an enemy. Stephen Prince further explores the American mechanisms of political demonization and centers on its manifestation in films from the second half of the 1980s. He remarks: 'As Reagan took office, détente and human rights were discarded as the discredited policies of yesterday, and a new Cold War commenced. As in the old Cold War, the major source of conflict and aggression throughout the world was held to be the Soviet Union...' (Prince 50). Prince examines a series of films such as *Red Dawn* (1984), *Rocky IV* (1985), *Invasion USA* (1985), *Top Gun* (1986), *The Delta Force* (1986), *Heartbreak Ridge* (1986), *Iron Eagle I* (1986), and *Rambo III* (1988), which reflect this post-cold war demonization (in political rhetoric) of the Soviet Union (49–81).

With the era of *perestroika* and especially after the collapse of communism, however, this situation changed on both sides of the Iron Curtain. Acknowledging this change, Prince points out that 'the recent changes in Eastern Europe and the breakup of the Soviet empire have begun to rearrange not only the map of Europe but also the shape of contemporary American politics' (49). He insists that the dogged anti-Sovietism of the previous era is transformed into 'more tolerant and cooperative international relationships' (Prince 49). From the mid-1980s, Russia also adopted a new direction toward the West, outlined in the concepts of *perestroika* (economic restructuring) and *glasnost* (openness). Gorbachev's period marked a transition towards new international relations, new political thinking, and a new global psychology.

As a result of Russia's attempt to (re)enter an active and intensive dialogue with the West, a relatively more realistic picture of the world developed. The previous construction of the (western) other as different and dangerous was replaced with an acceptance and welcoming of this difference. From a denounced system, the free-market economy became the preferred economic model. The West was no longer the forbidden and impossible fantasy and suddenly became an almost real opportunity for travel, relationships, or immigration. When the subject gets too close to fantasy, when the distance between subject and fantasy disappears, fantasy breaks down. Nancy Ries points out the sudden reversal of attitudes after the disintegration of the Soviet Union:

> Concomitant with the negation of everything Soviet came a celebration of everything having to do with the old capitalist nemesis, 'the West.' Where the Soviet media had regularly exhibited

images of the cruelty, unfairness, and contradictions of capitalist systems, in perestroika this practice was inverted, and images of poor people receiving medical care in U.S. clinics were juxtaposed with interviews with Russian mothers who could not obtain medicines or services their children desperately needed. Thus mythical images of the West (as one-sided as the previous hellish images of Western life had been) were used in the assault on the mythos of socialism. (174)

Or, in Kristeva's terms, this is a moment when an individual or a nation can develop the strength to realize and accept the strangeness within the self. The break of fantasy opens space for the subject or a nation to seek the other within the self. Does this, however, actually happen, or do other fantasies develop constructing new outsiders?

Contrary to Prince, Segal argues that the mentality of the West has not changed drastically after the end of the cold war. While the negativity is withdrawn, the recognition of ambivalence and guilt causes pain. Predictably, new defense mechanisms have arisen. The West developed new manic defenses such as triumphalism and megalomania.[11] This 'development' was inevitably bound to construct new enemies to replace the Soviet Union (Milošević and Saddam Hussein are two examples) and to continue the drive toward military superiority. Segal aptly pinpoints the new psychological conditions borne out of the Soviet collapse: 'At the time of perestroika, rather than face guilt we turned to manic defenses: in particular to triumphalism. Perestroika was felt to be the triumph of our superior system and power, and our nuclear mentality did not change' (1997, 166). Russia has also reacted and developed new defense mechanisms and fantasies, which, however, differ from those of the West.

Psychological Cost of the Transition

The collapse of communism advanced the process of globalization – an unparalleled expansion of international capital – and brought shocking surprises and disappointments for the West and the former Soviet countries. Žižek writes: 'The passage from actually existing Socialism to actually existing capitalism in Eastern Europe brought about a series of comic reversals of sublime democratic enthusiasm into the ridiculous' (2000, 205). The West impatiently waited for and instigated democratic changes in Russia and Eastern Europe because it wanted political pluralism and free-market economies – that is, new territory for the expansion of its capital. From the West's perspective, however, the implementation of democratic changes resulted in corruption, unstable economies, ethnic conflict, and nationalist obsessions. Eastern Europeans in turn, after idolizing and dreaming of prosperous democracies, have faced merciless unemployment and poverty as well as an invasion of western capital and culture.

After the collapse of communism, Russia's glossy magazines, such as *Money, Power*, and *Career*, lured Russian readers with temptations of the 'American dream'. Today they display advertisement presenting to the Russian consumer all of the 'enticements' available in the West – imported cigarettes, fashionable clothing, cars, computers, mobile phones, and cameras. Moreover, they tell stories of young successful Russians, almost always men, who in their mid-twenties become millionaires; they enlighten Russians on the pleasures of golf, teach them how to dress in a businesslike manner, and obsess over beauty, attractiveness, and style. They rank the best European colleges and universities where Russians could send their children to study and offer Russians housing that not long ago was only a distant fantastic dream. All the 'riches' of capitalism that were demonized by the Soviet regime – thereby stoking the fantasies of the people for those very things – now have been aggressively made available through magazines, films, and the Internet. Soviet/Russian citizens' dreams have almost come true.

Now that the demonized/fantasized extravagance of the West has been made available to Russians, is there access, and who has access to it? Russian reality pokes gaping holes in these voluptuous magazine pictures, which purport to fulfill Russians' formerly forbidden dreams of western excess. Dreams, in light of certain realities, morph into nightmares. The stories of overnight success and glittering extravagance usually obscure illegal manipulations, criminal activities, and violence. The vast majority of Russians had no financial access to the products made so readily 'available' to them, especially in the early 1990s and especially in the countryside.

In 1993, the new constitution of the Russian Federation gave Russians the right to entrepreneurship and other economic activities, and by 1996 the government had privatized or transferred to private ownership over 100,000 commercial entities (Grant 242). But in the first half of the 1990s the enthusiasm for taking advantage of these new opportunities began to fade away and, instead of *privatizatsiia* (privatization), the process turned into *prikhvatizatsiia* ('grabification').[12] Bruce Grant notes: 'The most common scenario was for managers [former leaders] of state firms to install themselves as *de facto* owners, using their influence to run their new companies as small satrapies' (242). A new merchant class emerged – aptly named 'New Russians' (*novye russkie*) – which took full advantage of the new rights and freedoms and quickly adopted a western lifestyle. Today they vacation in Turkey, Spain, or the Caribbean; indulge in luxurious goods from the Moscow stores of Gucci and Armani; and drive Mercedes and high-priced SUVs. At the same time, most Russians suffer from the increased crime rate as a result of loosened state control and international economic relations. Though apprehensive, some continue to dream of the West and its lifestyle. Others still hate the (western) other, but now internalized. The first disappointments of the transition to democracy were experienced in the early 1990s, but the Russian collective imagination was still fearfully holding illusions and dreams born out of the powerful pull of the West.

In these confusing economic and political conditions, former values such as social privilege, academic degrees, and party membership have disappeared and have ceased to shape the individual identity, which strives for new values. Michael D. Kennedy observes that 'identity formation after communism is ironic' (1994b, 3). Scholars, politicians, and economists restlessly reiterate the very fact of the end of Soviet-style communism. At the same time, individuals – all subjects of this drastic change – 'want to be normal. They wish to be who they "really" are, or who they ought to be. In short, they want to be something inconsistent with the system they recently overturned and the social relations it produced' (Kennedy 1994b, 4). In the midst of the burdened social, political, and economic heritage and a traumatic transition to democracy 'East Europeans want unproblematic identities' (Kennedy 1994b, 4).

The desires detected in this irony testify to confusion, uneasiness, and hesitation in identity formation, which require a search for and acceptance of new values and self-definitions (as well as the emergence of new fantasies). More importantly, they require the difficult integration of old and new values into the formation of identity, the painful acceptance of the idealized and demonized (western) other as a part of the self. It can be argued that this confusing economic and political state typical for a period of transition corresponds to a similarly confusing stage in the subject's individual development, the period of adolescence. During the transition from Soviet-style communism to democracy and a market economy, as during adolescence, value and belief systems clash with other value and belief systems, and society, like the subject, struggles to know what and who it is and to find its identity. The most important driving force during adolescence is the ability to process mental pain, confusion, and conflicts, and to integrate all of them. But at the same time there are impulses working to keep them apart. Margot Waddell, a psychoanalyst and consultant in the Adolescent Department at the Tavistock Clinic in London, describes the mental and psychological conditions of adolescents as follows: 'Adolescence can be described, in narrow terms, as a complex adjustment on the child's part to these major physical and emotional changes. This adjustment entails finding a new, and often hard-won, sense of oneself-in-the-world, in the wake of the disturbing of latency attitudes and ways of functioning' (1998a, 125). Adolescence, and the transition from one political and economic system to another, is a crucial period of time in which essential aspects of one's personality as well as the collective identity respectively are shaped.

Adolescents are tempted to quickly fulfill their dreams and to consume the forbidden fruit, but at the same time there are fears that slow them down and keep them sensible. Impatient waiting to realize one's fantasies and dreams marks both society's transition and adolescence. When control over impatience loosens and adolescents are unable to realize their dreams, they identify with an idealized object but assume only superficial signs of this object without really being able to integrate it. The future development of both the individual and society depend greatly on the capacity to relate to an idealized object and to manage choices, independence, and, most likely, disillusionment with life and the world.

As already noted, from a Lacanian perspective the relationship with an idealized object is governed by fantasy. When the Soviet Union crumbled and the distance between the fantasized West and Russia diminished, the fantasy of the West began to collapse as well. Here it becomes clear how fantasy sustains the subject's sense of reality. As Žižek contends: 'When the phantasmatic frame disintegrates, the subject undergoes a "loss of reality" and starts to perceive reality as an "irreal" nightmarish universe with no firm ontological foundation' (1997, 66). But before this happened in Russia after the disintegration of the Soviet Union, the possibilities to travel and live in the West became real, and yet it was difficult and often impossible for Russians to leave their country. They had to obtain foreign visas and prove financial stability, two difficult tasks considering the turbulent state of Russian economy at the very beginning of the 1990s and the lack of enthusiasm on the part of western countries to allow a great number of Russians (and other East Europeans) to visit or live in the West. Thus, although the fantasy of the West was moving closer and closer to Russia and its citizens, there was a certain distance between the subject and his/her fantasy which made it still effective. As argued earlier, when the subject gets too close to fantasy, when the distance disappears, fantasy breaks down and the subject is forced to face the (nightmarish) real. Russian films, produced in the first half of the 1990s, before the fantasy of the West broke down completely, reveal the imaginary nature of the fantasy apparent in clichéd and stereotypical images of the West as well as in supernatural remedies for the materialization of the fantasy.

Screening Temptations and Fears
Several films from the first half of the 1990s, such as Leonid Gaidai's *On Deribasovskaia the Weather is Fine, or, On Brighton Beach It's Raining Again*, Dmitrii Astrakhan's *Everything will be OK* (1995), and Alla Surikova's *Moscow Vacation* (1995), divulge the impatience of the adolescent to take

advantage of the newly arisen opportunities or, in the case of Russians, to communicate and eventually unite with the West. The films also expose how imaginary and fictional the fantasy of merging with the West is, for all of them offer *deus ex machina* solutions for the realization of the fantasy. In the last two films, visitors from the West (a Russian émigré with his son and a beautiful Italian woman respectively) arrive in Russia, and, after miraculously resolving numerous problems, they leave for other countries with a Russian partner.[13] About such films Christina Stojanova notes:

> [T]hey offer ample sociological evidence about the frustrations and contemporary mythology of ordinary Russians. In spite of their genre diversity, they basically fit in this generalised scheme: an emigrant (or a visitor) arrives from the West. He/she provokes – or witnesses – a string of melodramatic or burlesque events, and then resolves them as *deus ex machina*.

Conversely, other films from the first half of the 1990s, such as *Window to Paris, A Patriotic Comedy* (1992), *You are My Only One* (1993) and *American Daughter* (1995), vigilantly approach the new temptations presented by the dismantling of the Berlin Wall, and reject the possibility of exile in favor of rebuilding Russia. In these films (as well as others based on literary adaptations), Faraday notices a new trend in early 1990s Russian cinema, which he calls *national popular* cinema (183). All of these films foster a fantasy in which the protagonists are granted a possibility to leave Russia and settle comfortably in the West, but they refuse it for love of their country despite its myriad problems. These films unravel the dreamed 'privileges' and 'advantages' of the West, warn against the (often superfluous) corrupting temptations of such a western life, and finally conclude that the motherland is the only home for Russians. All of these films engage images of the West and, through the contact and relationship with the other, pose questions or offer solutions for the new Russian identity and place in the world. Elaborating on these films Lawton writes:

> Several films of the post-Soviet period treated the 'abroad' theme, depicting the disillusionment of those who attained, or were about to attain, the unreachable dream and had to resize their expectations. Often these films sounded a patriotic note, with the protagonists reevaluating their national identity and choosing the homeland over the promised land. (2005, 190)

Although this second patriotic category has attracted more discussion and interpretation, the two groups of films (suggesting either a seamless union with the West or its rejection) expose the shortened distance between the subject and fantasy, as they euphorically (and unrealistically) embrace the newly emerged opportunities of traveling to the West. The former divulge the fantasmatic nature of these opportunities, while the latter, although holding onto the fantasy of the West, reveal cautious and uncertain withdrawal from it. Passé and predictable images speak of the fantasmatic perception and understanding of the West. Because these images function as the foundation of the fantasy, Russian film characters feel that they know them intimately, but it becomes apparent that their knowledge is shallow and stereotypical.

In addition to these films, there are numerous others dating to the early and mid- 1990s in which the image of the West occupies a peripheral space. Films such as *Drum Roll* (Sergei Ovcharov, 1993), *Diuba-diuba* (Aleksandr Khvan, 1993), *The Foretelling* (El'dar Riazanov, 1994), *The House under the Starry Sky* (Sergei Soloyev, 1991), *Little Giant with a Big Sex Drive* (Nikolai Dostal', 1992), *Non-Love* (Valerii Rubinchuk, 1992), *Promised Skies* (El'dar Riazanov, 1991), and *The Time for Sadness Has Not Come Yet* (Sergei Sel'ianov, 1995) engage western characters or the western world at the level of plot and imagery. *The Foretelling* includes a French female protagonist (Irene Jacob) who appears to be the hero's muse and salvation. *Non-Love* employs a series of Marilyn Monroe images and a newsreel about the actress. In *Diuba-diuba*, after his death the male protagonist ends up in America: an ambiguous ending that can be interpreted as either his imaginary Eden or his nightmare. Sel'ianov demystifies the myth of the West alongside other myths of Soviet cultural icons (border patrol and railroad) in *The Time for Sadness Has Not Come Yet*. In his daydreaming, Ivanov, the main character, hijacks an airplane and commands a new destination – Paris. But after landing he realizes that he is not in front of the Eiffel Tower but in his home village.[14]

Since most of these films do not warrant a detailed discussion of their treatment of the western theme, for it is either integrated into the cinematic narratives only in passing or is inconsistently addressed, the following analysis focuses comparatively on only two films: Gaidai's *On Deribasovskaia the Weather is Fine, or, On Brighton Beach It's Raining Again* and Iurii Mamin's *Window to Paris*. They reveal different attitudes to the newly emerged opportunities to travel and live in the West, but at the same time they similarly betray the illusory nature of the fantasy or demonstrate how the fascination with the object-cause of desire is a chimera.

The former exemplifies the Russian enthusiasm and naiveté that characterizes the perestroika period. Using the genre of film comedy, Gaidai feeds and, at the same time, teases Russian expectations of a quick and warm friendship with America. Set in the later years of perestroika, the film presents the comic adventures of a KGB officer, Fedor Sokolov, and a CIA agent, Mary Star, and their shared efforts to combat the Russian Mafia in America. Their superiors follow the operation from Russia, where they have met to exchange information in a new spirit of cooperation. The political relaxation and friendship between Soviet and American leaders is demonstrated through the opening scene of the film, which presents the leaders of the 'free world' cordially talking on the hotline and expressing concern about the increased activities of the Soviet Mafia in the States. From the very beginning the director teases the viewer by showing the unimaginable friendly relationship between the two former cold war enemies.

A true product of the early transition period, when the fantasy of the welcoming West was still potent, the film's musical score and especially the song "Hello, America", which runs through the film as a leitmotif, betray Russian impatience to effortlessly engage in a new relationship with America or even a more daring fantasy of a perfect, cooperative world. The lyrics repeatedly reassure viewers: 'From the other coast, You seem like paradise, America, and You look OK...'

The film portrays America as a colourful and somewhat tasteless paradise in which Russians feel at home. Brighton Beach, off-screen marked by Russian culture visible in ethnic stores, is transformed on screen into a culturally exaggerated Russian neighborhood with the most superficial tourist manifestations: vodka, caviar, and Soviet souvenirs. Listening to the song's lyrics, viewers see Sokolov strolling along the streets of Brighton Beach, amazed at the Russian atmosphere of the American neighborhood. It seems that Russian fantasies and dreams of a prosperous and welcoming West have come true, and Russians have turned Brighton Beach into an affluent section of Russia. They have exported their culture, goods, and traditions, and while the director comically mocks this fantasy, one might say he also confirms it. In this seamless transformation of Brighton Beach into Russia and in the happy portrayal of Russians living there, one detects the impatience of adolescents taking the waiting out of the wishing. At the same time, matters are more complex than that.

Cinematically the gap between fantasy and reality is suggested through the technique of fast motion. Sokolov's quick and smooth adjustment to American culture is presented on screen as fast-motion movements in and out of stores, which he enters with boxes of Russian caviar, for instance, and then happily exits counting the cash he has obtained. Not only is this achieved through fast motion, but viewers can merely see the beginning and the result of Sokolov's bargaining (adjustment) process. The real encounter is off-screen. The fast motion and the off-screen operation destabilize the field of vision and suggest the impossible point of view of the gaze. In these scenes something defies the eye and it is there that one can locate the impossible free-floating Lacanian gaze.[15] From a fast-motion scene the director cuts to regular motion, where the vision is complete and normal. This cut or this transition from the destabilizing gaze to the normal eye shifts the passage from impossible to possible, from invisible to visible, from fantasy to reality. The clearly marked presence of the destabilizing gaze (in the fast-motion shots) transports viewers to western reality. The normal eye is deficient in following such a transition. Thus, the seamless nature of the transformation of America into Russia is exposed as an illusion and a new fantasy.

In addition to this cinematic technique, which in a way sustains the transition, American culture is reduced to stereotypical and emblematic constructions of otherness (which strives for sameness), represented only schematically and briefly in the film through background images of such traditional American symbols as the Statue of Liberty and McDonald's. They appear on the screen to show that the action takes place in America, but the life of Russians seems unaffected by the culture of the other. Such a portrayal of America hints at a superficial and shallow understanding of the other and suggests that even though new opportunities emerge for knowing and relating to the other, the distance between the object-cause of desire and the subject is still significant.

Similarly, the scenes in Russia blatantly deploy a stereotypical symbolism of Russia's uniqueness and exoticism. In these scenes the director presents the commanders' cooperation as amicable and joyful. He succumbs to the temptation of displaying hackneyed images of Russia, but with the comic manner of this presentation he also pokes fun at them. The exuberant and exotic edifice of a Russian bathhouse, Russian ballet, and the infinite quantities of vodka offered and consumed create a pleasurable (although difficult to fathom) experience for the American CIA agents. The overall portrayal of Russia as a tourist attraction for Americans exposes Russia's immature fantasies about its place in the world and especially its exotic culture, which the world has yet to discover.

While *On Deribasovskaia* teasingly constructs a positive global image for Russia and practically denies the differences of American culture by abridging it to stereotypical images, Mamin's *Window to Paris* attempts to recognize and respect cultural differences between Russia and the West. Yet the film reinforces rather than deconstructs cultural stereotypes. Because stereotypes keep the two worlds apart, the fantasy of the West, although altered by recent political and economic changes, retains its potency.

Epitomizing the theme of self/other (Russia/West) relations, Mamin's film visually and spatially constructs two worlds, Russian and French, and, unlike Gaidai, who presents Russian and American life as superficially compatible, Mamin poses many questions about the two worlds' differences and similarities. The main character, Nikolai Nikolaevich Chizhov (actor Sergei Dreiden), a teacher of aesthetics and music, is given a room in a communal apartment, where he meets the Gorokhov family and their friends, who enjoy life in a communal apartment with its atmosphere enhanced by vodka and songs. Much to their surprise, they discover a 'window' leading to the roof and soon thereafter realize that this 'window' takes them to the streets of Paris. The rest of the film portrays a series of absurd encounters between Russians in Paris and Parisians in St Petersburg.

Although the film rings a patriotic note and the director returns the Russian characters to Russia, the cinematic device of the 'window' functions not unlike the destabilizing gaze in Gaidai's film. Walking through the 'window' various characters appear fluid and out of focus. The window is needed to secure once again the transition from the impossible to the possible, from fantasy to reality. The cinematic device of the 'window' hinting at the presence of the gaze suggests that the distance between fantasy and reality is still there.

The Russian film critic, Irina Pavlova, argues that the director created two versions of the film – one for western and one for Russian distribution – because the two worlds are so different, and Russian and French people understand humor and sorrow differently. The film versions do not differ much, but the worlds represented in the film certainly do. The director shortened the western version and excluded several scenes that neither bring more information nor change the representations of Russia and France.

The film's cinematography – presenting St Petersburg's reality through grey and dim colours, run-down communal apartments, and decaying facades of building – constructs or reaffirms an image of Russia that the western collective imagination expects to see – an image of Russia as the other, which, Neumann and Wolff argue, Europe constructed over the centuries. The director presents this (Russian) other – emerging from long years of Soviet-style communism – to western viewers as uncivilized, irrational, ignorant, and violent. A scene shows Nicole, a French taxidermist who is the Gorokhovs' neighbor, by the 'window', in the streets of St Petersburg, where she is amazed and appalled at the dirt and the lack of civilized behaviour. There Nicole is cheated, made drunk, and arrested.

Mamin does not avoid stereotypes in the portrayal of Paris either. The streets of Paris appear on the screen as images from postcards: colourful, shiny, and beautiful. Such representation, reflected in the delight and astonishment of the Gorokhovs as they examine Paris's stores, meets the expectations of Russian viewers who have nurtured the fantasy of the western paradise.

At the same time, however, for many years the West was demonized as morally decaying, and the director does not avoid such a banal construction either. Nicole is a pretentious taxidermist and sculpts the favorite deceased pets of rich owners, bending over backwards to satisfy their caprices. When Chizhov, enchanted by Paris's spirit, lands a job, he discovers that he has been hired to play Mozart *sans pantalon*. The mercantilism of the capitalist system and the decadence of the established consumer culture have destroyed the true function of art and music. Unlike Gaidai, Mamin recognizes the disparity between the two worlds, but he succumbs to predetermined images of dissimilarities – easily recognized and accepted – of Russia and France.

Although Gaidai presents the two worlds as similar and compatible and locates the differences in tourist and symbolic representations, in the images of Sokolov and Mary he also pursues some preconceived ideas of distinction between Russian and American mentalities. While Mary is portrayed as practical, pragmatic, and reasonable, Sokolov is emotional (even irrational) but nonetheless effective in his methods as a KGB officer. Not surprisingly, the two develop feelings for each other, and at the end their love saves them as well as the rest of the world. While Mamin and Gaidai approach and construct the image of the other differently, the viewer still detects stereotypical representations of both Russia and the West in their films.

The two directors similarly chose to focus on problematic aspects of Russia's late- perestroika and early 1990s realities; but, again, their choices differ. Gaidai shows Russia's talent and ingenuity serving the nation's organized crime. Mamin, by contrast, exposes the clash of Russia's humanist tradition with the new vulgar consumerist style of life.

Gaidai ironically constructs the image of the Russian Mafia in America.[16] The Russian boss's nickname is the 'Artist' because he always assumes a new political face or a role and thus escapes all attempts by authorities to capture him. Viewers see him as Lenin, Stalin, and Brezhnev or Napoleon, Hitler, and even Othello when conducting meetings with his thugs, notably all from the Caucasus, Armenia, or Asia. The artistic perfection in the embodiment of the political figures speaks of artistic skills misguided and wasted or, even worse, employed for criminal ends.

Similarly, the scenes with the Gorokhovs in Paris, as well as the portrayal of the business school where Chizhov teaches, satirize the early entrepreneurial spirit of Russian society. The sardonic presentation of the transition from what Mamin perceives as a more spiritual Russian mentality (exemplified in the image of Chizhov) to a vulgar and empty consumerism (showcased in the Gorokhovs' dancing and singing Russian tunes in Paris and the new posters of foreign currency bills in the business school) exposes fantasies and fears produced by the drastic economic and political changes.

To soften the effect of such changes through cinematography and narrative, Mamin reinforces the idea that even though Russia experiences acute problems on the road to democracy, it is Russians' homeland and certainly has advantages over any western culture and society. Chizhov emotionally appeals to his students, who wish to remain in Paris, that they return to their 'bankrupt' country because it needs them. Film critic Karina Dobrotvorskaia doubts the sincerity of the appeal commenting: 'The wonderful actor, Dreiden, is not to blame for the unconvincing results' (85). She believes that the director tries to deceive the audience and perhaps himself.

The final scene raises even more questions about the decision to return to Russia. Back in St Petersburg, the cat that first showed them the 'window' to Paris disappears into a hole in a wall and the Russian characters desperately begin searching for a new 'window'. From a medium shot of the men drilling holes in the wall, the camera pulls back, showing them as insignificant figures at the bottom of a huge wall that spreads over the whole frame. There is no outlet, no sky, horizon, or hope.

Even though this film belongs to the category that rejects life in the West and tries to promote patriotic loyalty for the betterment of the country, many viewers, as well as critics, found the message unconvincing and superficial. The director's hesitation, which becomes apparent through the radical differences in the cinematic representations of the Russian and French worlds, as well as through the ending, parallels adolescent hesitation: the experience of the clash of different value systems and the temptation to taste the forbidden fruit (pleasure principle/id) that nonetheless is constrained by reason and ideals (reality principle/superego).

Conversely, in *On Deribasovskaia* Russians' enthusiasm for integration in the world after years of isolation manifests itself in the successful collaborative operation against the Mafia, the outcome of the relationship between Fedor and Mary, and the film's happy ending. Unlike other Russian films, which insist on the impossibility of such a union, this film suggests some problematic political and social ramifications of emerging globalization, but more visibly reveals the early naïve hopes of Russians who hastily embraced the opportunities to travel and live outside of the Soviet Union.

All the films discussed and mentioned above employ stereotypical cultural images, a combination of traits and symbols that viewers instantly recognize. Some ignore differences between Russia and the West, and eagerly embrace the West, offering magical solutions for a union between Russians and westerners. Other films focus more on the exceptionality of Russian culture in its encounters with the other and the world. But all of them employ clichéd images of the West that mask the ever-distant object of desire. Despite their differences, all the films reveal three entwined socio-psychological processes: 1) the uneasiness and hesitation in identity formation that require a search and acceptance of new values and self-definitions in a perplexing global world; 2) the continual attempt of the Russian collective imagination to seek out the other for its identity development; and 3) the still potent fantasy of the West (manifested in stereotypical images that either deny differences between the West and Russia or acknowledge differences but reinforce cold war perceptions of the world), which sustains the subject's sense of reality. Although Russia's political and economic conditions and consequently ideology changed after 1991, the fantasy still persists and structures existence in a confusing and turbulent time.

Employing the western cultural screen, the Russian collective imagination tries to build its new national image, which reflects and rejects, promotes and denounces western values and beliefs. These films reveal Russia's endeavour to find and construct a Russian national and cultural identity that corresponds to the new global world. Yet, the directors fall victim to predetermined thinking, images, and stereotypes. Even though the films' creators sometimes ironize cultural stereotypes, the films do not really deconstruct them. Rather, they achieve a very fragile balance between promoting and demoting cultural identity. Despite the understanding that stereotypes are considered notoriously unreliable in providing insight into other cultures, they reveal something important about the fantasmatic elements that support reality and ideology.

To return to the questions posed at the beginning of the chapter, Russian national identity during the period of transition is in flux. The space necessary for a dialogue between the self and the other is neglected by the impatience of the immature imagination to integrate old and new values. The idea of the other and the image of the other made easily available to the self are superficially perceived without the need to really know the other. Extreme and exaggerated portrayals of both the West and Russia speak of uncertainty, fears, and a still powerful fantasy.

Notes

1. Here I am guided by Kaja Silverman, who reformulated Jacques Lacan's concept of the mirror into a concept of a cultural screen, which offers a possibility of a distance between the individual and his/her projected image (1996, 31–36).
2. For more on this nineteenth-century division, its effect on the intelligentsia and the formation of Russian communism, see Berdiaev.
3. In his work *Inventing Eastern Europe*, Larry Wolff effectively pinpoints the cultural prejudice that drives contemporary pejorative West European attitudes towards Eastern Europe in general and Russia in

particular: 'Alienation is in part a matter of economic disparity, the wealth of Western Europe facing the poverty of Eastern Europe, but such disparity is inevitably clothed in the complex windings of cultural prejudice' (3). He studies the western construction of the idea of Eastern Europe from the eighteenth century to the present.

4. *New York Tribune*, 11 April 1853, 7; 12 April 1853, 4; 14 June 1853, 6; 19 August 1853, 5–6; 2 February 1854, 4; 20 February 1954, 4 (quoted in Bloom 154).

5. *Briefwechsel*, III, 127 (quoted in Bloom 160).

6. For a more detailed analysis of the media relations and images of the Soviet Union and the United States, see Zassoursky.

7. In 1925 Sergei Eisenstein's film *Strike* represented the fall of Russian capitalism, juxtaposing the empty life of the imperial merchant classes and their brutality with the hard conditions and the misery of the strikers.

8. Throughout the book I have spelled Lacan's names for registers (imaginary, symbolic, and real) with no capital letters, except the concept Other (the Law) when it is used in strictly Lacanian sense.

9. All Russian quotations are translated by the author unless otherwise indicated.

10. For more on anti-Americanism in Russian cinema, see 'Nightingales on 17th Street' (Stishova and Sirivlia).

11. Segal offers a very persuasive analysis of the western behaviour of splitting and projection in her book, *Psychoanalysis, Literature and War* (157–69).

12. Bruce Grant's English translation of 'prikhvatizatsiia' as 'grabification' captures well the spirit of the time when all state enterprises were up for grabs, or exposed to unprecedented and unlawful transformation of state to private property.

13. Other, even less remarkable, films that reflect the newly born Russian discovery of America include *American Boy* (1992) and *Alaska, Sir!* (1992), even though the latter addresses it by way of the past.

14. For plot summaries and brief discussions of these films, see Lawton (2005).

15. For more on the Lacanian gaze and its development and application in film, see Lacan (1981), Žižek (2001) and Vighi.

16. For more on Gaidai's comic style, see Aleksandr Prokhorov's analysis of the director's early comedies.

2

The Russian Hero: Fantasies of Wounded National Pride

Adolescence is a crucial period of time during which critical elements of the personality become shaped and various emotional and mental changes, as well as psychological defenses, occur. There are also different stages within adolescence such as puberty and early adolescence, mid-adolescence, and late-adolescence, confirming the complex nature of the period (Waddell 1998a, 141 – 175). It is not my goal to provide a complete and exhaustive study of adolescence and to seek corresponding psychological elements in the Russian collective imagination of the transition to democracy. At the same time, however, there are noticeable analogies that I find significant to point out in order to shed light on the psychological cost of the transition and of Russian national identity transformations. In analyzing the construction of both the main protagonist and the other as well as the formation of national aggressive sentiments in Balabanov's *Brother*, *Brother 2*, and *War*, this chapter draws attention to corresponding adolescent psychological states: acute projective mechanisms, increased aggressive urges, understanding of the world in extreme divisions of good and bad, and idealization of the self.

The second thread that runs through the discussion of Balabanov's films is the outline of the collapse of the old fantasy and the emergence of a new one, which structures identifactory relations. The chapter reveals how the fantasy of the demonized/idealized West breaks down only to evolve into another one that supports Russia's moral superiority over the commercialized and shallow West. Although the new fantasy in a way resembles cold war perceptions and sentiments, I point out how the focus of both the idealization of Russia and the denunciation of the West has shifted.

At the beginning of the 1990s western advisers, especially from the United States and the International Monetary Fund, preached liberalization, stabilization, and rapid privatization as the three pillars of radical reform strategy. The Yeltsin administration hurried to implement these capitalist conditions for creating a market economy without preparing the underlying institutions or institutional infrastructures (Stiglitz 139). As a result, the radical reform strategy fared less than well. Economic conditions worsened with each year, and by the middle of the decade enthusiasm for quick changes and expectation of swift improvement in the standard of living faded. The economy grew worse as lawless and unregulated capitalism settled in. Russian industrial production dropped nearly 60 per cent, an even greater loss than during World War II (Stiglitz 143). While national economic treasures dwindled, the disparity between the rich and the poor grew as whatever money remained was inequitably divided up among the rich and powerful. Oligarchs using political influence managed to secure assets in the billions, but the average Russian received a much smaller fraction of the national wealth. Big money was concentrated in the big cities, where companies such as Mercedes, Gucci, and Armani offered imported luxury goods. According to a survey conducted by the World Bank, while in 1989 only 2 per cent of Russians lived in poverty, in 1998 23.8 per cent lived on $2 per day and 40 per cent had less than $4 per day (Stiglitz 153). Joseph Stiglitz pinpoints the economic discrepancies and problems when he writes: 'The traffic jam of Mercedes in a country with a per capita income of $4,730 (as it was in 1997) is a sign of a sickness, not health' (154).

Despair and depression replaced the energy and illusions that had been prevalent at the end of perestroika and the beginning of the transition period. Aleksandr Etkind remarks:

> When wild capitalism replaced cradle-to-grave security, many people were frightened by the revolutionary forces they had helped unleash. Blue and white collar workers now faced unemployment; intellectuals found their spiritual bonds threatened by inequality; artists lamented their lost state subsidies; the once pampered military forces saw their prestige take a nose dive; collective farmers felt reluctant to strike out on their own as private producers; and nearly everybody felt the void inside. (1996, 122)

As Freud maintained, the basic function of fantasy is to fill the void between desire and satisfaction (1953, 12: 215–26). But the fantasy of the 'bright future' of socialism or of the demonized/idealized West, which had kept Russians satisfied with their social reality evaporated as Etkind's quote aptly demonstrates. The distance between the subject and fantasy shrank to a minimum and when Russians had to face the tempting and threatening West (which in a way infiltrated Russian life), the imaginary nature of this fantasy became readily apparent. Almost everyone became disillusioned with the present and the immediate future, which offered nothing promising or glamorous. The West and its economic and political system neither welcomed Russians abroad nor assisted effectively in improving living standards in Russia. On the contrary, as already noted, the conditions worsened drastically. The fantasy, which had served as a screen against the direct intrusion of the real, broke down. The trauma of the real, perceived as a nightmarish reality (or as the 'void inside' Etkind describes), threatened to overcome people's lives. In other words, Russians experienced 'reality after reality is deprived of its support in fantasy' (Žižek 1997, 66).

Balabanov's *Brother, Brother 2*, and *War* came to the rescue to fill this void and offer a new fantasy to protect viewers from the intrusion of the real. Balabanov uses a variety of narrative, stylistic, and thematic techniques in his films to construct a fantasmatic and idealized model of a national(ist) hero, a defender of everything Russian. Critics such as Daniil Dondurei (1998), Andrew Horton (2001), Elena Stishova, Irina Liubarskaia, and Natalia Sirivlia have already discussed the ideological nature of the films and the socio-psychological effect they had on Russian viewers. I position my argument in the cultural and psychological dimensions of globalization in general and Russian westernization in particular. I argue that while in *Brother* there is still some ambiguity about the nature of the hero and the identity boundaries of self/other, this ambiguity disappears in *Brother 2* and *War*. Furthermore, the latter films construct masculinity perceived as moral strength beyond physical qualities. Masculinity is also a key element for the resurrection of national pride and identity and for the construction of a new fantasy that structures power and identifactory relations. In the creation of a moral masculine identity (different from the western physical type and morally superior to it), Balabanov's films introduce a new fantasy of a feeble and inadequate West, against which Russian national identity sustains and defines itself. In the discussion of masculinity and how it operates in later Russian action films, I evoke other film and television examples (Egor Mikhalkov-Konchalovsky's *Antikiller* (2002) and Aleksei Sidorov's *Brigade* (2002)), which support my argument.

In Search of a National Hero

After the disintegration of the Soviet Union, the Russian film industry declined drastically.[1] In 1992, Dondurei, chief editor of the Russian film journal *Iskusstvo kino*, urged film-makers to work on a national cinema and create a 'national hero', attributing part of the decline to weak cinema mythology:[2]

> There is no such thing as a national hero and nobody cares to create him...What must be done is to create a national mythology instead of wasting time on creating films that are not even mentioned, let alone attended...The Soviet masters of culture depict their own society as one of criminals and in a masochistic way reopen its wounds. (1992, 27)

In 1997, Balabanov created a present-day Russian hero, although perhaps not exactly the kind Dondurei had in mind. Beginning his career with literary adaptations such as *Happy Days* (1991) and *The Castle* (1994), Balabanov claimed that he wanted to 'take intellectual material and make it a thriller' (Faraday 168).[3] In this peculiar genre of 'intellectual thriller' the emphasis fell more on 'intellectual' than on 'thriller', but Balabanov soon found better-suited material for the thriller in his *Brother* films. In an interview with Faraday about the direction in which Russian film-making was moving, Balabanov says:

> Mostly emotional and energetic. It's not intellectual anymore. The time of Bergman and Fellini and Tarkovsky is over: they're very boring now. People want to see real feelings and energy. They don't want to think. Filmmaking is a mass industry and people want to see films that are stimulating and interesting. (Faraday 168)

In *Brother* and *Brother 2*, Balabanov moved away from the 'intellectual thriller' and created in its place an action thriller using material from present-day Russian reality. Russians define the genre as *kriminal'nyi boevik* (crime-action). The gaze of the Russian imagination indulges in visual pleasure awakened by anti-western (and in *Brother 2* more specifically anti-American) feelings and energy that the films evoke. The two films – record-breakers for the time – wildly appealed to viewers (perhaps effectively containing their anxious gaze), pleasantly surprised the distributors, and inspired heated debates among critics. *Brother* received the Grand Prize at *Kinotavr*, the most important Russian film festival, as well as compliments and praise in Cannes. *Brother 2* was one of the early Russian box office successes, collecting over a million dollars from the first few months in theatres, which is nothing compared to western returns, but was a history-making sum for the post-Soviet film industry.[4]

Since *Brother*, Balabanov has shot *Of Freaks and Men*, *Brother 2*, *War*, *River* (2002), *Blindman's Buff* (*Zhmurki*) (2005), and *It Doesn't Hurt* (*Mne ne bol'no*) (2006), which belong to various genres. While the *Brother* films and *War* address present-day problems, dexterously construct a Russian hero, and share a like-minded cinematic style, *Of Freaks and Men* and *River* turn viewers' attention

Sergei Bodrov, Jr (as Danila) in Balabanov's Brother.

to the past and display different screen properties.[5] Employing Russia's best actors and stars even for the supporting roles, *Blindman's Buff* (*Zhmurki*), a criminal comedy, exposes the stupidity and cruelty of the criminal world.

I focus here mainly on *Brother, Brother 2*, and *War*, which created a cult character and turned actor Sergei Bodrov, Jr into a cult figure in Russia mythologizing aggressive and xenophobic masculinity that marginalizes women.[6] Openly expressing anti-western and nationalistic attitudes, the three films share similar cinematographic and editing styles as they tackle contemporary issues. But while the *Brother* films more closely follow the genre of the western action, *War* combines action with techniques of the war film, an approach with a strong Russian tradition. Balabanov, it would seem, has adopted a socio-psychological angle and utilized a genre in which the social and psychological anxieties of his nation have found perfect expression.

Brother introduces a young man, Danila (Sergei Bodrov, Jr), who has just finished his military service in southern Russia. His mother sends him to St Petersburg to live with his older brother, Viktor (Viktor Sukhorukov), who, viewers soon discover, is a hit man. Without any hesitation or scruples, Viktor involves Danila in the criminal world, causing Danila to risk his life. The younger brother, however, having just returned from war, cannot be easily trapped in Viktor's plan and effectively deals with his assassins. After discovering that his brother has set him up, Danila spares Viktor's life, gives him some money, and sends him to live with their mother before himself leaving for Moscow.

Aleksei Chadov (Ivan) delivering justice in Balabanov's War.

In *Brother 2* viewers follow Danila from Moscow to Chicago, where he travels to avenge the brother of a fellow soldier from the Chechen War. In the sequel the narrative, characters, and cinematography become more one-sided and flat, whereas the anti-western and anti-foreign ideology deepens and grows more aggressive – a move that, disturbingly, secured the film's huge success with audiences.

In *War*, Ivan (Aleksei Chadov), a young Russian, while in prison awaiting a sentence, describes his experience as a soldier in Chechnya. Captured by a Chechen warlord and released, he returns to Chechnya to help a British actor, John, locate the warlord and pay ransom money for his fiancée, Margaret, also captured by the warlord.

Brother introduced a new type of hero in post-Soviet film: the hit man who follows his own moral standards and becomes a Russian Robin Hood under the new social and political conditions.[7] The hero protects the poor (usually only ethnic Russians) and delivers justice, yet he upholds no coherent moral principles and kills callously. The Russian critic Evgenii Margolit compares Danila in *Brother* to Chapaev, a revolutionary hero and film character from the 1930s (*Chapaev* 1936, dirs. 'Brothers' Vasiliev) with almost mythic popularity (58). Andrew Horton defines Danila as a 'geeky-looking youth' who has just finished his mandatory army service (2001). In similar terms, Julian Graffy characterizes him as 'experienced yet unformed, a killer with the innocent face of a Young Pioneer' (2000, 44). While the Russian critic is preoccupied with the character's huge success and popularity among Russian audiences, Horton and Graffy describe him in less than flattering terms, as a killer who looks like a nerd. Accustomed to the exceptional physique of the hero (often the bodybuilder) in Hollywood action films, these western scholars respond accordingly to the average and unimpressive appearance of Danila. In her study on masculinity in film, Yvonne Tasker insists: 'The white male bodybuilder as star has been one of the most visible aspects of recent American action cinema' (73). This aspect, however, appears to be irrelevant for the box office success of the *Brother* films, which emphasize different character qualities that I shall discuss later.

Viewers of *Brother* know nothing with certainty about Danila's past. He claims to have served at 'the Headquarters', but his skills in assembling handmade guns make one question the accuracy of this information. One may argue that Danila seeks guidance and is even concerned with existential and philosophical questions. He listens when his brother Viktor advises him to buy better clothing and mentions that Moscow is a bigger city than St Petersburg, with better opportunities. After being wounded, Danila asks Hoffmann, his German friend, about the meaning of life: 'Listen German, you're smart. Tell me, why do we live?'[8] In *Brother*, Danila's character suggests a romantic philosopher.

Following the popularity of the film and its main character, and perhaps attempting to better serve the anxieties and fantasies of the Russian collective mind, Balabanov deprives Danila of intricacy and ambiguity in *Brother 2*. In this sequel, a confident and omnipotent male character replaces the romantic philosopher. The character's past and his participation in the Chechen War are plainly spelled out. His best friends now are his fellow soldiers. It is Danila who advises, even issues orders, to Viktor, who this time assumes an inferior role. The hero no longer asks questions about the meaning of life because he knows the answers: 'Power is in justice, not in money.' The painful problem of money for impoverished Russian viewers becomes marginalized. While money is still a significant dilemma in reality, the film offers a fantasy to effectively deal with it. Truth and justice (not money or physical strength) make people like Danila powerful. Whistling a patriotic song he heard at a school celebration in Moscow, Danila climbs the emergency staircase of a Chicago skyscraper and, after confronting an American criminal boss, delivers justice.

Balabanov similarly constructs the major characters in *War*. Masculine moral qualities – decency, loyalty, and love for Russia – are emphasized and promoted at the expense of complexity and depth, two features typical for three-dimensional cinematic characters. The Russian Captain Medvedev (actor Sergei Bodrov, Jr), a captive of the Chechen warlord Aslan, is portrayed as the ideal Russian: stoic, spiritually strong, and honourable. As a continuation of Balabanov's depiction of the Russian hero that began with Danila, the Captain is wounded and almost immobile, but irradiates strength and calmness. His image – stillness, physical incapacity – visibly contrasts with the American image of the bodybuilder hero: the pointedly named Captain Medvedev possesses moral and spiritual power superior to any physical strength.[9] Part of his idealized image stems from Ivan's references to him, invariably in terms of admiration and loyalty. When Ivan tries to explain to the journalist his motives for returning to Chechnya, he insists that money, unlike revenge, was not a motivation. Most likely, however, he went back for the Captain.

Ivan is also portrayed in a positive light, his courage highlighted by its juxtaposition with John's weakness and inadequacy. Telling the journalist about their adventures on the way back to Chechnya, Ivan emphasizes with bewildered aversion the fact that John was shooting a film while they were trying to survive and rescue John's fiancée. Even worse, after their success, thanks to Ivan and Captain Medvedev, John becomes famous and rich selling his story, whereas Ivan awaits his sentence for killing Russian citizens while a civilian. *War* revives the familiar theme of western mercantilism projected against the superiority of Russian morals.

Balabanov's type of hero – physically average but morally superior – no doubt assuages anxieties provoked by Russia's complex economic and political conditions and by difficulties in the development of the Russian collective identity during the period of transition. Economically and militarily marginalized in today's global world, the Russian collective imagination finds consolation in the superiority of its values.[10] Though Danila's persona differs physically from heroes of American action films such as those portrayed by Sylvester Stallone, for instance, the films *Brother* and *Brother 2* alleviate anxieties and fears the same way that 'Rambo is seen to cinematically correct the national humiliation of the defeat in Vietnam' (Tasker 93).

Also not very muscular is the body presentation of other Russian film stars who owe their reputations to the roles of cops or criminals. It is interesting to outline how the example of masculinity set by Balabanov's films is utilized in later Russian action films. Mikhalkov-Konchalovsky's *Antikiller* and *Antikiller 2: Antiterror* (2003) outdid the box office success of the *Brother* films and created an opposite type of hero: morally very different from Danila. *Antikiller* offers Russian viewers an ex-cop-superman (actor Gosha Kutsenko) as the main protagonist and, judging by the ratings, convincingly satisfies the desire for control and order. The character from *Antikiller* so much contradicts Danila's philosophy to take the law into his own hands that a Russian critic called it 'antibrat' (antibrother) (Komm 20). Accused of unlawful investigation techniques, Major Korenev, the antikiller ex-cop, served jail time and after being released he returns to Moscow to find a new world governed by criminals and gangs. Shaken by the death of his friends, he opts to reinstall law and order.[11]

A highly rated television miniseries, *Brigade*, challenges the viewer's desire for order and control and offers instead romanticized criminals, who stand in opposition to the Robin Hood nature of Danila or the cop Major Korenev. Four high-school friends reunite after Sasha Belov (actor Sergei Bezrukov), their lead man, returns home from serving in the army. The young men, 'victims of

Sergei Bezrukov (as the criminal boss Sasha Belov) in Brigade.

circumstances', engage in criminal activities and become a thriving criminal organization in the underground world. Actors Gosha Kutsenko, the antikiller cop, and Sergei Bezrukov, the charming criminal boss, do not have the bodybuilder muscular physique of Hollywood action-thriller stars. Undoubtedly there are differences in the appearances of Danila, Major Korenev, and Sasha Belov. Danila (Sergei Bodrov was 26 years old when shooting *Brother*) is the youngest of them and appears innocent and youthful without well-defined manly characteristics. Major Korenev is lean and strong; Sasha Belov appears boyish and full of energy. But none of them show any evident muscularity and their masculine performativity, while powerful, is not exactly hypermuscular.

Discussing Viktor Erofeev's novel *Russian Beauty* and especially its failure to inspire the interests of Russian critics and readers, Nadezhda Azhgikhina and Helena Goscilo contend that Russian readers have a different hierarchy of values from western readers, placing inner life higher than appearance (Azhgikhina and Goscilo 94). Even if these remarks concern the perception of female beauty, the popularity of physically average Russian action-film actors suggests that Russians value strong spiritual qualities rather than physical strength. Interestingly, such priorities persist even after ten to fifteen years of massive Hollywood presence in the Russian movie theatres, which has undoubtedly shaped the tastes of Russian viewers. The Hollywood aesthetic powerfully evokes a link between muscularity (hardness) and phallic power. Scholars associate the hardness of the muscular body (or poses that mimic hard lines and angular shapes) with symbolic phallic power (Walters). This association, however, does not ring true for Russian viewers, at least when Russian actors are displayed on the screen.

I have already suggested that Danila derives phallic power from his commitment to a very personal and subjective justice. It is particularly significant that Russian viewers associate phallic power not so much with imagery but with values enforced and defended by male characters. Major Korenev also pursues justice, though in a different way, trying to restore law and order and fighting against the killers of cops. Sasha Belov is concerned with justice, too, justice that would guarantee survival and success under the circumstances of a murky economy and corrupt politics. When campaigning for a political office, Belov addresses Russian viewers at a televised political debate and 'honestly' admits that not all of his activities are legal but insists that he believes in and fights for justice. Firm and unconditional commitment to justice compensates for the physical (and moral) 'imperfection' of Russian action stars and their bodies.

The 'Russianness' that unites all three characters also functions to offset the lack of muscular bodies. They share the same turbulent recent history of the Soviet Union's disintegration and the period of transition. At the films' openings Danila and Sasha Belov have just finished their military service and embark on their lives in a society that offers them neither present security nor future promises. *Antikiller* opens with a medium shot of Korenev pledging allegiance to the Internal Affairs Services of the Soviet Union against the background of a red flag with the hammer and sickle symbol. The personal history of all three heroes becomes intertwined with the (military) history of the Soviet Union and Russia. In the context of the tumultuous and traumatic national history, their struggle for justice defines the ideological configurations of nationhood and masculinity.

However, in Russian action thrillers justice is never achieved solely by an individual character but is a result of a collectively negotiated masculinity that positions brotherhood above individualism.[12] All of the discussed films' narratives subordinate individualism to collective action and fraternal bonds.

Gosha Kutsenko (Major Korenev) in Egor Mikhalkov-Konchalovsky's *Antikiller*.

Although not to the same degree, Danila, Major Korenev, and Sasha Belov all cherish their friends. The elevated and revered brotherhood that Susan Larsen notices in the *Brother* films applies to the others as well. 'The film conflates family and national bonds as the basis of Danila's impromptu vigilante justice throughout the film, yet Victor's many betrayals of Danila's trust suggests that brotherly love – like its national equivalent patriotism – is only a convenient fiction, not a moral absolute' (Larsen 2003, 504). Yet this fiction, extended to the bonds of fraternal unions, operates effectively in Russian action films and evokes powerful identification with the male heroes.

All films discussed in this chapter, but especially the *Brother* films and *War*, consolidate the dominant aesthetic and cultural priorities of national politics that emphasize the superior position of the heterosexual Russian male over other ethnic or gender manifestations. Balabanov's films establish a cinematic structure based on consistent hostility and aggression toward the other and on the marginalization of women. Danila's resentment of Jews, 'darkies' (Russian citizens with non-Russian ethnicity, usually from the Caucasus), Americans, and the French is clearly spelled out in the *Brother* films. 'I'm not your brother, black-assed worm', Danila quietly but rather determinately says to Southerners who dare to ride the tramcar without tickets, as he forces them to pay the fine at gunpoint. The visual presentation of the group of men in the train also constructs Danila as a superior specimen. While Danila is confidently standing and pointing a gun at them, they are begging for mercy as they almost fall on their knees.[13]

Danila's sexual potency inflates the construction of heterosexual masculinity in the *Brother* films. He casually engages in sexual relations with all women whom he meets and effortlessly wins over all of them. In *Brother* he sleeps with Kat and Sveta, very opposite and yet ordinary young women, while in *Brother 2*, his mere appearance (although insignificant) is enough to infatuate the pop star Irina Saltykova (played by Irina Saltykova herself). In Chicago he saves the Russian prostitute Dasha, who decides to follow him and go back to her country. He even has a sexual encounter with the African American television reporter Lisa Jeffry (also playing herself). The weak female presence in the cinematic narrative and the objectification of the female bodies enhance Danila's manly power, and, through his sexual conquest in the United States, the director objectifies and feminizes black America. Hence Danila's masculinity assumes national proportions and consolidates national identity desires.

A rhetorical strategy operates in these films to enable a construction of masculinity that detracts attention from undesirable characteristics. The male characters' Russianness, commitment to the cause of justice, membership in larger fraternal communities, and protective attitudes toward women are all perceived as positive traits of the masculine and national ideal. This strategy leaves their dominance over women, their xenophobia, and, last but not least, their violent behaviour unquestioned. Extreme violence in these films is redefined as acceptable and even necessary. The violence, which is not there only to please the audience, increases in the sequels to *Brother* and *Antikiller* and becomes an important part of the films. Violence also becomes rampant in the later part of the *Brigade* miniseries.

These somewhat contradictory elements of masculinity and national identity correspond to the profound sense of contradictions and inadequacies that confront the adolescent when adjusting to the world – an adjustment that requires achievements, recognition, and accepting responsibilities. Adolescents often feel confused and unequal to the task (of adjustment), as their state of mind often oscillates between inadequacy (feelings increased by the rivalry of peers) and 'feelings of omnipotence (which gives them an exaggerated sense of their abilities)' (Dubinsky 99). The construction of moral masculinity, evoked to answer a sense of inadequacy and to oppose the presumed dominance of the West, and enacted to project omnipotence manifested in super-heroes' violent conquests, suggests a parallel with the adolescent state of mind. The rivalry of peers, or in this case, the newly emerged supremacy of the West, evokes both a sense of inadequacy and, as a reaction to it, a feeling of omnipotence, which is secured in the creation of the new hero. Feeling inadequate to the task of matching the financial and military power of the West (America in particular), the Russian collective imagination conceives a morally superior and omnipotent male character.

Interpreted from another angle, the construction of moral masculinity becomes a conduit of nationalist, racist, and sexist sentiments (as has been already noted in the discussion of Danila's portrayal and will become even more clear in the rest of the chapter). These sentiments became more powerful, paradoxically, after the collapse of the Soviet system, when the former Eastern bloc embarked on the road to democracy and political ideology was expected to overcome the hostility of the cold war. Elaborating at length on the deficiencies of today's democracies, Žižek explains:

> Here we have again an exemplary case of the Lacanian logic of not-all where the universal function is founded upon an exception: the ideal leveling of all social differences, the production of the citizen, the subject of democracy, is possible only through an allegiance to some particular

national Cause. If we apprehend this Cause as the Freudian Thing (*das Ding*), materialized enjoyment, it becomes clear why it is precisely 'nationalism' that is the privileged domain of the eruption of enjoyment into the social field: the national Cause is ultimately the way subjects of a given nation organize their collective enjoyment through national myths. (1992, 165)

The Thing of materialized enjoyment produces the fantasy of Russian moral superiority and organizes members of the Russian nation around collectively recognized national myths. This process also exposes the very nature of fantasy as national and particular; fantasy always resists universalization. Žižek argues that the failure of democracy lies in the eruption of particular (national) sentiments and fantasies. These sentiments surpass identifications with social or human rights values that reach beyond ethnic and national borders (1992, 162–69). The identification with national myths, constructed against the myths and enjoyment of the other, is further revealed in the construction of the enemy and the explosion of national pathos manifested in Balabanov's films.

The Enemy

The perception of masculine (national) identifications in Balabanov's films is defined against the background of self/other (re)evaluation. The *Brother* films and *War* present simple and realistic narratives that unfold chronologically. *War* employs an on-screen narrator, Ivan, who talks to a journalist from his cell while his voice-over frames the story. Dondurei, a critic who closely follows Balabanov's film career, argues that the director approached *Brother* as a small-budget film. The director held little pretence about elegance and cinematic quality and hardly anticipated the phenomenal process of identification that occurred for Russian viewers (Dondurei 1998). In *War*, however, the director obviously wanted to secure this identification and used both *mimesis* and *diegesis* in structuring the story; hence the narrator has a vested interest in helping to convey the message and to portray the situation from his point of view, that is, from the 'true' Russian point of view.

In *Brother* the story takes place almost entirely in St Petersburg and only once shows Danila's hometown in the provinces. St Petersburg is marked in the Russian imagination as the Russian 'window to the West'. Embarking on the crucial process of westernization of Russian culture, history, and identity, in 1703 Peter the Great built the city with western architectural style and ambience. In this city, Danila meets Kat, who hangs out at McDonald's and takes him to a party with foreigners. On his first day in the city, Danila befriends Hoffmann, a German who stayed in Russia after World War II to disprove the Russian proverb: 'What is good for Russians is death for Germans.' Here Danila also encounters Hoffmann's friends at a Lutheran cemetery, a reminder of the other in the predominantly Russian Orthodox tradition. Here Danila's brother acquired the nickname 'the Tartar'. Danila is hostile to all other non-Russians but feels comfortable with Hoffmann and his friends. In his article "I'm not your brother, worm...," Dondurei mentions that Germans are pitied in the film: having lost the war, they now live in the cemetery. In other words, they are weak and can be Danila's friends even though as Germans they are outsiders (Dondurei 1998, 66).

Following Anne Norton's insistence on studying boundary markers, where self and the other ambiguously overlap, one can look into this unusual companionship between Danila and Hoffmann and can address the role of the 'liminar' groups for collective identity formation. Russians today, given their economic and political marginality in the world, can afford to compare and define

Balabanov's War.

themselves in relation to Germans living on their territory. In *Universe of the Mind: A Semiotic Theory of Culture*, the Russian thinker Yuri Lotman discusses a similar example for collective identity formation. Russians in the seventeenth century referred to people at their territorial borders as *svoi pagany* (our pagans) and thus defined themselves, among other ways, in relation to people perceived as inferior in a religious sense, and yet who were close and familiar. On the one hand, this comparison boosts the perception of the self; on the other hand, it complicates the categories us/them and self/other. This ambiguity appears only in *Brother*; in the other two films the boundaries of self/other become clearly marked as Balabanov attempts to place the other in various locations.

Unlike in *Brother*, which is largely limited to St Petersburg, the events in *Brother 2* take place between Moscow and Chicago, and in *War* between Chechnya, London, St Petersburg, Moscow, Tobolsk, and Vladikavkaz. The stronger the hostility against 'outsiders' grows, the more geography is employed to localize 'outsiders'. In these two films Russian resentment toward the other acquires spatial expression. Balabanov noticeably divides the space into 'ours' and 'theirs', localizing Russian animosity to anything foreign and giving it a geographic setting. Nationalistic fervor demands the spatial construction of all outsiders, be they Americans, British, or Chechens.

In his provocative study of the cultural dimensions of globalization, Appadurai advances the idea that globalization is acutely historical, irregular, and, paradoxically, a localizing process. He understands locality to be a structure of feeling caused by forms of international activity. He argues further that 'all locality building has a moment of colonization...in the sense that it involves the assertion of socially (often ritually) organized power over places and settings that are viewed as potentially chaotic or rebellious' (Appadurai 183–84). Even though Appadurai is concerned more with the 'production of neighborhoods', one can detect a similar process of producing locality in Balabanov's films, especially in *Brother 2* and *War*. To be more precise, Balabanov constructs localities not so much in the colonizing sense as in the differentiating sense – a differentiation threatened by international activities, by globalization. Russian localities, established in *Brother 2* and *War* with shots of Red Square, an Orthodox church, or the Kremlin, are represented as neutral or, one can argue, evidence of Russian superiority. By contrast, the foreign localities are saturated with negative connotations and sentiments. In *Brother 2* Viktor calls the personnel at airport control 'morons' and, as Mark Lipovetskii has noted, most scenes in Chicago depict African Americans as uncivilized, primitive, and threatening (2000). Likewise, in *War* the Chechen scenes are filled with the most gruesome cruelty against Russians and with 'barbarous' customs, such as the slaughtering and skinning of sheep. I do not claim that Balabanov's production of locality has a distinct moment of colonization, although there are certain similarities. The scenes mentioned above, trivial cultural stereotypes that exploit the shallow and often inaccurate perception of the other, mainly attempt to divide the world and thus localize it. Today the collective Russian experience lacks the confidence of a great colonizing power of the sort it might have felt during the Soviet period and even further back during the times of the Russian Empire. In this context, Balabanov's attempts at localizing indicate a reaction to the lack of confidence and a need to create boundaries to guard identity under the volatile conditions of cultural and economic invasion.

Margolit points out that in *Brother* all characters are clearly divided into 'ours' and 'non-ours' (59). Even though one can agree with this division, the criteria for such a distinction are not quite clear; they are based on neither entirely national nor social characteristics. The German is 'good'; the Russian thugs, Jews, and Southerners are 'bad'. Viktor – 'good' or 'bad' – is saved only because he is Danila's brother. Kat's drug problems and taste for McDonald's make her 'bad', but at the same time she is Danila's friend, and he cares about her. In *Brother 2* and *War* the characters are not only divided into us versus them, but the division is drawn by national identity and social status. People lack individuality or psychological substance and are presented on the screen as ciphers. No one resists Danila, no one attacks him or shoots at him, because none of the characters are 'real people', but, rather, 'ideological phantoms' (Lipovetskii 2000, 57). Evgenii Gusiatinskii compares the construction and representation of the 'enemies' in *Brother 2* to the representation of Germans in Soviet films about World War II. They were all stupid and looked like complete idiots (Gusiatinskii). In *War*, which Horton calls 'Balabanov's most nationalist film to date', the variations and the division of characters become even more simplified and clear (2002). All non-Russians, Chechens, and British are bad; Russians are good, with the exception of a corrupted translator in the Foreign Ministry and a couple of crooks.[14]

In *Brother*, Danila declares that he is 'not wild about Jews' and refuses to have anything in common with Southerners, while he despises and even recognizes no difference between Americans and the French. Expanding the boundaries of resentment, in *Brother 2*, Viktor does not like Filipp Kirkorov, a contemporary Russian pop singer, because he uses make-up and is Romanian. When corrected about Kirkorov's nationality (Bulgarian), Viktor answers in the usual way, 'What's the difference?' The hatred in the first film directed only against such 'traditional enemies' as Jews, Chechens, and westerners spreads over in the second to include all non-Russians – Romanians, Bulgarians, and Ukrainians. When Viktor runs into Ukrainians in Chicago he refers to them with a pejorative ethnic term and calls them Nazi collaborators. Viktor's aggression resonates with Russian viewers' anxieties, which can be explained as a kind of mourning process that has not been worked out.

Romanians, Bulgarians, and Ukrainians were perceived as part of the Soviet empire, but these parts were lost after the collapse of Soviet communism. Now the unconscious wish to restore these lost appendages of the imagined empire constructs them as enemies and generates aggression against them.

Explained in other terms, the stronger the feeling of the imagined threat to national identity and the experience of national marginalization, the more intense the need becomes to create clear boundaries that protect identity. The anxieties are registered as a rigid insistence on difference, although this difference is deprived of any convincing substance. The other is condemned as different and, even worse, as evil for no reason other than its otherness. Arguing about a similar construction of otherness in the film *Something Wild* (1961), Jameson writes: 'The modern gothic, in other words – whether in its rape-victim or its political paranoid forms – depends absolutely in its central operation on the construction of evil...Evil is here, however, the emptiest form of sheer Otherness (into which any type of social content can be poured at will)' (1991, 290). Balabanov's films endorse a shallow and trivial idea: Russians have high moral standards, love their motherland, and are not corrupted by money; therefore, they are better than anybody else in the world. Apparently, the collective mind experiencing an imagined invasion needs no credible proof or explanation. A naked statement of difference suffices to pass moral judgment on the other and to allay anxieties.

In his study *The Conquest of America: The Question of the Other*, Todorov sheds light on how one may locate the problematics of alterity. He suggests three approaches:

> First of all, there is a value judgment (an axiological level): the other is good or bad...Secondly, there is the action of rapprochement or distancing in relation to the other (a praxeological level): I embrace the other's values, I identify myself with him; or else I identify the other with myself...Thirdly, I know or am ignorant of the other's identity (this would be the epistemic level). (185)

Todorov operates here within a mode of thinking grounded in the premise that if communities and nations come to know one another better, they will also avoid animosity and act less violently. However, it seems that Balabanov, adjusting to mainstream anxieties, completely ignores the praxeological and the epistemic levels of the problematics of alterity and positions his characters only at the axiological level. What provokes such anxieties, which reject the other without any attempt to know it better or comprehend it?

According to Klein, the ego employs a variety of defense mechanisms to protect itself against the overwhelming fear of obliteration; one such technique is to introject the good and to project negativity onto an object, thereby creating a 'hateful object' (Segal 1974, 158). Negative experiences and characteristics are attached to the bad object. In a state of permanent anxiety the split is widened in an attempt to keep the good and the bad worlds as far apart as possible, while having them under control. This split is observed in Balabanov's increasing attempts to localize and thus keep the 'hateful outsiders' as distant as possible. Splitting allows the ego to deal with chaos and to order its experiences. The need to know the other better or to identify with the other is denied, and a split picture of the world appears with a good self and a bad other. Waddell observes the frequent use of this psychological mechanism in the turbulent age of adolescence. 'Characteristically,' she asserts, 'the adolescent draws on projective mechanisms in his desire to get rid of uncomfortable feelings. This unconscious process of attributing to others what are really aspects of the self means that somebody else can then become the problem' (1998a, 131).

Rogin's *Ronald Reagan: The Movie* uncovers a similar process noticeable in America's construction of the other during various periods of American history. The author argues that the history of demonology in American politics consists of three stages: 1) racial division places white people against people of colour; 2) class and ethnic divisions attack working-class 'savages' and alien 'Reds'; and 3) during the cold war the 'Soviet Union replaces the immigrant working class as the source of anxiety' (Rogin 237). Cold war cinema, he argues, '[a]s conscious anti-Communist propaganda and as an unintentional register of anxiety...reflected, shaped, and expressed the buried dynamics of a repressive political consciousness' (238). In the films he discusses to illustrate his viewpoint, Rogin identifies layers on which the domestic anxiety is centered, such as family, state, and society. Balabanov's films reveal a kindred mechanism, but a different focus of anxieties: Russian national identity and class membership.

According to Salecl, '[i]n the fantasy structure of the homeland, the nation (in the sense of national identification) is the element that cannot be symbolized. The nation is the element in us that is "more than ourselves"' (1994, 15). In the case of Balabanov's films, moral masculinity and national superiority are the fantasy that fills the empty place of the nation and that organizes the symbolic structure of society. This fantasy, positioned against the other's fantasy, provokes aggression, which in turn strives to defy the perceived dominance of the other. Salecl argues that '[t]he aim of war is to dismantle the fantasy structure of the enemy country. The aggressor tries to destroy the very way the enemy perceives itself, the way it makes national myths' (1994, 15). In all his conquests in America, Danila aspires to obliterate the enemy's identity structure: He achieves his goal by downplaying the western belief in its supremacy, by physically eliminating his American enemies and all others who stand in his way, and by emasculating America as he sexually wins over the African American journalist. His triumphs challenge America's own fantasies of its moral, military, and financial leadership in the world. Balabanov's films create others and target their fantasy structures, as they isolate and localize them as well as destroy their perception of themselves. Thus, these films effectively redefine Russian as well as western identifications, deconstructing old national myths and reinventing new ones.

National (Mis)apprehensions

Three major characteristics define Danila in *Brother 2*: 1) he loves his motherland; 2) he does not care about money; and 3) he is a superman (though his average physique and boyish appearance point to no superior physical qualities). National identity and social insecurity appear to be the most vulnerable sides of the Russian collective imagination today. Capital and consumer culture (to which most Russians have no access) threaten them, as does the invasion of foreign culture. In this globalization-exposed world, which is perceived by the Russian collective imagination as annihilating national culture, anxieties mobilize defense mechanisms to protect from the sense of a threatened national identity and the overwhelming power of money. The strength of the superman, in this case Danila, comes from his unconditional love for his country and his protection of the weak and the poor. The character functions as a powerful fantasy defense against the external reality of deprivation.

Lipovetskii remarks that the film advances the love for the motherland, spectacularly contrasting

Danila's love for his country with African Americans' lack of morals, a contrast revealing the destruction of the other's fantasy. 'I particularly liked how he [Danila] was shooting...blacks with the poem on his lips (such a contrast: he – about the motherland, and they – about motherfuckers)' (Lipovetskii 2000, 58). In *Brother*, love for the homeland is advanced indirectly through statements made by Viktor ('Today Russians are pressured because they know we are weak') and Danila ('Soon it will be the end of your America'). In the sequel, love for Russia is a persistent leitmotif that manifests itself in direct as well as indirect discourses. To the first category belong the patriotic poem and Danila's vow to the Russian cab driver in New York City that he will return home because he loves his country. The second category includes the song "Good-bye, America" by *Nautilus Pompilius* and Dasha's obscene gesture to the American officer when boarding the plane for Russia.

Unlike the film's crude and unsubstantiated division of characters into 'good' and 'bad', love for the motherland in *Brother 2* is supported by a racist attack on American democracy, with its political correctness and 'hypocritical' regulations. Viktor is shocked when a policeman wants to arrest him for drinking from an open bottle in public because he has seen others drinking in front of the store. (He failed to notice that they were hiding the bottles in paper bags.) Danila looks bewildered when Dasha tells him that one is not supposed to use the 'n' word when addressing or talking about African Americans. In school he was taught that Chinese live in China, Germans live in Germany, and Negroes (sic!) live in Africa. Dasha, after living eight years in the United States, claims that African Americans possess a primitive strength, which is why white people are afraid of them. Horton remarks that her tone of voice when uttering this statement might be appreciative, but the statement itself sounds suspiciously related to the fascist idea of the 'noble savage', which clearly advances racial hierarchy (2001). To this disturbing perception of African Americans by the Russian characters the film adds negative images of African Americans and their supposed lifestyle (Lipovetskii 2000, 56–57). As Danila wanders through Chicago's poor neighborhoods, the camera captures African Americans exclusively as criminals, pimps, and the homeless. The predominant image of the United States shown to viewers is that of problematic realities subject to selective, overemphasized, and exaggerated treatment in the interests of negation.

During the cold war, Soviet ideologists attacked western capitalism for its inhuman nature, manifested in the working conditions that produced the two polar classes of the rich and the poor. Now, with a capitalist economy as the preferred economic model in Russia, that polarization is a fact of post-Soviet life; therefore the attack on America has shifted to create a new fantasy. Focusing on America's efforts to teach tolerance and to secure equal rights for minorities, Balabanov mocks political correctness and exhibits racist attitudes towards African Americans.[15] His films aspire to damage the fantasy structure of the West by attacking democratic values and notions that the West perceives as its own identifactory marks. Explicating latent drives behind the aggression and war in the former Yugoslavia and the notion of 'homeland' (territory) as a fantasy of national identification, Salecl writes: 'Thus when the Serbs occupied a part of Croatia, their aim was not primarily to capture Croatian territory but to destroy the Croatian fantasy about that territory. The Serbs forced the Croats to *redefine their national identity*, to reinvent national myths' (1994, 15). Balabanov's films attack not a territory but the notion of democratic values, which are mocked and exposed as inefficient.

The Russian collective mind, being intolerant itself and perceiving minorities either as an imminent threat or as subhuman, rejects such democratic attempts as ineffective, finds comfort in its own aggression, and denies the consequences of such an attitude. More significantly, the underlying message in *Brother 2* is that Russia must follow its own unique way and does not need inefficient, hypocritical American democracy, which is inappropriate for Russia. A new fantasy of Russian identity is being constructed, positioned against the other's fantasy of democracy (attacked and deconstructed).

Not only democracy, but also cash seems unnecessary for the morally strong: Balabanov portrays Danila as a person who succeeds because he fights for justice, not for money, which he needs only

Chechen children abusing Russian prisoners in Balabanov's War.

for the barest necessities. Though lacking a job or any other apparent source of income, Danila possesses confidence and strength and radiates tranquility – characteristics prized in today's Russia. Ivan in *War* is similarly indifferent to money, explaining to the journalist that he returned to Chechnya for reasons other than the financial payment offered by John. In short, Balabanov's films construct a fantasy around the meaning and function of money. The money that has corrupted the West is unnecessary for the survival of the true Russian spirit, and this irrelevance of things material renders Russia superior to the western mentality.

While *Brother* reveals a tension between narrow solidarities with certain others and a complete 'egocentric' nationalist approach, *Brother 2* and *War* easily alleviate this tension by granting an absolute victory to the latter. If Danila is guided by his own 'moral' point of view in *Brother* by befriending Hoffmann and protecting the weak, in the sequel and in *War* he follows only the interests of Russia, giving no reason why these interests are more important than those of other nations.

War in a sense justifies aggression against the other and pushes it a step further by portraying the Chechens as cardboard characters who embody inimical cruelty and inhumanity. Chechen cultural differences (like skinning sheep) are exaggerated and connected to purported everyday cruelty and violence. Just as *Brother 2* attacks western identifactory notions of racial equality and political correctness, *War* aims to destroy Chechen cultural and ethnic marks of identification by inflating the presentation of violence in Chechen culture. More interesting is the fact that the Chechen War is depicted as a conflict between Russians and Chechens, and while non-Russian ethnic citizens of the Russian Federation also participate in the war, they do not appear in the film. Through such an omission Balabanov indirectly advances the fantasy of the 'pure' Russian nation, though when questioned on this point, he denies it.[16] The film, however, unveils a different attitude. The oversimplification of characters and plot, the creation of clear boundaries of us versus them (rehearsed in *Brother 2*), as well as the endorsement of the direct discourse of love for the homeland and hatred for all outsiders, on the one hand reveal a complete rejection of an ethical point of view and, on the other, attempt to destroy the other's sense of ethnic (national) identification.

Interestingly, the less sophisticated and stylistically intriguing *Brother 2* and *War* become, the more ideological they grow. The characters lose their dimensionality and become one-sided, the plot flattens out, and the slight philosophical nuance present in *Brother* disappears in *Brother 2*. The style becomes more trivial and the films more closely resemble the western genre of the action-thriller. This process is accompanied by an ideological, increasingly vehement rejection of everything western and American. Ironically, the cinematic style of the Hollywood action-thriller does not diminish the identification process and anti-American sentiments.[17]

Cinematic Resistance and Submission
In *Brother*, Balabanov deviates from the rules of the action genre, and, through periodic fading-to-black, punctuates the pace of the action and creates a unique rhythm. This technique ruptures the plot and relates to the unstructured and inconsistent character of Danila. Balabanov has turned the periodic fading-to-black into his signature technique, which appears again in *Brother 2* and *War*. Similar to silence in literature, which has various literary functions, and the use of pauses by other film-makers such as Jean-Luc Godard and Robert Bresson, the black screen in *Brother* secures space and time, a quiet moment of reflection away from the action. Balabanov often uses the black screen to imply brutal violence or gratuitous sexuality without actually showing it. With the fading-to-black technique and

quick-cutting from one scene to another, the director avoids the on-screen representation of cruelty. The spectator sees neither the rape of Sveta (Danila's girlfriend), nor the beating of his brother – scenes, one might say, typical for the action-thriller. Thus, Balabanov attempts to distance the film from the rules of the genre and, to a certain degree, he succeeds. At the end, however, when Danila murders the Mafiosi who have captured Viktor, the shooting is caught on screen and achieves the uncanny feeling of meaningless violence, which establishes the mode of violence for the sequel.

The fading technique also serves to portray the city as an anonymous force in the film: 'The city is a terrible force. The bigger the city, the stronger it is. It sucks you in. Only the strong could resist it.' This philosophy, pronounced by Danila's German friend, is captured on screen by the yellow-greyish colours that make the city sad, cold, and forceful. The camera tracks the city's facades, the street crowds, street kiosks and open markets, and dilapidated communal apartments. With tight frames and tight editing, Balabanov achieves an intimate look at the city and pulls in the gaze of the spectator to make him/her connect and identify with the characters and the place.

Although Balabanov continues to use the fading-to-black technique in *Brother 2*, here it does not work as effectively. The technique is used less and appears only before or after an important episode. In the sequel, viewers do not perceive Moscow or Chicago through the shades of St Petersburg as in *Brother*. The colours here are much brighter: the red flag in the former Lenin museum, the use of yellow in Irina Saltykova's apartment, and the beautiful autumn tree colours in America on the way from New York to Chicago (Sirivlia). Along with the shades of the first film, the philosophy and mystery about the meaning of life and death disappear. Everything comes into view all too clearly: the enemies and the meaning of life (the lives of Russians are valuable; the lives of everybody else are deprived of any value).

Balabanov also brings more violence to the screen and thereby moves closer to the conventions of the genre. In two scenes more typical of the action genre, Balabanov presents a car chase on the streets of Moscow, in which Viktor uses the machine gun he took from the Lenin museum, and a scene in Mennis's club where Danila shoots randomly at everyone along his way to the safe-box.[18]

In *War* the fading-to-black and use of colour techniques function similarly as they do in *Brother 2*. The black screens emphasize episodes rather than punctuate the rhythm as they do in *Brother*. *War*'s colours are again brighter than those in *Brother*. The Chechen landscape, with its southern mountain shapes and pale yellowish tones, contrasts with the green Siberian hillside.

Similar to the function of the fading technique, the use of music in *Brother* and *Brother 2* is engaged as a reflexive and organizational principle.[19] The songs of Viacheslav Butusov, the lead singer in *Nautilus Pompilius*, enhance the action (Sirivlia 28). Infatuated by the rhythm and the words, Danila is constantly seeking *Nautilus*'s "Wings", using the music to literally and metaphorically escape from reality. In one scene the CD player literally saves his life when a bullet breaks the player but does not harm him. In *Brother 2* the music loses its multifunctional role. *Nautilus* music is heard rarely, and there are other pop songs performed mainly by *Bi-2* and the pop singer Zemfira, which are deprived of any philosophical subtext. Only *Nautilus*'s "Good-bye, America" sounds powerfully ideological as it plays at the end of the film, but this is an exception to the empty but popular melodies that dominate the film. In 2002, "Good-bye, America" forcefully rejects the enthusiasm of the 1992 film *On Deribasovskaia*, which comically welcomed Russian-American relations with a repetitive 'Hello, America! You seem like paradise and you look OK.'[20]

A process is noticeable in the production of the *Brother* films and *War*: these films narcissistically negate the West, yet inadvertently strive to achieve the western model for success manifested in the popular action film genre. Although one has to clarify that these films do not blindly follow the western genre and often subvert it, they are ultimately grounded in it. There are two conflicting processes visible in adolescence: 'pressure towards conformity on the one hand, and individuation on the other' (Waddell 1998b, 128). In other words, what one notices in this contradiction of Balabanov's films – to conform more and more with the western genre of the action film and to be simultaneously different from it – is similar to the adolescent's desire to follow other models for identification but at the same time to be his/her unique self. The same paradox is addressed by Paul Upson who, using the prevailing economic order and its measures for success, argues that the adolescent's aspirations to become a quick economic success often lead to a 'narcissistic "short cut" solution' (171).

National Paranoia

The process of identification, fueled simultaneously and paradoxically by both anti-western ideology and the western style of representing this ideology, has already been noted and compared to similar adolescent anxieties, but the paradoxical process deserves further elaboration. Stylistically speaking, *Brother 2* remains Balabanov's most western film and, ideologically speaking, his most anti-western and anti-American film. Dondurei reveals this paradox:

> This is why the million dollars collected by *Brother 2* for the first three months of showing only in the movie-theaters speaks about something really important: Balabanov and Selianov [the producer] managed with their openly anti-Western film to conquer precisely these viewers who have grown up with popcorn and biographies of Hollywood stars and who speak English fluently. This is not a paradox but a first rate symptom of the value system of our society. (2000, 68)[21]

Russian viewers have grown up consuming American and western culture; they have almost exclusively watched Hollywood films, as the Russian cinema industry came to a near halt by the mid-1990s; and they have learned English, motivated not by Shakespeare but by Eminem. In a way, they develop an imaginary global mentality, both pleasing and extremely frustrating. In the Russian social, political, and economic conditions, western capital and culture offer something pleasing because they fill a cultural and consumer vacuum created by the decline of the economy and film industry and by Russia's long isolation during the cold war in which western culture was fervently idealized and desired.

But, more important, the western presence is frustrating for Russians for two reasons. First, it remains an unattainable imaginary world to which most viewers have no access, except in its virtual forms and cheap manifestations. Second, with its overwhelming presence, it threatens feeble attempts to reconstruct the Russian national culture and identity. This frustration deepens depressive anxieties and unlocks paranoid defenses against the West. Thus, on the surface, a western presence can be an enjoyable experience, but on an unconscious level, threatens annihilation. To defend against these threats, the Russian collective imagination develops paranoid anxieties and seeks defenses in the backlash of nationalism.

In the extreme conditions of globalization, in which individuals as well as Russian society as a whole experience the acute feeling of obliteration, the people are apt to defend themselves against

THE RUSSIAN HERO: FANTASIES OF WOUNDED NATIONAL PRIDE | 59

uncertainty and threat. They do so by looking for someone to blame, by idealizing the Russian subject as morally and spiritually superior, and by projecting negativity onto an outside object. As observed in *War*, the enemy is not only the West or the US, but also Russian minorities from the South, such as the Chechens, because they are also perceived as threatening stability and challenging ethnic Russian superiority. They are blamed for a whole range of problems: from violence on the streets to the weak economy and the unstable political situation. The enemies are also Romanians, Bulgarians, and Ukrainians, all imagined as subhuman.

Rancour-Laferriere contends that 'projection is a typical feature of nationalism and ethnic hatred' (189). He writes: 'The Russian nationalist who feels hated *by* Jews ("Yid-Masonic conspiracy") is projecting outward a fragment of himself, namely, his own hatred *of* Jews. The Jew is confused with the self' (189). In other words, when Russians feel threatened by western and particularly American superiority (in most instances rightly so), they nonetheless project part of their own wounded feelings of superiority. Furthermore, in Balabanov's films they project their fears toward undeserving others (Ukrainians, Romanians, and Bulgarians) who politically and culturally are unable to threaten Russian national identity. This exposes the workings of what I term *national paranoia*. To connect such feelings to the adolescent's experience, I evoke Waddell again. Waddell argues that the paranoid state of mind often bothers the adolescent, who relates and experiences the other in extreme terms of love and hate, opposites felt to be irreconcilable (1998a, 135). Yet love and hate fuse in the Russian viewers' appreciation of Balabanov's films. The *national paranoia* and love-hate infatuation with the West observed in the films reflect an adolescent's state of mind that is disturbed by the presence of the other.

Driven by paranoid attitudes, manifested in aggression, racism, and sexism and addressed against the other, Balabanov's characters idealize Russian national characteristics as they dismantle the other's fantasy and reinvent a new fantasy of Russian national identity. Nationalism, experienced as resistance to globalization in Russia as well as in Africa and Asia, is appropriated through actors, film-makers, soccer matches, and athletes (Diawara 110–14). National culture and the state create the framework for cultural and political discourses that absorb nationalist sentiments and passions.

In this context, Appadurai's insistence on the disappearance of the nation-state and its sentiments fails. He is convinced that the nation-state, as a complex modern political form, is disappearing. The system of the nation-state is not equipped to deal with the flows of peoples and images that mark the here and now (Appadurai 19). But my argument so far shows that the collective imagination as social practice, even though grounded in international *mediascapes* (for example, the international acceptance of the conventions of the action genre), cannot exist independently of national passions constructed and carried around in the idea of a nation-state. On the contrary, the collective imagination is powerfully driven and fueled by nationalism. Appadurai's argument creates the misleading impression that everyone can take equal advantage of global cultural flows. However, in the economic and political conditions of Russia after the collapse of the Soviet system, global cultural flows, more often than not, are experienced as damaging by the majority of Russians who suffer under the conditions of globalization. The widening gap between the obscenely rich Russian oligarchs and the average Russian complicates the effect and perception of globalization. While the Russian elite takes full advantage of global mobility and culture, the average Russian experiences only the frustrations, presented by Hollywood films, and is left to imagine the advantages of globalization. In reverting to national passions, the anxious Russian imagination finds security and rehabilitation of its wounded existence. Thus, while there are conditions preventing people from taking advantage of global cultural flows and global human mobility, while a nation is unable to integrate bad and good experiences into its own national body, and while it reverts easily to paranoid anxieties that require an enemy, the idea of the nation-state and its sentiments is alive and well regardless of how inadequate it is to deal with the global flow of people and images.

Here Žižek's insistence on the deficiencies of the capitalist and democratic model, which is often perceived as able to overcome national passions and unite people beyond national borders, appears again helpful. He recognizes that '[i]n recent decades, the striving for universality has been given a new thrust by a whole series of economic, technological, and cultural processes' (Žižek 1992, 162). Continuing his discussion with the exploration of the universal and particular features of democracy, Žižek notes: 'The problem is not that this abstraction proper to democracy dissolves all concrete substantial ties, but rather that *it can never dissolve them*. The subject of democracy is, in its very blankness, smeared with a certain "pathological" stain' (1992, 164–5).

Thus, the particular construction and idealization of masculinity that defines national identity, the objectification and aggression directed toward the other (Americans, African Americans, Brits, Ukrainians, Bulgarians, Jews, and Chechens), the intense perception of a divided world ('us' versus 'them') all point to a certain pathological stain, a certain materialized enjoyment, a national Cause that organizes Russians around the collective myth of their moral (masculine) superiority

Notes

1. Beumers states: 'The ensuing crisis in the film industry has become fully evident only since 1995, when the number of new films plummeted to a new low in the history of Russian and Soviet cinema, matched only by the lows reached during Civil War and under Stalin' (1999c, 871). Susan Larsen speaks of this decline too (1999, 192).
2. A few years later Mikhalkov, too, advocated for a creation of a positive film hero in his speech at the Filmmakers' Congress, May 1998. For more, see Mikhalkov (1999).
3. While *The Castle* is clearly based on Kafka's novel, the literary sources of *Happy Days* remain vague. Many scholars believe that *Happy Days* is tenuously based on Beckett (Dondurei 1998, Larsen 1999). With the exception of the identical title and the absurdity in Balabanov's film, I find nothing in common with Beckett's play *Happy Days*. In my view Beckett's female protagonist Winnie expresses an existential quest for serenity and finds pleasure in the limited world of her objects, whereas Balabanov's Sergei Sergeevich seems destined to wander eternally and to not be able to find tranquility. For more on my interpretation of Beckett's *Happy Days*, see "Winnie: The Woman Who is Not-All /Beckett's *Happy Days*/" (Hashamova 2001). The *War* DVD's extra material states that Balabanov's film *Happy Days* is based on D. Kharms. I was unable, however, to identify any particular Kharms story as a literary source of the film.
4. *Brother* and *Brother 2* were some of the first films to show the increased interest of Russian viewers in their national cinema. In the last few years, the Russian film industry has undoubtedly picked up speed. *Novyi ekran* publishes the ratings for domestic and foreign films and while *The Lord of the Rings: The Two Towers* (2003) and *Harry Potter and the Chamber of Secrets* (2003), for example, have collected $8 and $7 million, respectively, from ticket sales, the Russian films *Antikiller* (2002) and *Oligarch* (2002) grossed $1.31 and $1.05 million. Balabanov's *War* grossed $0.83 million ("Reiting Otechestvennogo prokata" *Novyi ekran*, no.1/2, February - March, 2003, 85 and no.3–4, May - June 2003, 77). Even though the domestic earnings are much less than those from foreign films, the numbers are still encouraging especially compared to ten years ago. The July 2004 release of the Russian fantasy-thriller *Nochnoi dozor* (*Night Watch*, dir. Timur Bekmambetov) broke all previous figures, earning $5.3 million during the first week of screening (and much more since then) (Gladil'shchikov).

5. For more on *Of Freaks and Men,* see "The Gaze of Power, Impotence, and Subversion in Balabanov's *Of Freaks and Men*" (Hashamova 2003).

6. Tragically, on 20 September 2002 Bodrov, Jr died in Osetia while shooting his latest film. More than one hundred cast and crew members and local citizens died when a glacier suddenly shifted and caused a massive landslide. Using an Internet forum on Balabanov's film company site, hundreds of fans spoke of the unconditional love and support Bodrov had. They even disavowed the possibility of his death.

7. Beumers defines Danila as a romantic knight (1999b).

8. This philosophical inquiry evokes a scene from the 1957 film *Cranes are Flying,* in which the female protagonist, driven by guilt for having married another man after her fiancé volunteered and left for the front in World War Two, asks a roommate: 'You're an intelligent woman. Tell me, what's the meaning of life?'

9. The Russian word 'medved'' means 'bear'.

10. Mark Lipovetskii similarly remarks that the ideology Balabanov instills in *Brother 2* tapped into the collective unconscious of contemporary Russia that nobody respects and nobody fears (2000). Lipovetskii does not develop this thought but (like Gusiatinskii) furthers the idea that *Brother 2* explored images and techniques from the Soviet past and socialist realism, which increased the process of identification awakened in the Russian audiences. I, however, decided to seek the psychological mechanisms in the context of the concrete political and economic circumstances that allow films to serve as political fantasies and psychological manifestations of hopes and fears unveiling actual and imagined relations that determine social and national identity.

11. In the sequel, the main character joins the state anti-terror forces.

12. Although the Hollywood tradition knows the 'buddy film', I believe that in general Hollywood action films operate more around protagonist individualism, whereas recent Russian action films demonstrate more affinity toward fraternal heroism.

13. A more detailed discussion of the construction of the enemy follows later in the chapter.

14. Notably, it is the Russian-English translator (no doubt contaminated by the West) who is portrayed as a corrupt individual.

15. During the spring and summer of 2003 in Russia a real media wave and even a campaign mocking American political correctness and Affirmative Action took place. On television and in the press every example was used and manipulated to show the inefficiency of these institutions. Russians indulged in reading pejorative articles about a scandal with an African American *New York Times* journalist who was exposed as having fabricated data and stories, which according to the Russian media, happened only because of Affirmative Action.

16. In an interview after the premiere of *War,* he announced that not all Chechens are enemies, clarifying that he considers everyone Russian who speaks the Russian language and who accepts Russia as his country (Balabanov, 46–47).

17. For similar sentiments and contradictions, see Dina Iordanova (1999).

18. Elena Prokhorova argues that the machine gun scene is different from car chase scenes typical for the genre. Although she does not elaborate much, I think that the very presence of the scene, however, even if it vaguely resembles the genre chase scenes, already brings the sequel closer to the action film, whereas *Brother* does not present any such scenes.

19. For a more detailed analysis of the function of music in Balabanov's film, see "National Identity, Cultural Authority, and the Post-Soviet Blockbuster: Nikita Mikhalkov and Aleksei Balabanov" (Larsen 2003).

20. American films (from *Scorpio Rising* in 1963 to the present) have used popular tunes to enhance the identification process.

21. In a conversation between Natalia Sirivlia, a Russian film critic, and Vida Johnson, an American film scholar, Sirivlia turned her attention to the same paradox. The Russian critic pointed out that Russians keep their money in dollars, endlessly watch American films, and, at the same time, endorse vehement anti-Americanism (Johnson 20). Johnson contended that Russian-American relations have always been very complex when the US and the USSR existed as equal powers, but today America has alarmingly become the only superpower. Johnson looked for explanations for the anti-American sentiments in the position the US holds in the world today, while Dondurei saw these sentiments as a symptom of the Russian value system.

3

MOBILIZING INTERNAL FORCES: THE IDEALIZED PAST AND CULTURE

One of the most difficult undertakings of adolescence is the capacity to establish a mind and identity of one's own, distinct from models and sources available in the family, school, community, or society. The struggle for separation and uniqueness determines the adolescent's entry to adulthood. In this process, many defense mechanisms and fantasies are awakened to aid the adolescent's effort at achieving exceptionality. Instrumental in this stage is the ability to find sources within the self that can assist the transition from late-adolescence to adulthood. This chapter explores the Russian struggle to establish itself as a unique nation against the background of the intense globalization changes that mark Russian identity formation with the unease of the adolescent forced to seek self-determination. Aspects of Mikhalkov's *The Barber of Siberia* and Sokurov's *Russian Ark* unveil the Russian collective imagination's search for unique Russian characteristics that outline Russia's cultural exceptionality.

Alongside defensive splitting and paranoid sentiments (observed in Balabanov's films) and contrary to them, the adolescent also begins to recognize the complexity of the world and to position/compare self to other in order to establish the parameters and the specific qualities of the self. In the course of this quest for self-definition more moderate and reflexive ways of understanding and knowing the self emerge. A more mature vision of the world lessens negative projective processes demonizing the other and intensifies introjective processes. The self (as well as the other) is seen as one body, both frustrating and gratifying, loved and hated. This change in the state of the subject and the other brings a change in the focus of the subject's anxieties. Reparative fantasies arise in connection to loved objects, internal or external.

Explaining the ways the adolescent relates to the other and the ways s/he tries to positively absorb (internalize) external models, Waddell writes: 'Intrinsic to the introjective process is the capacity to relinquish external figures of dependence and attachment and to install a version of them within as sources which inspire and encourage the independent development of the personality' (1998a, 157). The present chapter explores how and to what degree Mikhalkov's *The Barber of Siberia* and Sokurov's *Russian Ark* renounce external values and images (the West) and how the films simultaneously internalize them. The chapter also centers on the two films' quest for national internal sources (past and culture) that secure Russian cultural independence and uniqueness.

From a Lacanian theoretical perspective, these films' engagement with Russian past and history and their search for unique Russian characteristics that distinguish them from the obliterating globalization reveal yet again the workings of fantasy and desire. To put it in Lacan's terms, Mikhalkov's *The Barber of Siberia* and Sokurov's *Russian Ark* seek the *object a* of Russianness: what is in Russianness more than Russianness, or what in Russian national identity stays the same and is thus irreducible.[1] It is this object, as Salecl argues, that 'embodies the surplus of demand over need, the object that stands in for the emptiness which the subject encounters when its demand remains unsatisfied' (1994, 125). Paradoxically, the *object a* fills a lack in the Other (or represents this lack), but at the same time it 'prevents any object from really filling this lack' (Salecl 1994, 126). Thus, desire is always unsatisfied, as one object substitutes another.

In a way, Mikhalkov's and Sokurov's films, although still preoccupied with the West, shift their focus to another object – Russian past and history. By uncovering and changing the symbolic representation of history, the films attempt to find the unalterable in Russian national identity. The films supply historical signification and thus undertake to exercise (ideological) control over viewers. The symbolic power manifests itself in the effort to determine the past and (re)write history. The films' resistance to globalization indicates desire to uncover the *object a* – something that defies globalization, something that stays the same despite constant changes in symbolic national identity. The two films, however, significantly differ in their endeavours to provide historical signification (or in their venture at symbolizing the *object a* that ultimately cannot be symbolized).

Reparative fantasies and the search for positive internal forces as well as efforts to supply historical signification to the kernel of Russianness develop against the backdrop of Russian cinema's revival. In December of 1997, Dondurei, chief editor of *Iskusstvo kino*, spoke about the state of Russian national cinema. He pointed out that all signs suggest a resurrection of the Russian film industry: in 1997 the production had risen 250 per cent; television companies were producing seven miniseries for a total of 100 hours of transmission time; Russian films and miniseries accounted for 45.5 per cent of film screenings on television; and the reconstruction of cinema theatres like the Pushkin, the Arts Cinema, and the Cine-Center stimulated three powerful financial groups to invest $100 million each into the creation of multiplexes and into the Russian film industry (Dondurei 1999, 46–47). He insisted, however, that film-makers had to change their focus and their portrayal of reality if they wanted their production to be successful. A long list of Russian films from the first half of the 1990s, offered by Dondurei, presents only violence, crime, and poverty: 'But surely we cannot seriously think that films immersed in an ocean of unpunished violence will arouse delight and identification in any sensible spectator. Who likes to see the hero defeated, or all government structures shown as totally criminal?' (1999, 49). 'Art,' Dondurei stresses, 'above all, is a means to model the future successfully" (1999, 50). Pressured by changes in Russia – the development of a market economy, the increase of western presence, Hollywood films included, and by the viewers' demands and augmented expectations – Russian directors seem to have abandoned bleak films (*chernukha*) from the first years following de-Sovietization and have instead offered Russian viewers more positive emotions, models, and events. These more optimistic and constructive changes reflected on the screen undoubtedly speak of the Russian collective imagination's awakened reparative fantasies resulting from the complex feelings toward the West, as well as unconscious attempts to locate and symbolize the kernel of Russian national identity focusing on past, history, and culture.[2]

Glorious Past Resurrected

Recently, scholars have noticed the nostalgic longing for the values of the past. In his work on 'cults' and postmodernism in post-Soviet Russia, Eliot Borenstein argues that on the one hand the ideological struggles of the new religious movements and the old establishment (government and Orthodox Church) lead to further relativism, but on the other to an unexpected unity: 'All parties to the debate speak the same language: a language that combines nostalgia for a long-lost, mythical past and strong faith in the supernatural...' (1999, 456). While I agree with Borenstein's observations and findings, I insist that along this path of the nostalgic longing for the past Russia has begun to construct a cultural space, manifested partly in films, containing symbolic representations of national fears and fantasies, and helping in the process of adjustment in the context of global economy and culture.

In 1992, Lawton also recorded the involvement of perestroika Russian cinema with the past: 'The past has been dug out and presented from every possible angle and in many different forms' (1992, 166). During the 1990s Russian directors fervently persisted in revisiting Soviet as well as the imperial past. Ten years after her first observation Lawton reiterated it: 'the search for Russia through the revival of her past will continue to be a subject of interest to film-makers until a new identity is established' (2002, 106). Examining the dialogue of post-Soviet film with its Soviet traditions and the ways recent Russian cinema returns to the past in order to 'set the record straight', David Gillespie writes: 'Originally seen as a means of legitimizing the (Soviet) present, the cinematic investigation of history has tended in recent years not only to debunk past ideologies, but also to create new myths as pointers to the future' (14).

Two overall tendencies can be noticed in the return of Russian interest to the past.[3] The first one revisits the Soviet past and especially Stalin's terror. Ivan Dykhovichnyi's *Moscow Parade* (1992) is the first post-Soviet film exposing Stalin's period. Pavel Chukhrai's *Thief* (1997) offers another interesting view on Stalin's reign and his legendary but fraudulent role as Russia's Father. In 1998, Aleksei German's *Khrustalev, my car!* explored events that unfold a few days before and after the dictator's death. *Encore, Once More, Encore!* (Piotr Todorovskii, 1992) reexamines post-World War II consequences and realities.

The second tendency reveals film directors' preoccupation with more distant Russian history. Two films dealing with the last Russian tsar, Nicholas II, framed the 1990s. In *The Assassin of the Tsar* (Karen Shakhnazarov, 1991) the action takes place in a Soviet mental institution, in which a patient believes he killed the tsar, and the doctor, too deeply involved in the case, assumes the role of the tsar. While Stanislav Govorukhin's *The Russia We Have Lost* (1992) nostalgically celebrates pre-revolutionary values as a chance for salvation, Gleb Panfilov's *The Romanovs: An Imperial Family* (2000) presents the last days of the royal family and boldly attempts to rehabilitate its image and role in history. Viewers also saw Aleksandr Proshkin's *The Russian Rebellion* (1999) based on Pushkin's novel *The Captain's Daughter* (1836). The film recreates Pugachev's revolt intensified on the screen with violence and sexuality. All of these films, part of the historical discourse, testify to the impatient desire of the Russian collective imagination to rethink and reconfigure its national identity under the new post-Soviet conditions by engaging and reconstructing Russia's historical events and figures and by revising and recreating historical myths.

Two prominent and stylistically very different directors of Russian cinema, Mikhalkov and Sokurov, play an interesting role in this search for new identity symbols through a return to Russia's past. The Oscar-winning *Burnt by the Sun* (1994) by Mikhalkov exposes Stalin's purges through the arrest of a respected and well-liked hero of the revolution. But interestingly, the director creates an idyllic picture of a Russian family in the 1930s living happily in the countryside – a tranquil and beautiful life suddenly disrupted by Stalin's orders.[4] After *Burnt by the Sun*, Mikhalkov continued his attempts at myth-making, returning further back in history – late nineteenth and early twentieth centuries – with his film *The Barber of Siberia*, which is the main focus of my investigation here. Sokurov, on the other hand, far from idealizing the past, recreates historical figures and events in his *Moloch* (2000) and *Telets* (2001). While the former is a psychological examination of historical figures of fatal consequence like Hitler, Borrmann, and Goebbels, the latter portrays Lenin, the dynamic and revered leader of the revolution, as a sick man losing control of his mind. More important for my study is Sokurov's *Russian Ark*, which compared to *The Barber of Siberia* offers an intriguing view on Russian national identity.[5] Both films idealize Russia's imperial past, but they still convey different attitudes towards the past. Both directors explore the nature of Russian culture vis-à-vis the West but they differently imagine this relationship and consequently Russian culture. These differences shed light on the maturity of the Russian national identity marked by sentiments of the adolescent's development. Simultaneously, the comparative analysis reveals the elusive nature of the kernel of Russianness (Lacan's *object a*) functioning in the two films as historical time (*The Barber*) and historical non-time (*Russian Ark*) as well as place (*The Barber*) and non-place (*Russian Ark*).

Using Bakhtin's ideas about the fullness of time in national narratives, I suggest that a linear monolithic representation of history and a concomitant representation of fixed identity fall short of expressing modern identity in flux.[6] Such a Bakhtinian analysis uncovers the stumbling blocks in Mikhalkov's and Sokurov's efforts to supply historical signification (or to symbolize the kernel of Russian national identity) and poses questions about the candid search for positive internal sources. In expanding and looking beyond Bakhtin's thoughts I am guided by scholars such as Kristeva and Homi Bhabha, who adopted Bakhtin's theory and developed it further in order to deconstruct its limitations. Although Bakhtin applied his concept of the chronotope to literature, it is nonetheless helpful in cinema studies. With the introduction and the skillful use of montage, a film director is able to avoid the restrictions of time and space, yet their interplay (or interreliance in more linear and traditional narrative) remains important for the comprehension and effectiveness of the film narrative. While editing allows directors to manipulate time through classical cuts (which keep continuity) or intellectual montage (which awakens associations and emotions), the preservation (and alternatively the manipulation) of real time and space are integral to any cinematic structure.

The Barber of Siberia

Mikhalkov's latest film skillfully constructs a positive model reacting to the complex conditions of the Russian collective imagination during the last years of the twentieth century. The film manifests a new stage of the complex and endless love-hate romance between Russia and the West. As a French-Russian production, the film reveals the French infatuation with an exotic and mysterious (unknown) Russia and the longstanding desire of Russians to impress the West with Russia's magnificence and uniqueness.

The setting is Springfield, Massachusetts, in 1905, and Jane Callahan (Julia Ormond) writes to her son, a cadet in a military academy. Her memories take viewers back twenty years, when she was in tsarist Russia on a mission to help her friend, the desperate inventor McCracken (Richard Harris), raise funds to finish building a steam-driven forest-harvesting machine. There she met two men: a passionate, sensitive, and handsome young cadet, Andrei Tolstoi (Oleg Menshikov), and a powerful tyrant of a general, Radlov (Aleksei Petrenko), both of whom were enchanted by her beauty. Andrei and Jane spend a night of passion together. Later, at a performance of *The Marriage of Figaro*, Andrei overhears Jane denying her interest in him to the general, who, she hopes, would secure the finances for her friend's forest-harvesting machine, the 'barber'. Distraught, Tolstoi attacks the general, who arrests his young rival on false charges and exiles him to Siberia. Years later Jane accompanies McCracken, whom in the meantime she has married, on a trip to Siberia, and there she looks for Andrei.

Viewers have had numerous difficulties with the representation of history in this film, but the most problematic one concerns the idealization of Alexander III, whose reactionary politics is entirely ignored, or silently approved. With gusto and pride Mikhalkov himself acts as Alexander III, constructing the image of an ideal tsar and an affectionate father. In a grandiose scene representing the graduation of Russian cadets, the camera shifts from panoramic views of Moscow cathedrals to the appearance of the tsar and his son riding together on a white horse.[7] In the dignity with which Alexander III greets the cadets and the attention he pays to his son, Mikhalkov attempts to fuse the patriarchal tsar's greatness with his love for his son, family, and nation. What is disturbing in this representation of history is not only the slanted outlook on historical figures but also 'President' Mikhalkov's own persistent pretensions at greatness and the keenness of his desire for personal glory. The portrayal of Alexander III becomes a conduit for Mikhalkov's narcissistic inclinations and political aspirations, as well as for his hope to invigorate Russian national identity. [8]

Mikhalkov (as Alexander III) in The Barber of Siberia.

Film critic Nikita Sokolov pinpoints many historical inaccuracies in the film, starting with the early film scene of an assassination attempt, which could have been historically accurate only if set before 1883. By that year the military organization *People's Will* (Narodnaia volia), responsible for such attacks, had been entirely liquidated. The film, however, opens with the year 1885 and thus neglects historical precision (Sokolov 48). Further, Sokolov uncovers a casual mixture of epochs and their traditions and recounts numerous historical fabrications, of which I will mention only a few: 1) the voluptuous presentation of the Russian spring festival, Maslenitsa, with grandiose fireworks, which in the film is shown to be prepared for the common folk but which in reality (because of its extravagance and expense) could not have been dreamed of even in Peterhof or Tsarskoe selo; 2) the nineteenth-century Russian population (even prison guards) appears to be all fluent in English; 3) the graduation of the young Russian cadets and their promotion to officers was a strict military ritual, radically different from its presentation, with champagne toasting, in the film; 4) the nature of Tolstoi's sentence and the train expedition of prisoners reminds Sokolov more of article 70 of the Soviet Penalty Code and the gulag than of late-nineteenth-century punishments and their execution (Sokolov 48–49). And the list goes on. Notably, Mikhalkov constructs the historical mystification as reality and transforms illusion into truth. Such transformation of selective and manipulated historical episodes into real history and the insistence on truthfulness and credibility underlie the ideological discourse of the film and its teleological orientation.

The historical inaccuracies and manipulations are backed by colourful epic screen images. Following his desire to boost Russian national self-esteem and to impress western audiences with Russia's wonders, the director portrays beautiful scenery consisting of vast forests (the opening scene of Jane's train [symbolizing the West] moving through winter birch forests [that is, Russia]) and historically famous Moscow attractions such as Kremlin's cathedrals.[9]

Mikhalkov effectively combines the panoramic views of Russia's landmarks with more intimate and detailed close-up shots of cadets' boots and a little sparrow jumping and chirping around the boots blissfully ignorant to the most solemn occasion of the cadets' graduation and the tsar's appearance.[10] In a muted scene, in which only the sparrow can be heard, the camera cuts to a shot of the Russian flag and back to cadets' boots and the sparrow. One can associate this detail, transforming the small and the insignificant of everyday life into profound history with Bakhtin's chronotope, in which national time becomes concrete and localized. Bakhtin observed such construction of historical time not only in Russian contexts but also in Goethe's national vision, in the German writer's *Italian Journal*:

> Against the background of these times of nature, daily existence, and life, which are still cyclical to one degree or another, Goethe also sees interwoven with them signs of historical time – essential traces of human hands and minds that change nature, and the way human reality and all man has created are reflected back on his customs and views. (Bakhtin 1986, 32)

For Bakhtin the spatialization of historical time reveals 'a creative humanization of this locality, which transforms a part of terrestrial space into a place of historical life for people' (Bakhtin 1986, 34). In this case, Russian culture is shown to encompass both the mighty collective and the 'minutest creature', the national and the human, the whole and the detail – in short, the culture of *sobornost'*.

Throughout the film – for example, when Alexander covers his son's mouth when the boy wants to provoke the cadets to shout out yet another greeting to the tsar at a time important to and dedicated to them – viewers observe a similar transformation of the insignificant personal act belonging to the realm of everyday life (*byt*) into national history. Such scenes reveal a national space that is achieved only in the fullness of time and history. The construction of a glorious and unquestionable past is connected to everyday human experience and the impression of patriarchal power with a human face is cemented by these details, which create the effect of truthfulness.

Historical time in this film, then, is constructed as linear time, as progression, project, and teleology, as national history inseparable from everyday life. Nothing in the film betrays any hesitation in the linear and teleological understanding of history. On the contrary, historical realities from various times and even centuries (as pointed out by Sokolov) are pieced together in a cinematic narrative of twenty years in order to create a monolithic vision of national history with its 'creative humanization'. Thus, the film attempts to advance a national identity that is rooted in the certainty of a celebrated mythical past presented as reality, thereby avoiding the dilemmas confronting the present.

Lacan's theory uncovers contradictions and problems in such a presentation of history: the mythical past constructed as concrete time and reality aims to present reality and appearance as one, a strategy which attempts to leave the viewer in ignorance as to what is there beyond appearance. Lacan insists that what we see is always-already a consequence of the invisible (object a) (Lacan 1977, 226–280). Therefore, the redundancy of Mikhalkov's images, his 'too visual' reality veils latent elements that control them. What Mikhalkov offers is a surrogate of object a, of the kernel of Russian national identity.

Mikhalkov's desire to hide reality behind positive images is seen in his presentation of positive national ideals in the historical context of late nineteenth and early twentieth centuries. Not infrequently he has expressed his disappointment with the recent state of Russian film production, which focuses on violence, sex, prostitutes, and killers – that is, on the 'ugly present'. He insists that cinema should promote ideals and create heroes as he refers to Lenin's famous definition of cinema as the most important art: 'Cinema was nominated as the most important of all arts because it was capable of shaping the consciousness of the masses. It was an art, because it was clear even then that it was not only a document, but an artistic illusion, a myth, if you like, capable of facilitating the creation of a model for a new society, and for a hero which the state and the authorities needed at a particular time' (Mikhalkov 1999, 50). Mikhalkov continues clarifying that serving the Fatherland does not necessarily mean serving a regime. His approving quote of Lenin, for example, does not mean that Mikhalkov endorses his political views.

A cultural theorist, Bhabha, aptly articulates the importance of the presentation of the nation as a temporal process and, in so doing, directs attention to Bakhtin, who also emphasizes 'the necessity of the past and the necessity of its place in a line of continuous development...finally the aspect of the past being linked to the necessary future' (Bakhtin 1986, 36). Mikhalkov, being disappointed in the dark and hopeless filmic representation of Russia's current reality, certainly offers aspects of the past, but he does so only to idealize it and, in turn, constructs a more optimistic necessary future. In other words, Mikhalkov creates a mythic visual world, in which viewers cannot conceive of the present and the future without the symbolic configuration of the past.

Russian Ark

In a dream-like continuous take that lasts ninety-six minutes, Sokurov takes viewers on a tour of thirty-three rooms in the Hermitage (the Winter Palace), one of the world's largest art museums. Alternating

Sokurov's Russian Ark.

presentations of the museum's collection with the appearance of Russian historical and cultural figures, the director covers three centuries of Russian history. The film offers an unusual experience, utilizing an innovative cinematic technique that rejects the theory of the montage so brilliantly developed by Sergei Eisenstein, and conveying a kind of 'reverie presentation' of time and place in which the spectators encounter, in a fractured way, the many visitors who came to the Hermitage over the years and glimpse the masterpieces of European art displayed on the walls of the museum.

Russian Ark, like many other Sokurov films, opens with a black screen, no image, and only sound. Viewers hear the narrator's whisper: 'I open my eyes and see nothing.' At the end of the film, after a journey through Russia's history and culture, partly guided by this denial of vision in the introduction, one is forced to ask such questions as 'How much do we see when we look back into history?' and 'What do we learn from it?'

This beginning invites further elaboration in psychoanalytic terms through the concept of *object a* and the dialectics of the gaze. The blind spot of the film's opening and its ambiguity evokes Lacan's claim that the gaze *qua object a* prevents the subject from knowing what is there beyond appearance (Lacan 1981, 77). The free-floating gaze ultimately attached to the visual is there to unveil the unreliable nature of appearance. As Italian film scholar Fabio Vighi contends, 'cinema's own reflexive/self referential nature offers us a unique chance to investigate the correlation between what we see and permeate with meaning and the displaced element that governs it most secretly' (34). In other words, if one applies this argument about the nature of cinema to *The Barber of Siberia* and *Russian Ark*, one may infer that while Mikhalkov's film insists on offering only the 'seen', Sokurov complicates matters from the very opening scene and hints at the presence of the 'displaced element' which orchestrates the visual. While Mikhalkov denies (and avoids at all costs the workings of the free-floating gaze that suggests the invisible mastery of the unconscious), Sokurov shoots his film in a way which implies that the excluded remains operative in what is seen, a cinematic strategy underlying the whole structure of *Russian Ark*. The next instance, governed by this strategy, appears in the function of the film's two guides.

Two men take viewers on the tour through the rooms of the Hermitage: the invisible contemporary narrator (the voice of Sokurov himself), and a nineteenth-century Frenchman, the historical Marquis Astolphe de Custine (Sergei Dreiden), who visited Russia in 1839 and wrote *Russie en 1839* – a travel account that was banned in Russia several times before and after the October Revolution. In the two guides' continuous dialogue expressing attitudes toward art and history, viewers witness Custine's ongoing critique of Russia's history and cultural adoption of European models, as well as the narrator's responses. This dialogue (visible and invisible) frames the tour through Russian history, in which the viewer stumbles upon Peter the Great, Catherine the Great, and Pushkin; participates in a royal presentation, in which the Shah of Persia's emissaries apologize to Nicholas I for the murder of Aleksandr Griboedov (diplomat and playwright); observes Nicholas II and his family; or peeks into a room where a carpenter makes coffins for the victims of the Leningrad siege during the Second World War.

In addition to the major sensations that the film achieves – floating in time and the constant (dis)orientation in space – one comes away with an impression of four main concepts often presented in an interdependent manner: past, present, Russia, and Europe. In the film, contemporary visitors interpose between historical episodes. The contemporary narrator and the nineteenth-century French visitor together explore Russia's history and the Hermitage's mostly European art collection. Thus, the film employs a temporal framework that weaves together past and present, and a space in which Russia and Europe merge. Needless to say, the main concepts (past and present, Russia and Europe) lie at the heart of the ongoing process of the formation of Russian national identity.

One can argue that with his sumptuous presentation of Catherine's Winter Palace and his emphasis on imperial luxury and power, Sokurov, like Mikhalkov before him, glorifies and idealizes Russian imperial history. Unsurprisingly, the film received mixed reactions at its world premiere at Cannes 2002. Some criticized it as 'an exercise in czarist nostalgia' (Hoberman 54). Matters are more complex than this, however. On the one hand, Sokurov constructs a romantic and idealized portrayal of tsarist Russia, but on the other, he unveils repressed and hidden aspects of Russian history, thereby deconstructing stereotypes and myths.

The idealization of imperial Russia begins with Sokurov's decision to shoot the film in the Hermitage. In choosing the location – Catherine's Winter Palace – the director inevitably comments on Catherine's rule as a great epoch for Russia, one that was open to European influences. German-born Catherine assumed the throne after a court rebellion against her husband, Tsar Peter, a grandson of Peter the Great. She decisively increased Russia's power and political presence in Europe and established a new state policy, collecting European art.

A romanticized perception of tragic royal destiny is conveyed in a scene with Nicholas II and his family, all dressed in white at table, with one of his daughters holding a doll. Sokurov has voiced his romantic view of the last Russian tsar: 'When we're speaking about the Hermitage museum, we're inevitably speaking about the people who lived in this palace. Certainly, there's a romantic approach to these people, but I prefer romanticism to an aggressive research into something I can't access – their personal lives' (quoted in Macnab 20). Similar to Mikhalkov's blind idealization of Alexander III, Sokurov expresses nostalgic longing for the lost epoch of Russian tsarism. Historians Pamela Kachurin and Ernest Zitser rightly criticize the director for removing 'all personal responsibility from the Russian Imperial elites' for the war and the revolution, and for constructing 'a nostalgic vision of Nicholas II, the last Romanov tsar, as the saintly forgiving father – not as the "Bloody Nicholas" whose troops fired upon unarmed demonstrators calling for an end to an unjust war' (18).

One of the final sequences, presenting the last royal ball in the Hermitage in 1913 just before World War I, enthuses viewers with its representation of cultural achievement, imperial exuberance, and a powerful feeling of apparent approval. Sokurov hired two thousand actors and extras who rehearsed for six months in order to achieve the desired effect: one long shot without montage and the perfection of the mazurka dance at the ball. The camera gently glides among the dancers, recording their elegance, and unnoticeably climbs up on the orchestra's stage to float among the musicians. The Mariinsky Orchestra conducted by Valerii Gergiev (the present director of the Mariinsky Theatre) at the 1913 Winter Palace ball creates an anachronistic impression yet again uniting past and present. The prolonged applause at the end of the ball registers the enjoyment and the satisfaction in the extraordinary celebration of harmony and perfection. Although a more critical eye can notice flaws in the realization of the shot (occasionally extras do not know which way to move), no doubt this presentation of the ball contributes to the film's overall effect of promoting nostalgia for a lost but idealized imperial past.

To express such sentiments has become popular in recent years, despite the fact that very few historians support a positive view of Russia's autocracy and its belated modernization. Analyzing the contradictions of the enduring fascination with the idea that tsarism might have survived given a chance, historian Christopher Read concludes that 'when looked at closely, even optimists did not hold much hope for tsarism as it existed' (210). Read suggests that this groundless fascination is rooted in popular wishes and desires rather than in historical facts and their interpretations by historians.

Infatuated with Russia's imperial past, Sokurov avoids a detailed presentation of Soviet history and suggests its devastating consequences only in passing. While encountering a gloomy room, in which coffins are prepared for the victims of Leningrad, the narrator quietly but determinedly informs Custine about Russia's victory over Nazi Germany and about the one million victims lost in the Siege of Leningrad. At the same time matters are always more complex than is immediately apparent in Sokurov's film. Soviet history and culture are present in the film through numerous intertextual references and allusions. As Dragan Kujundzic points out, 'the movie operates as a colossal attempt to do the impossible: to erase the historical period that has in turn obliterated the tradition represented in the film. Soviet art insistently pushes through in the repressed references to Eisenstein, Malevich or Vertov' (233).

More important, Sokurov, unlike Mikhalkov, is not afraid to uncover an unfamiliar and not always positive and 'proper' side of Russian history and to challenge Russia's increasingly selective view of the past. Even though the director romanticizes imperial Russia and attempts to justify his romantic approach, he also voices ambivalence toward Russia's history, pointing out that Nicholas II was murdered by his own people: 'The sadness of the final scene is connected to the fact that all these people will be killed. And I want you to pay attention to the fact that they will be killed by their compatriots' (quoted in Macnab 20). Numerous scenes in the film reveal controversial and unofficial episodes of Russian history. The marquis in his erratic journey passes by a theatre production enacted before Catherine, who interrupts it by running around looking for a pot to relieve herself in, finally finding a vase. Later on in the film, viewers see her again in her old age, appearing frail and unpredictable. While these scenes merely add a 'human touch' to majesty (not entirely unlike the father-son scenes in Mikhalkov's film), the narrator also encounters a scene in which Peter the Great beats up one of his generals. Nicholas I's insensitive treatment of the Persian emissaries presents an unsympathetic portrait of the 'iron emperor', and, once more on the lighter side, Alexander Pushkin, a mythologized literary figure for the Russian mind, runs around chasing and pinching a young Russian lady, or perhaps it is Natalie, his capricious wife. Even though the nostalgia and the idealization of Russian history are there, Sokurov suggests that history has yet another face and brings mythologized figures from Russian history or literature down to their controversial human manifestations.

Exceptionally revealing of the repressed and hidden aspects of Russian history are the episodes with silent men dressed in black suits and wearing white gloves; they closely follow Custine and do not allow him to enter certain rooms. The authoritarian style of the Russian state, which dates back before the Revolution, is effectively unveiled in the film through the omnipotent presence of these men who, in a way, direct Custine's journey through Russian history. Although Mikhalkov too hints at Russia's repressive apparatus in Tolstoi's scarred face at the end of the film, the presence of the men in black in *Russian Ark* is more consistent and unquestionably speaks of the old history of Russia's secret police.

A close observation of the film's exploration of time and space, or of Bakhtin's concept of the chronotope, suggests a complex presentation of historical temporality different from the one constructed by Mikhalkov in *The Barber of Siberia*. The space is limited to the numerous rooms of the Hermitage museum, framed by the opening scene in which viewers see a crowd entering the museum and the final scene with guests of the last ball descending the stairs of the Hermitage to face a tormented sea (or the overflowing Neva) at the exit. Sokurov's choice of space has a special symbolic dimension. It brings a range of connotations pertaining to the Russian cultural identity. The presentation of time in the film, both reel and real, unavoidably challenges the limits of Bakhtin's concept of the chronotope. A ninety-minute continuous shot of reel time reveals three hundred years of Russian history. The presentation of history, however, does not flow in linear historical time: the viewers see Catherine, followed by a scene with two contemporary visitors to the museum, followed by Pushkin, then by a victim of the Leningrad siege, followed by Catherine, and Nicholas I. And the feeling of cyclical historical time is cemented by the continuous shot, which leads viewers in and out of the Hermitage's numerous rooms representing various (nonchronological) epochs and cultural achievements.

In addition, there is no attempt to transform everyday settings and daily existence into historical time. The representation of historical time in Sokurov's film is abstract and deprived of any attempt to achieve the creative human locality and thus to convey a constructed truthfulness. Even in the scenes with Nicholas II and his family, the vision of time is romanticized but escapes the concrete natural setting of *Localität*, discovered by Bakhtin in Goethe's narrative. The fullness of time that Bakhtin insisted upon and that one can detect in *The Barber of Siberia* occupies a different narrative and cinematic space in *Russian Ark*. The fullness of time, which sustains a continuum between past, present, and future, although visible in Sokurov's film, is punctuated by doubt, hesitation, and reflection, and, more important, by a suggestion of the existence of double temporality.

This implies an approach to historical time different from Mikhalkov's monumental presentation of the fullness of narrative time. In *Russian Ark*, one perceives a certain 'doubling' of time, a concept advanced by Kristeva and later by Bhabha.[11] The nation's time, according to Kristeva, always borders on double temporality: 'In short, with socio-cultural ensembles of the European type, we are constantly faced with a double problematic: that of their *identity* constituted by historical sedimentation, and that of their *loss of identity* which is produced by this connection of memories which escape from history only to encounter anthropology' (1986b, 189). In other words, Kristeva writes about two temporal dimensions: the time of linear history and that of another time and another history. The latter represents repetitive, cyclical modes and encloses supranational and sociocultural entities. While the former constitutes identity, the latter unveils loss of identity or difference. In *Russian Ark*, the intersection of the contemporaneous flow of linear reel time in one long shot and the feeling of cyclical historical time (achieved by the representation of nonchronological, almost repetitive, historical episodes) in the same (dual) cultural space uncovers another temporality, that of difference, and proposes to rethink the sign of history in literary or film discourses, which designate that history as one. The film, therefore, also avoids the temptation to present reality and appearance as one.

Sokurov, in my view, seeks (consciously or unconsciously) to unravel precisely the double temporality in the process of national identification. Unlike Mikhalkov, who advocates a fullness and singularity of national narrative time, Sokurov proposes a process of cultural identification that occurs on the brink of identity hesitation. The persistent floating in time and space and the feeling of cyclical movement that his camera achieves, combined with the presentation of unpopular (or even never mentioned) episodes of Russian history, suggest a more performative temporality of difference rather than the linear monumental time of history.[12]

Elaborated in psychoanalytic terms, this difference between the presentations of historical temporality in the two films reveals the dialectics of *object a* (the irreducible kernel of Russian national identity). Both directors attempt to locate it or materialize it in history, but while Mikhalkov offers its visual symbolization in linear time and constructed history (excluding the invisible hesitations of history and reality), Sokurov, despite his desire to find an image for its symbolization, senses and cinematically suggests the impossibility of its symbolization in the presentation of double historical temporality and the constant dialogue between the visible and the invisible.

Through the Looking Glass of the Past: Culture, Identity, and Difference

Russian Ark

While analyzing the temporal framework of *Russian Ark*, Beumers observes the chronological presentation of the Romanov dynasty ruptured by scenes with several directors of the Hermitage and various contemporary visitors to the museum interpreting this double temporality as 'the collapse of past and present' (2003b, 56). Later on, after scrutinizing the spatial structure of the film (and more precisely the 'choice of the art, the culture, the historical figures, as well as Sokurov's lens'),

Beumers locates Sokurov's sentiments on the side of the westernizers in their nineteenth-century debate with the Slavophiles: 'In ignoring, rejecting, annihilating the here-and-now,' she writes, 'Sokurov cannot hope for a positive reception of his film by Russian audiences, beyond the admiration for a technical achievement... Like Custine, Sokurov denies Russia the right to its own culture, its own voice and its indigenous tradition' (Beumers 2003b, 58–59).

My argument so far follows Beumers's understanding of the 'collapse of past and present' in the film with its two temporal frames, but her statements that Sokurov annihilates the 'here-and-now' and denies Russia its own culture invite closer scrutiny. Sokurov's choice of art (all West European), the historical periods, and the location hardly mean that he ignores the present. On the contrary, as Bakhtin would argue, the past is there to serve the present and the future. Today, western (especially film and pop) culture has infiltrated Russian life no less than during the time when the Romanov fascination with western art inundated it with its products, but this does not suggest that Sokurov denies Russia its culture. Moreover, as Kujundzic argues, Soviet (non-western) art can be detected in various cinematic references in the film.[13]

Unlike Mikhalkov, who boldly and unconvincingly promotes Russia's cultural uniqueness, Sokurov rather proposes that one of Russia's national and cultural missions is to reevaluate and guard western art and culture, a mission tenuously resembling the idea of the 'Third Rome' – in which it is Russia's mission to be the saviour of Christianity. To Custine, who recognizes the style of the Vatican in one of the Hermitage's halls, the narrator replies: "No, this is not the Vatican. It is better, it is St Petersburg."

The film offers numerous scenes in which Russian visitors to the museum perceive western art rather differently from Custine. For example, the hands of El Greco's *Peter and Paul* speak and move Russian youth with the power of their expressiveness. Their perception, different from Custine's appreciation of the picture filtered through his knowledge of the biblical story, is no less valuable than his. On the contrary, the reaction of the Russian young visitor reveals the unusual role of Russian culture vis-à-vis western culture: to reassess it and revitalize it.[14]

At the same time, Sokurov does not accept Russia's engagement with the West unquestioningly. By using two guides, one Russian and one French, for the tour through history and culture, Sokurov once again secures a dual approach to Russian history and culture, but also a Russian reaction to the West. After his *Russie en 1839*, Marquis de Custine became an important figure – a spokesman of the official western perspective on Russia. In his observation of Russia he was deeply influenced by the already existing construction of Russia as the European other of the eighteenth century, and he passionately continued and intensified this tradition. He warned his readers that they could be easily deceived by Russia's appearance of civilization, whereas underneath a real barbarism existed: 'The circumstance which renders Russia the most singular State now to be seen in the world is that extreme barbarism, favoured by enslavement of the church, and extreme civilization, imported by an eclectic government from foreign lands, are there to be seen united' (Custine 15). In 1946, Custine's book became available to the American reader and was reprinted in France. Custine's discoveries and observations about Russia and the Russian character sadly became the most valuable knowledge the West acquired on all things Russian. After World War II, the US ambassador to the Soviet Union wrote that its 'political observation' was 'so penetrating and timeless that it could be called the best work so far produced about the Soviet Union' (quoted in Wolff 365).

Even during the cold war, Zbigniew Brzezinski recommended the book for the 'insights into the Russian character and the Byzantine nature of the Russian political system' (Wolff 365).

Such a prolonged construction of Russia in fixed formulas as the European (un)civilized other, which began even before the eighteenth century and which Custine's book carried effectively to the very end of the twentieth century, prompts Sokurov to challenge the flatness and superficiality of this tradition and to expose its shallowness. It is no accident that the director uses Custine as his opponent during the tour through Russian history and culture. Often, instead of defensively opposing the marquis, the narrator is silent, and Custine unveils his shallow superiority on his own accord. When Pushkin passes by, Custine remarks that he has read him in French and finds nothing extraordinary in Russia's national poet. The assumption that one can know everything about the other's culture, while not knowing the other's language, reveals Europe's failure to make an effort in learning more about the other, as well as its self-deceit about its own cultural supremacy. Their conversation about music similarly exposes Custine's pretences and false preeminence. Custine confidently insists that a German must have composed the music they hear because Russians have no good composers, in response to which the narrator utters simply, 'No, this is Glinka.' Is there a need for an argument here? Certainly, the narrator is not as arrogant and self-absorbed as Custine is, but the narrator's more modest and reflective tone does not imply that he agrees with Custine. The difference in the way the two perceive art and comment on history exposes Custine's (Europe's) megalomania and often deceptive self-confidence. When the marquis and the narrator discuss Russia's participation in World War II and the losses Russia suffered, Custine's denigrating remark is: 'Too high a price.' The narrator calmly and quietly answers that 'in Russia, it is said that freedom knows no price.' The sympathies of the viewer are clearly steered toward the narrator's absolute belief in freedom and his acceptance of people's sacrifices rather than with Custine's relativism. These few examples (among others) counter Beumers's understanding that 'often he [the narrator] repeats Custine's words with an ironic tone in his voice, yet he never contradicts, argues, or offers an alternative view to Custine's assessment of Russia' (2003b, 57). More significant, however, is the fact that the two guides in the film persistently approach the historical and cultural process of identification from different perspectives and unveil its complexities and contradictions.

At the very end of the film, when Custine senses the journey's descent into chaos and refuses to continue, the camera leaves him behind and focuses on the massive exit of all the guests, who retain the glow of pleasure on their faces while descending the stairs of the Hermitage only to face cloudy, gloomy, and stormy waves at the doors of the museum. The view of the grey waters conveys the threat of the unknown and the unpredictable, but the calm and confident voice of the Russian narrator assures viewers that Russia is destined to sail forever and live forever. Powerful and disturbing in its visual representation of the tormented waters, the final scene alarms viewers and simultaneously comforts them with the narrator's voice-over proclaiming Russia's eternally surviving spirit ensuing from Russia's world-class culture and rich history. This doubling of the scene, in which the visual and the vocal opposing each other unite to create one overall impression, again illustrates Sokurov's complex approach to Russian history and national identity. The ending presents the Hermitage in terms of Noah's ark and becomes a metaphor of Russia's strength and perseverance.[15]

The integration and internalization of western models as sources of independent development into Russia's national identity reveal more reflexive and mature sentiments about Russia's uniqueness and independence. Sokurov's view allows the recognition and absorption of foreign influences into the exceptional configuration of Russian culture. Mikhalkov's denial of influence and insistence on a pure national culture at the beginning of the twenty-first century appears questionable.

If Mikhalkov is clearly a neo-Slavophile and an unquestioning patriot, Sokurov reveals considerably more complexity, closely examining the westernizers' approach to understanding Russian national and cultural identity, while also conveying a national pride in Russia's abilities to 'live forever and sail forever'. Mikhalkov perceives faith in one's country as unqualified affirmation, whereas Sokurov affirms in spite of critique.

The Barber of Siberia

Mikhalkov uncritically advances the portrayal of positive traits attributed to the Russian state and its national institutions, such as the royal family and the country's military might and glory, exemplified in the royal military academy. The film is dedicated to the values represented by the royal cadets – their honour, fraternal bonds, and loyalty to tsar and country – their elite status. The scene of Tolstoi's departure for Siberia portrays the devastated cadets seeking out their friend Andrei for a last farewell. The train carries Andrei away, but he is again united with his fellow cadets in singing Figaro's aria from the Mozart opera he performed in when he was arrested, thus demonstrating his ability to transcend personal misfortune.[16] Although General Radlov is portrayed as a complete idiot

Mikhalkov's *The Barber of Siberia*.

and a drunk, Captain Mokin, the cadets' immediate superior, is ready to sacrifice his rank and himself to protect his cadets. Numerous scenes in Mikhalkov's film – the cadets' graduation ceremony, Andrei's attack on the General, and the Forgiveness Day – promote an understanding that the Russian national identity might be bound by irrational feelings but also by loyalty, honour, and high moral standards.

In addition to the demonstration of the cadets' high values and brotherhood, in his desire to resurrect the national ideal, the director attempts to reinforce traditional family values (nurtured by Russian characters). Jane's seduction and consequent betrayal of Andrei's feelings ruin his life. Tolstoi's irrational attack on the general during the performance of *The Marriage of Figaro*, even though serving the purpose of exposing the daring, committed and extreme nature of the Russian character so much emphasized by Mikhalkov, plainly determines the sad outcome of Tolstoi and Jane's affair, as well as of Tolstoi's future troubles. He is exiled to Siberia, but this might actually prove to be a blessing in disguise: Duniasha (Tolstoi's family maid) reveals her complete devotion to her master and her unconditional love for him. Viewers learn that she has followed him to Siberia and they are married with three children. Her devotion clearly appears stronger and more steadfast than Jane's passion for Tolstoi. Beumers argues that Duniasha (representing Russia and her simple folk) is endowed with solely positive characteristics, unlike Jane (the West) 'who is a liar' (2000, 200). The film offers enough evidence to support Beumers' conclusions that western culture is denigrated while Russian culture is elevated: Jane is portrayed as a mercantile and treacherous woman; Andrew's American captain, O'Leary, is ignorant and shallow; the forest-harvesting machine is a monster that destroys nature and threatens Russian people's lives.

Yet there are a few details that upset the clear-cut perception of the destructive and corruptive West and the morally superior Russia. Jane's horrible past as an abused and molested child on the one hand speaks of corrupted western family values, but on the other hand it could explain her failure to be honest with Andrei. Also, one of the last scenes shows Duniasha ready to strike Jane with a sickle to prevent her from meeting Tolstoi again. This may be seen as a sign of Duniasha's willpower, positive at first glance, which, however, can also be interpreted as a destructive obsession. Mikhalkov's desire to simultaneously flirt (financially and aesthetically) with the West and resurrect Russian national pride has resulted in a few mixed and confusing constructions of western and Russian images, but no doubt the overall perception of these images positions Russia's cultural values as superior to those of the West.

At the end of the film, Tolstoi's responsibility as a husband and a father appears stronger than his previous passion for Jane. In the last few scenes of the film Mikhalkov shows Jane leaving Tolstoi's house after she has failed to find him. Realizing that she has arrived too late, she chases her horses down a dusty Siberian road angrily shouting: 'Go!' Another shot cuts to Tolstoi in the forest who abruptly abandons his occupation and starts running feverishly. He appears on the edge of a field, sees Jane's carriage, and hears her shouting. At this crucial moment he stops to catch his breath, looks at the carriage, and lights a cigarette. A close-up of his face and the hand reveals a rather rough and dirty hand of manual labor with a shining golden wedding ring. After this shot it becomes more than obvious that he will let Jane leave without seeing him. His responsibility and devotion to his family prevail over any infatuations of the past.

Oleg Menshikov (as Andrei Tolstoi) looking at Jane's carriage at end of The Barber of Siberia.

The place of Tolstoi's exile, Siberia, although a well-known exile location in Russian history, in this film carries additional weight and signifies Russianness more than anything else, more than even the Kremlin perhaps. This is the place where Russian nature has accepted Tolstoi; he has created a Russian family, and the characters are at peace with themselves and their environment. The symbolic power of Siberia guards him, rejects the intruder, Jane, and guarantees his family happiness.[17]

Mikhalkov imperceptibly weaves faith and religion into the resurrection of Russian national identity too. Many panoramic shots of landscape contain typical silhouettes of Russian church domes. The presence of Russian Orthodoxy can be perceived at many levels in the film: from the religious service Jane overhears when she visits Tolstoi in the hospital, through a celebration (Maslenitsa) of the last week before the long Easter Lent, to the priests' blessing of prisoners on their way to exile. The representation of positive Russian characteristics and the image of the fatherland become linked to Russian Orthodoxy. In interviews, Mikhalkov often insists that faith and religion are 'like air: you don't notice it, but you cannot live without it' (Mikhalkov 2000, 24). He believes that today's children of Russia should be brought up in a way that they feel a natural necessity to go to church and attend services (Mikhalkov 2000, 27). The film unmistakably tries to cultivate this natural necessity for faith and religion. The persistent but not overemphasized presence of religion in his film confirms his beliefs that faith is like air. Mikhalkov does not focus on religion *per se* but imperceptibly intertwines religious images in the shots so they become an essential part of Russian landscape and everyday life. With their serenity and their natural presence in Russian life these images become part of Russian cultural identity, testifying to its spirituality as they stand in contrast to western symbols (the forest-harvesting machine or the army camp in Massachusetts) stripped of any signs that hint at an existence above the material world. In the Massachusetts camp, Andrew stands out as an oddity because he is stubbornly faithful to Mozart's music. Notably, he has inherited this love from his Russian father, Tolstoi. The only hope for the mercantile and materialistic western world is the cultural and spiritual influence of Russia (although Mozart is a western composer).

Even though Sokurov also engages religious and cultural images, he is preoccupied first with art and only through it with religion and spirituality. Analyzing the scene, in which the narrator talks about the victims of the Leningrad siege and implicitly points to the fact that Russians saved the treasure of world art from the Nazis, Kachurin and Zitser believe that 'Sokurov presents Russia as the Christ of modern nations and as the only hope for salvation for a materialistic, bourgeois, and decadent West' (19). Further, Kachurin and Zitser discuss the presence of El Greco's *Peter and Paul* and Rembrandt's *Prodigal Son* and *Danaë* in the film. They remind readers that St Peter is a patron of both Peter the Great and St Petersburg as they argue that 'Peter was not a just another monarch, but a ruler whose creation fits into the largest scheme possible – the story of the world's redemption' (19). They interpret the camera's long shots of the *Prodigal Son* as another example of Sokurov's interest in a story of redemption through repentance (20). Although *Danaë* depicts the ancient myth of the virgin, Danaë, impregnated by Zeus through golden rain, Kachurin and Zitser see implicit references to the Virgin Mary and St George (Danaë gives birth to Perseus, a dragon slayer) (20). Even if one finds all these interpretations a bit exaggerated, no one can argue that Sokurov's choice of these particular paintings is accidental. I think that for Sokurov art comes first and through it religious stories and messages which are disconnected from their original purely religious form and which can speak to contemporary viewers in various ways, as it was mentioned that the perception of *Peter and Paul* by contemporary visitors of the museum is already aestheticized.

Mikhalkov attempts to create two distinct worlds: the West – shallow, ignorant, and corrupted; and Russia – passionate but rich in cultural and moral values. Such division and differences uncover insecure national identity. Conversely, Sokurov unravels the complexities of Russia's involvement with the West through the Hermitage's collection and the Russian perception of it as well as the Russian role in its preservation. Through Custine and the narrator, whose ideas often clash, Sokurov challenges any one-sided comprehension of Russian national identity versus the West.

The films analyzed in this chapter seek internal positive forces such as past, culture, and religion in order to promote Russia's cultural independence and uniqueness in the global world, a process resembling the adolescent's struggle for separation and exceptionality that determines her/his entry to adulthood. Sokurov, in my view, is more impartial than Mikhalkov in his quest for Russia's cultural uniqueness and national identity. *Russian Ark* idealizes the past but also attempts to reveal the complexities of the past's interpretations. The film engages the West in a more dialectic relationship, internalizing it as a source for inspiration and simultaneously exclusivity. Mikhalkov, unlike Sokurov, deems the western models unsuitable and rejects them, seeking at the same time positive energy in a mythologized and manufactured past and a hyped Russian culture. Mikhalkov, believing in his infinite power to alter reality, tries to find cinematic expressions, to symbolize the kernel of Russian national identity, an attempt that results in confusing and unconvincing images and in a surrogate of the *object a*. Sokurov, on the other hand, intuitively senses the complexity of Russian national identity and the impossibility to symbolize its essence, creating a more complex engagement with past and culture. Salecl argues that '[t]he *object a* is the substitute the subject gets when it is subjected to castration upon entering the realm of symbolic mediation' (1994, 126). Following this thought, one can infer that in these two films Russian viewers saw substitutes of 'true' national identity in times when they are subjected to frustrations upon entering the global world.

Notes

1. According to Lacan, the object of fantasy can be any item that supports our subjective perception of reality. This item (mother's gaze or voice in child's development) is both the cause of desire and the object of desire. It is irreducible and ultimately cannot be symbolized. The fantasy relation to the object involves some opposition to speech, knowledge, and the symbolic.

2. In addition to history, post-Soviet cinema turned its attention to Russian literary classics. Rudol'f Fruntov's *All of Which We've Dreamed so Long* (1997), for example, intrigues with numerous references to *Crime and Punishment*, references at work on multiple levels. The storyline offers a modern interpretation of Raskolnikov's murders and Sonia's spiritual influence over him. For contemporary cultural and literary references to Dostoevsky, see "Igraia so slovami klassiki: Dostoevskii v sovremennoi literature" (Mochizuki). Other films from the last decade of the twentieth century, based on Russian literary sources, include: Sergei Bodrov's *The Prisoner of the Mountains* (1996), founded on a story by Lev Tolstoy; Valerii Todorovskii's *Katia Izmailova* (1994), which followed Nikolai Leskov's *Lady Macbeth of Mtsensk*; Nikolai Dostal's *The Little Demon* (1995) dramatized Fedor Sologub's novel by the same name; and Sergei Gazarov's *Inspector General* (1996), created after Nikolai Gogol's play. Most recently the adaptation of Dostoevsky's *Idiot* (dir. Vladimir Bortko, 2003) became unexpectedly popular and producers are continuing to rely on Russian literary classics. Viewers expect to see Gogol's *Dead Souls* (dir. Pavel Lungin), Pasternak's *Doctor Zhivago* (dir. Aleksandr Proshkin), Bulgakov's *Master and Margarita* (dir. Vladimir Bortko), Tolstoy's *Anna Karenina* (dir. Sergei Solov'ev), and Lermontov's *The Hero of Our Time* (dir. Dmitrii Meskhiev).

3. In briefly summarizing post-Soviet cinema's exploration of the past, I follow Gillespie's and Lawton's observations (Gillespie; Lawton 2002).

4. The director is working on a sequel in two parts.

5. For other noteworthy readings of the films, see Birgit Beumers (2000), Susan Larsen (2003), Nikita Sokolov, Birgit Beumers (2003b), Pamela Kachurin and Ernest A. Zitser, Nickolas Lupinin, Tim Harte, and Dragan Kujundzic.

6. See Bakhtin (1986). In analyzing and explaining Goethe's vision of historical time, Bakhtin admires the German writer's mastery over the creation of a 'fullness of time'. Two major components craft the fullness of time in national narrative. First, history must be understood and presented as a linear monolithic movement, a conclusive continuum of past, present, and future (as the past must have its 'effect' on the present and on the future). Second, 'the past itself must be creative'; that is, 'must be revealed as necessary and productive under the condition of a given locality, as a creative humanization of this locality' (25–54). In other words, national history represented as a linear movement of historical time is inseparable from everyday life, its settings and occurrences.

7. One would assume that this son is the future Nicholas II, but he was born in 1868 and would have been seventeen years old in 1885 and thus too old for the little boy shown. Alexander III's other son, Mikhail, was born in 1878, and it would seem that it is he who is portrayed in the film, although it is clear that Mikhalkov ignores historical accuracies.

8. For more on the political aspirations of Mikhalkov, see Georgii Bovt. Susan Larsen comments on the attempted fusion of film and politics: 'Held in the Kremlin Palace, which was specially equipped for the occasion with up-to-date projection equipment, a new wide screen, and Dolby surround sound, the premiere of *Barber* was packed with high-ranking government officials... The screening was followed by a fireworks display over Red Square, as if it were a national holiday, and several observers speculated that Mikhalkov was opening not only his new film but also a campaign for the presidency' (Larsen 2003).

9. Beumers notes that Mikhalkov removed the red stars from Kremlin's towers 'to allow for the film's setting in pre-Revolutionary Russia' (2000, 195).

10. Moskvina and Beumers notice the scene of the sparrow but mention it as an evidence of Mikhalkov's mastery of the small detail. Moskvina argues that Mikhalkov advances a monumental picture at the expense of the dramatic detail and pulls the story in a rather linear way. Conversely, Beumers believes that 'Mikhalkov never neglects the small at the expanse of the grand' [Moskvina 1999, 33; Beumers 2000, 201.]

11. While Bhabha acknowledges the importance of Bakhtin's observation on the fullness of time in the national vision of Goethe, he questions the effect of such a presentation in the present: 'We are led to ask whether the *emergence* of a national perspective – of an elite or subaltern nature – within a culture of social contestation, can ever articulate its "representative" authority in that fullness of narrative time and visual synchrony of the sign that Bakhtin proposes' (213). Bhabha draws on Kristeva's ideas (among others) about the nation's temporality to question the fullness of narrative time (advocated by Bakhtin) and to suggest 'narrative ambivalence of disjunctive times and meanings' (213–16).

12. Kujundzic offers an intriguing reading of the historical temporality in the film as 'counter-temporality'. The encounter between Custine (gaze) and the narrator (voice-over) enriches the narrative structure with spatio-temporal doubling. 'The narrative actually starts in the mode of this *contre-temps*, counter-temporality, whereby the beginning, the origin of filming is split between the two narrators' (224).

13. 'The endings of Pudovkin's *The Last Days of Petersburg* (1927) and Eisenstein's *October* (1927) end in the same place, the Jordan Stairwell in the Winter Palace. The two endings of the two classics of modernist cinema are quoted at the end of *The Russian Ark* but in a semantically and ideologically reversed direction' (Kujundzic 233).

14. While my reading of Sokurov's understanding of Russian cultural identity considerably differs from Beumers', it is more in accordance with Kachurin and Zitser's views. They argue that Sokurov presents himself as a patriot in the film and 'the mutually contradictory opinions of Custine and Sokurov are actually two sides of the same coin', that is, national sentiments (Kachurin and Zitser 20).

15. Sokurov often insists on the vital function of the ending for the success of the film. In an interview, he says: 'To me, if there's no ending, there is no film what so ever; it didn't happen.' (Sokurov 21–25).

16. Susan Larsen claims that this scene is 'a musical demonstration of persecuted heroism' (2003, 500).

17. In Siberia, when the forest-harvesting machine is tested, people are portrayed to be terrified by this monstrosity, a product of western civilization. For more on the conflict between nature and civilization, see Larsen (2003).

4

(Im)possible Relationships: Looking for the Other

Connected to the process of separation and the search for uniqueness is the formation of intimate partnership. Freud placed central to the achievement of adolescents the tasks of forming sexual identity, finding a sexual partner, and fusing the two stems of sexuality: the sensual and the tender. Developing an internal capacity for intimacy is one of the important goals of the adolescent who is approaching adulthood. The establishment of a deep and lasting emotional relationship depends on various internal as well as external factors: how love and loss have been experienced in the past and how parents have helped their children in such experiences, for instance, can reinforce the capacity to contain passions and to think rather than to act hastily and irrationally, which in turn equips them to have healthy relationships.

In a study of the fatal familial and social structures in the romance between Romeo and Juliet, Rustin insists, on the one hand, that the capacity to 'contain impulse in the form of thought' distinguishes well-functioning individuals and, on the other, that the social institutions and symbolic forms that might effectively contain such thoughts are the necessary preconditions for functional relationships (232). In this way Rustin calls attention to both internal and external conditions that determine the capacity to contain emotions and to transform them into thought. Here he departs from a strictly psychoanalytic view and points to a fruitful connection between psychoanalysis and social theories in their approaches to culture. Emphasizing the role of society, he writes: 'I also suggest that one criterion of the adequacy of a society for the development of those who live in it lies in the "cultural" or "symbolic space" it provides for members at different stages in their lives' (Rustin 234).[1]

How efficiently family, schools, and society can facilitate the capacity for thought among their members determines certain conditions for healthy and functioning individuals, their relationships, and society as a whole. Effectively drawing on these ideas in his analysis of Shakespeare's *Romeo and Juliet*, Rustin concludes:

> The play emerges at a historical transition point, in which both the emergent romantic individualist conception of sexual love of modern times and the authoritarian structures of patriarchal authority could be seen to exercise great power over the lives of representative dramatic figures. Both these structures are represented in *Romeo and Juliet* as fragile and unstable; hence the tragic outcome of the play. (235)

The romances, affairs, and the sexual passions examined in this chapter differ from the relationship of Romeo and Juliet and their social conditions, and yet one can observe similarities in the instability of the social and political conditions that define the Russian-western love affairs as well as in the fragility of the love relationships themselves. The changing political and economic climate after the collapse of the Berlin Wall, which presented new opportunities for East-West cross-national relationships, defines the very conditions and, consequently, the outcome of these relationships as seen in film examples.

This chapter examines the ardent but failed love affairs between western and Russian characters represented in some of the films already discussed, such as On Deribasovskaia, Window to Paris, and The Barber of Siberia, as well as in Gods' Envy and The Frenchman. Emotions and sexual passions occur amidst a historical context that appears unprepared for them. Social and political difficulties as well as powerful urges to preserve a unique national identity undermine characters' desire to unite with the West. The construction and unfolding of these Russian-western love and sexual relationships mirror challenges to the Russian national identity during the transition period in that they inevitably become entangled in the (gendered) desire of the Russian national identity for masculine dominance in these relationships.

Except the couples featured in Gods' Envy and The Frenchman, in which the women are Russian and the men are French, the male figures in the relationships are Russian and the females are western (American or French). In the context of this work's previous discussions about the fantasies and fears caused by threatened national identity and the loss of Russia's position as a world power, the Russian collective imagination compensates in film by displacing national anxiety into Russian male dominance in international romances.

In exploring the gender dynamics in cross-national relationships, I utilize two interrelated terms, 'gaze' and 'look', introduced by Laura Mulvey to film theory and more specifically to feminist film theory in her ground-breaking essay, "Visual Pleasure and Narrative Cinema". Since then other theorists have developed and differentiated the two terms. Here, I follow in the steps of Judith Mayne and Ann Kaplan who were interested in the 'looking relation' and its historical, cultural, and psychoanalytic implications (Mayne 1990 and 1993; Kaplan 1997). In this chapter, I use the term 'look' to indicate a relation and a process implying desire to know and curiosity about the other, while the 'gaze' designates the extreme anxiety and fears that preclude knowledge (Kaplan 1997, xvi-xxi). The look, driven by curiosity and desire for relatedness, is more interested in the object, whereas the gaze, consumed by its own anxieties, impedes (the learning) process and prohibits a relationship with the object. In the context of studies that explore how white men gaze at white women within the western world as well as how inter-racial look works, this chapter asks questions about the cross-national look (Kaplan 1997). What happens when Russian men travel to the West and gaze at western women? And how are western women looked at when they are in Russia?

The use of the gaze in this chapter differs from its utilization until this point as Lacan's de-essentializing force, as the free-floating gaze connected to object a and situated beyond appearance. Feminist scholars have drifted from such function of the gaze, for they claim that 'Lacan's gaze cannot be used to analyze sexual difference because it allows no differential analysis of mastery and subjection – everyone is subjected to a gaze which is outside' (Doane 55).[2] Since this chapter explores sexual/romantic relationships constructed predominantly as Russian (masculine)/western (feminine), distinguishing between gaze and look and, moreover, associating the gaze with the masculine/imperial position proves helpful in pointing out the desired privileged status Russia assumes in the imagined relationship with the West.

"Hello, America."

Gaidai's 1992 film *On Deribasovskaia the Weather is Nice, or, On Brighton Beach It's Raining Again* and Mamin's 1993 film *Window to Paris* are two of the early popular films after the destruction of the Berlin Wall to present romantic involvement between Russian and western characters.[3] *On Deribasovskaia* constructs an optimistic and hopeful relationship between Fedor Sokolov, a KGB officer, and Mary Star, a CIA agent, as well as a triumphant outcome: their love overcomes all difficulties and saves the world from an outburst of deadly chemical gas. Being a true comedy, the film allows itself unrealistic plot twists to result in a happy ending. As already mentioned, the Russian KGB officer is dispatched from Kharkiv to the United States to combat the Russian Mafia there. Love at first sight springs up between him and the American CIA agent, who is assigned to assist and protect him. The operation follows and reaffirms a myth: the Russian Mafia abroad can be neutralized only by Russian forces because the specificity of the Russian mentality defies the logic and rationality of the West. This myth of the unique and unfathomable Russian mind also governs the very nature of Sokolov and Mary's love relationship: he is portrayed as often irrational and easily tempted by his love impulses, whereas Mary is cold-hearted and practical, not allowing her emotions to determine her actions. The scene of their first encounter is typical: Sokolov is waiting for his American partner in a coffee shop, when he is approached by Mary (whom he takes as a curious woman eager to strike a conversation). He quickly tries to discourage her from sharing his table since an important meeting awaits him. For a few moments Sokolov cannot comprehend the possibility of having a female professional partner. After Mary proves to him that she is his CIA contact, his serious look changes into an objectifying and sensual gaze. Sokolov's attempts to ignore sexual temptations fail: he is determined to have a pleasurable time with Mary in his new apartment, while she soberly examines the place for possible traps. This gender dynamic granting Mary the more rational, business-like behaviour and Sokolov a more irrational and impulsive one, however, does not deprive Sokolov of having the upper hand in the overall operation. When matters reach the seriousness of 'saving the world', Sokolov unquestionably usurps the leadership position with Mary right by his side. Although Sokolov appears like a clumsy adolescent in love in his early contacts with Mary, the camera still positions him as an agent of the gaze full of sexual fantasies. More fundamentally, his gaze incorporates sexual and national fantasies and fears.

People travelling (or immigrating) to the United States at the end of the twentieth century were usually driven by the myth of the 'American dream'. They, however, soon realized the limitations and restrictions (constructed as looking relations) that negatively defined them. Sokolov is blissfully ignorant to such looking relations as he himself does not look but gazes at American culture and lifestyle, not interested in knowing it. His eye familiarizes all sites and people immediately upon contact (as already discussed in chapter one). Sokolov does not see any Americanness in Brighton Beach but recognizes only signs of Russianness. In his character, the male gaze and the Russian (national) gaze collude with one another. Sent to America on a mission, the KGB officer is not interested in learning more or knowing America better, but in romantically engaging his female American partner, in neutralizing the Russian Mafia, and in confirming Russian superiority in methods and tactics of intelligence.

Similar is the structure of the gaze in *Window to Paris*. After discovering the 'window' and walking the streets of Paris, Nikolai Chizhov and the Gorokhovs see and experience the fantasized West. But the teacher in music, Chizhov, and the trivial entrepreneurs, the Gorokhovs, relate to western reality differently. When admiring stores of electronics, fur coats, and liquor, Chizhov looks with curiosity and amazement, whereas Gorokhov gazes at what he considers the signs of decedent capitalism. In the fur coats he sees the fur of his Siberian animals, and liquor stores reassure him that the French drink more than the Russians. The film is replete with stereotypical images and tropes of the mythic construction of the West.

These Russian film characters' (Sokolov, Chizhov, and the Gorokhovs) trips to the West resemble western films about the travels of westerners to unknown Asian or African countries. Although the nature of the encounters is reversed, the structure of the gaze is similar. The western travellers, always agents of the imperial western gaze (representing culture and civilization), usually meet nature and barbarism in these encounters. Conversely, the Russian visitors come upon and are fascinated by western consumer culture and wealth. They (like westerners in Africa), however, refuse to establish a looking relation with the other but instead gaze and objectify the other. In Paul Glaser's 1994 *The Air up There*, the main protagonist, Jimmy Dolan, travels to Africa in search of the perfect basketball player physique. In one scene, he is so thrilled by the landscape and wild animals that he pulls out a video camera and begins filming. The shot resembles a carefully designed postcard (Kaplan 1997, 75–77). Although the Gorokhovs encounter the abundance of consumer culture and not the wild landscape of Africa, the way they gaze at Paris's stores is much like Dolan's fascination with Africa. In both cases individual anxieties are transformed into condescending paternalism; the gaze objectifies the other and prohibits mutual relation and recognition.

Only Chizhov, especially in his romantic contacts with Nicole, is a curious Russian visitor who is open in his encounters with western culture. Chizhov and Nicole sincerely follow their hearts in their mutual attraction, but when it comes to being faithful to one's homeland, Chizhov chooses Russia. The film rejects the possibility of effectively combining love for the homeland and love for a foreigner. Interestingly, Nicole understands Chizhov's dilemma and silently supports him in his decision. *Window to Paris* clearly subordinates the romantic relationship to patriotic feelings and loyalty to one's country. Chizhov is also disappointed by French realities, which do not adhere to the Soviet mythic construction of the western world. Unlike Sokolov, he recognizes the limits of mercantilism and consumer culture.

Despite their differences, *On Deribasovskaia* and *Window to Paris* unveil the hidden Russian desire to help or rescue the West. In both relationships, the male Russian characters save their romantic partners from difficulties. In *On Deribasovskaia*, Sokolov wins the battle with the Mafia and (in)directly saves Mary several times, while in *Window to Paris*, Chizhov rescues Nicole from prison when she finds herself tricked by the Gorokhovs in St Petersburg.

The upper-hand position of the Russian male protagonists in these relationships is also suggested by the naming of the characters. While Russians are given full names (first, patronymic, and last), their western partners are addressed mainly with their given names, a tactic which familiarizes them and reflects their archetypal nature. The French woman is stereotypically named Nicole and the American is Mary. Similar stereotypes are applied to the professions of the two women: Nicole is a pretentious taxidermist whose work is motivated by pragmatism and appears alien and even repulsive for the Russian collective imagination, and Mary is a CIA agent – a symbol of the professional gender equality and American 'feminism' often mocked in Russia. This approach to the female characters' stereotypical names and professions differs from the construction of Chizhov and Sokolov, who are more individualized in their dramaturgical characteristics. Both films' scripts deprive the female characters of multi-sidedness and offer full and interesting male characters.

The same gender dynamic granting the Russian males more cinematic visibility and power and the western females less character development is evident in *Quickie* (2001). In this film, Sergei Bodrov, Sr constructs an image of Oleg, a Russian Mafia boss in Hollywood, who has achieved undoubted financial success and lives in a multimillion-dollar mansion, but is tormented by the meaning of life and is eager to retire and leave the business to his younger half-brother, Alex. Experiencing similar sentiments to those of the music teacher in *Window to Paris* who realizes that consumer culture obliterates art, Oleg is indifferent to the luxury that surrounds him but brings no meaning to his empty life. The triviality of the western culture that Chizhov finds repulsive is also rejected here but only after being conquered. Oleg has the wealth and opulence that the Gorokhovs and Chizhov discovered with amazement.

At a New Year's Eve party, where Oleg announces his retirement, he is threatened several times on the phone and realizes that his days are numbered. In the morning a young American woman comes to clean the house and exterminate cockroaches. Oleg, fully aware that she might be his assassin, develops feelings for her (which seem to be mutual), and after spending a romantic day with her, asks her to drive him to his favourite beach where he meets her bullet. The profound exceptionality of the Russian soul, which does not fit into western culture, makes any relationship between the characters impossible.

In all the films mentioned so far in this chapter, a Russian man meets a western woman.[4] Despite differences in the construction of the romantic relationships, he rarely develops a true/lasting relationship with his partner (or the West), but gazes at her (it), as his national (Russian) desires appear stronger than his sexual passion. All these films reveal anxious fantasies and social unease about cross-national relationships.

"He is Russian. This explains a lot."
Although *The Barber of Siberia* differs in form and content from the previously discussed films, it shares with them the construction of the love affair between the Russian character cadet Andrei Tolstoi and his American flame Jane Callahan. Again, the Russian male character reveals his superiority over his American partner in his firm loyalty first to his values and second to the tsar and the country. If in *Window to Paris* viewers can notice a certain sadness and hesitation in Chizhov's decision to return to his homeland, in *The Barber of Siberia* Andrei's behaviour is the only possible solution for a true Russian. Andrei's honesty and his sincere emotions lead to his exile and a life of difficulties he bears with dignity.

The Barber of Siberia presents one very significant difference in the structure of the gaze. Jane, an agent of the western gaze, travels to Russia and is at first presented as a western explorer visiting the exotic and unknown Russia. The film opens with a scene in which she writes a letter to her son describing her experiences in Russia twenty years ago. It is interesting to ask here, how does the looking relation work in this different context, presenting the westerner as owner of the gaze?

At the beginning of the film, Jane's strong position as the subject (agent) of the gaze is evident in her first experiences in Russia as an observer of an assassination attempt and as a visitor to a spring festival. Her puzzlement while witnessing these events betrays the western construction of Russia as the other. As the narrative unfolds, however, Mikhalkov replaces her as an agent of the gaze with Tolstoi, whose male gaze takes priority and in turn objectifies her, blending male and national anxieties. If there is an initial impression that Jane gazes at the Russian object, Mikhalkov reverses the roles, and the 'subaltern' not only looks back, but also appropriates the gaze.

Mikhalkov portrays the love story a little better than he does the epic representation of Russia, for his talent lies in building dramatic tension and focusing on details. Despite hostility toward the westernization of Russian culture demonstrated in the director's previous films (*Close to Eden* [1991] and *Anna from Six to Eighteen* [1993]), Andrei and Jane represent not only two human beings seeking romance and happiness, but also two countries in search of a relationship.[5] Many critics remark on Mikhalkov's attempt to extend the mere romance between Andrei and Jane into a symbolic relationship between the two countries. Dmitrii Bykov's remark is typical: 'Mikhalkov shot an honest account of the affair between Russia and America' (50). Iurii Bogomilov, focusing on the significance of the romance in the film, suggests that Mikhalkov creates love relations not only between people and countries, but also between continents (63).

The very title of the film, *The Barber of Siberia*, contains the West-East relationship in the form of a pun, as the title recalls Rossini's opera *The Barber of Seville* (1816), based on Beaumarchais's play of the same name. The numerous film references to Mozart and the cadets' performance of Mozart's opera *The Marriage of Figaro* (1786), also based on Beaumarchais's sequel to *The Barber of Seville*, reconfirms the Russian ties to the West that the film attempts to (re)establish. The Seville from the title of Rossini's opera is replaced with Siberia, indicating Mikhalkov's intentions to show both the similarities and the differences of the two worlds. Mikhalkov's script introduces two major changes to Beaumarchais's play and the famous opera: the love affair unfolds in Russia, and it involves an American woman who travels to Russia and meets a Russian man. These changes inevitably position the film beyond the level of a simple love story and allow it to explore the complexity of cultural and social differences between the West and Russia.

Viewers first see Jane's image through a train window, on which the images of a wintry Russian forest and Russian cadets are also reflected. The double exposure of the two shots fuses the two worlds – one of the outsider (intruder) arriving on a train, and the other of authentic Russian natural life. Although she is still the agent of the gaze here, the scene hints at her role as an imposter and foreshadows her future objectification. Jane and Andrei's romance is destined to stumble onto obstacles, which only prove the candour of their feelings. Not surprisingly, Jane is presented as more manipulative, secretive, and deceptive. With each scene of her deception and betrayal, Andrei becomes the agent of the male (Russian) objectifying gaze.

The major conflict and misunderstanding between Andrei and Jane emerges when Andrei overhears Jane denying her interests in him to General Radlov. General Radlov's amorous pursuit of Jane and her promise to help her friend the inventor secure funds for his forest-harvesting machine complicate the situation and force Jane to manoeuvre between Andrei, for whom she begins to develop feelings, and the General, whom she needs to manipulate in order to achieve her goal. This conflicting situation tests the characters and uncovers Andrei's uncompromising nature and Jane's more pragmatic inclinations.

After an outburst and an attack on the General during the performance of Mozart's *The Marriage of Figaro*, Andrei is falsely accused of attempting to assassinate the Grand Duke and is exiled to Siberia. He remains true to his passion and his principles, unlike Jane who is tormented by these developments but accepts them and leaves Russia. Jane, however, carries with her a living reminder of Andrei, for she has given birth to his son, Andrew, who has inherited from his father a stubborn loyalty to his beliefs and principles. The film unambiguously focuses on the strangeness and greatness of Andrew's character, no doubt due to his Russian origin.

Mikhalkov's anti-western sentiments overpower his intensions to flirt with the West, and this almost fairy-tale love story between the West and Russia does not end in a happy marriage. The loving relationship between Andrei and Duniasha (his family's maid, representing Russia), who devoted her life to him and followed him to Siberia where they live and raise their children, remains the only lasting relationship in the film.[6] National anxieties and fantasies exercise great power over the role and the place of a foreigner (the West) in Russia; hence the impossibility of Jane and Andrei's feelings to develop into a mature relationship.[7]

Some parallels can be drawn in the structure of the gaze between *The Barber of Siberia* and the Hollywood film *Out of Africa* (dir. Sydney Pollack, 1985) exploring the story of Baroness Karen Blixen who travels to Kenya to seek adventure and fortune. Initially, she is patronizing and imperialistic toward the people on the plantation but begins to care about individuals and develops a genuine fondness for her main servant. Gradually, however, she falls in love with Denys Finch-Hatten, a hunter and organizer of safaris. And thus, by inserting a white man, the film deprives Blixen of the subject position, as she assumes the traditional feminine role. She is the desiring one who needs a commitment the powerful white man cannot make (Kaplan 1997, 88–93). The same shift from the subject to the object of the gaze occurs in Jane's role. She travels to Russia to use Russians and realize her plans but her affair with Andrei exposes her deceptive, unreliable nature and weakens her position. Kaplan suggests that *Out of Africa* 'displaces American anxieties in the wake of Vietnam and other challenges to American imperialism' (1997, 81). Similarly, *The Barber of Siberia* reacts to challenges to Russian national sentiments and fears in the wake of the collapse of the Soviet Union. The female westerner is objectified and sent back to America, as she has no place in Russian life and culture.

"What was that?"

Menshov's *Gods' Envy* presents different gender dynamics in the romantic relationships between the West and Russia. *Gods' Envy* offers viewers a passionate love story between a male French journalist, Andre, and a female Russian TV editor, Sonia. This film also adds to the already familiar romantic international relationships by presenting the passionate and erotic entanglement of the two characters. No other film that treats the theme of cross-national love dares to expose openly the erotic nature of such involvements. This lack of eroticism in most films is hardly surprising considering the long Russian puritanical tradition as well as the Soviet years when the existence of sexuality was denied.[8] Igor Kon, a prominent Russian psychologist and sexologist, writes: 'For many decades Soviet society hypocritically portrayed itself as utterly asexual, even sexless; it eventually even convinced itself of such drivel' (15). Communist ideologists saw sexual relations as disruptive for people who needed to give their whole lives to the only goal of human existence: the bright future of communism. However, this bright future never came, and the collapse of the Soviet system commenced a sexual revolution, among numerous other changes and social challenges. The transition period after 1991 certainly changed attitudes towards sexuality. Scholars of sexuality and pornography in Russian society all agree that the sexual scene in Russia has drastically changed over the last fifteen years, though they differ in their opinion as to the degree of this change.[9]

Russian films (beginning with Vasilii Pichul's *Little Vera* [1988]) showed nudity and sex acts with shocking frequency, suggesting the 'rehabilitation of flesh..., a reaction against asceticism of the still recent past.'[10] More than twenty years after *Moscow Does Not Believe in Tears* (1979), in which Menshov turns off the light when the female protagonist Katia (Vera Alentova) (unwillingly) kisses a TV cameraman, the director shot his fifth film *Gods' Envy* with Vera Alentova again playing the leading female role. One would expect to see a different presentation of the erotic in this later film. In fact, early in the film the director heightens the viewer's expectations of the erotic by having the main characters participate in a risqué, private screening of Bertolucci's *The Last Tango in Paris* (1972). It seems the director was impressed by Bertolucci's exploration of sexuality, which scandalized Western European viewers. Interestingly, this risqué scene is immediately preceded by scenes from the TV studio of *Vremia* (The First Channel news program from the Soviet era still present today) and documentary footage presenting the achievements of the Soviet Union: Soviet leaders' speeches, scenes from the arts and sports, and parades. These images are followed by the Bertolucci scenes, which alternate with shots of enormous stone heads of monuments or facade decorations that are watching over everyone and everything. The most intimate moments of human life are exposed to the omnipotent power of the Soviet gaze.

Gods' Envy tells a story about a woman's self-discovery and late awakening to sexual passion. The film is set in the early 1980s, when Sonia is in her forties. She is married to a famous writer and has an adolescent son. With the authorities' permission, she invites a French pilot to her home, and he arrives accompanied by a French journalist (Anatolii Lobotskii). The journalist, Andre, is instantly taken by Sonia's beauty and does not hesitate to pursue his desire. His gazing at her, more than suggestive, embarrasses her at the dinner table. Sonia is very much troubled by the sensual feelings she recognizes for the first time, but she is also sensitive to her neighbors' judgment, to her son's opinion, and to her mother-in-law's curiosity, or in other words, to the presence of the Soviet gaze. New feelings and old fears come together in Sonia's mind and psyche as a passionate and impossible affair begins between her and Andre.

Having placed the story in the early 1980s, Menshov is bound to address the necessity for secrecy in such an affair unfolding under the watchful gaze of Soviet power. Sonia accepts Andre's invitation to meet, first on a crowded street in front of an enormous Dzerzhinsky monument (Dzerzhinsky was a Bolshevik leader and the first chairman of the Cheka (secret police), which transformed into the KGB after World War II). Sonia looks fearfully at the statue and signals to Andre that they had better meet in the street's underground pass, away from Dzerzhinsky's glance. The chronotope of the public space with the monument of Dzerzhinsky reinforces the tension and conflict of their private relationship, which is set to unfold in the open, under the omnipresent gaze of authorities.

Viewers are gradually exposed to erotic scenes as Sonia awakens to her own sexual desire. At the beginning of the film, she is so shocked by some of the scenes in *The Last Tango* that she walks away from the screening and even refuses to talk to her husband about what they saw. Later with Andre, however, she discovers the pleasures of her body.

In two or three erotic scenes, Menshov actually invites viewers to an unusual voyeuristic experience of arousal and frustration. Viewers' expectations are set high, and the director teases them. In a truck scene – presenting the first sexual encounter between Sonia and Andre and exposing Sonia's naked body – Menshov directs the camera to the characters' entangled bodies, but before showing too much, the camera moves away to show a landscape of Soviet architecture. He repeats this technique twice. This scene culminates in Sonia's orgasm, shown through her surprised face asking 'What was that?' The furnishings in the apartment they rent for their secret meetings are all covered in plastic. On their first visit there viewers again see very little since the characters cover themselves with plastic sheets. Viewers can perceive the silhouettes of their excited bodies but not much nudity, presenting incomplete revelations. The technique blends aesthetic censorship with censorship in a Freudian sense. These scenes gamble on the arousal of desire and its non-fulfillment. The camera bars the look, ends the 'seen', and invests in the 'un-seen'.[11] These erotic scenes seemingly governed by Andre's gaze displace the erotic into Soviet public spaces or into the 'un-seen', the forbidden.

In his two films, *Moscow Does Not Believe in Tears* and *Gods' Envy*, Menshov explores the theme of the sexual awakening of adult women (among others), while unsurprisingly dwelling more on the erotic representation of this awakening in the more recent *Gods' Envy*. What is surprising here is the idea of introducing a French man who enables Sonia to experience the pleasures of the flesh. This change prompts important questions: Does Andre, as a real French libertine, actually help Sonia to overcome her inhibitions and puritanism? Or, does he overpower her, ruin her family, and cause her tragedy? Extending these questions beyond the immediacy of the sexual relationship, one might also ask, do western values influence Russia positively at the time of democratization? Does the West liberate Russia from its communist inhibitions, or does it introduce alien and possibly fatal values to Russia's culture and traditions?

Erotic representations on the screen, and especially the cinematic portrayal of female sexuality, have already attracted the attention of feminists and film scholars. They have turned the focus of film analysis away from content to how meaning is produced in film, while critically addressing the link between psychoanalysis and cinema. Arguing that psychoanalysis may have indeed oppressed women, Kaplan, in her seminal work on women and film, asserts that it is important to know how and why psychoanalysis has functioned to repress women's potential to become autonomous subjects and not passive objects (1983, 24). She writes:

> [T]hen psychoanalysis becomes a critical tool for explaining the needs, desires, and male-female positionings that are reflected in film. The signs in the Hollywood film convey the patriarchal ideology that underlies our social structures and that constructs women in very specific ways – ways that reflect patriarchal needs, the patriarchal unconscious. (Kaplan 1983, 24)

Exploring the psychoanalytic model of male-female relationships that elicit Oedipal traumas, Kaplan studies how sexuality has been constructed in patriarchal discourse to produce pleasure in two major forms: male dominance and female submission (1983, 23–35). She observes: 'We can say that locating herself in fantasy in the erotic, the woman places herself as either passive recipient of male desire or, at one remove, as *watching* a woman who is passive recipient of male desires and sexual actions' (Kaplan 1983, 26).

These observations undoubtedly pertain to the sexual presentation of Sonia in *Gods' Envy*. The erotic scenes position her as the passive recipient of Andre's desire and his dominant and more experienced sexual involvement with her. In these scenes, Sonia is objectified by the male gaze not only by her positioning in the sexual act, but also by the camera, which exposes more of her body while showing only Andre's bare back. However, this cinematic construction of Sonia – which clearly appears to subjugate her – together with her sexual awakening, invites questions. Sonia gradually becomes an active participant in the relationship, initiates their sexual encounters, and most importantly derives pleasure from them for the first time in her life. Does her awakening, as poets and critics suggest, empower her? 'Recognizing the power of the erotic within our lives can give us the energy to pursue genuine change within our world', claims the poet Audre Lorde (282). Contemplating the possibility of a woman assuming a more active/dominant position in the erotic, Kaplan also questions the dual pattern of the dominance-submission structure, which translates into masculine-feminine positions: 'Or is there merely the possibility of both sex genders occupying the positions we now know as "masculine"' and "feminine"?' (1983, 28).

In her work on sex in Russian cinema, Lynne Attwood, after unveiling the objectification of women in Russian films of the perestroika and post-perestroika periods, observes that the heroine in *Little Vera* is the only one who, though she has little control over her life, 'does at least seem to control her own sexuality' (82). Similarly, Sonia seems to enjoy her sexuality, although she too has little control over her life. In the end, however, both heroines are presented as sexual spectacles and each pays the price for her enjoyment. Both *Little Vera* and *Gods' Envy* expose the social constraints and limitations that the traditional family values impose on women, while simultaneously teaching women to accept these limitations; otherwise their lives would end tragically, as do Vera's and Sonia's. Thus, although Sonia is allowed to be active for a while and to experience sexual enjoyment, Soviet society punishes her in the end. The transgression is only temporary. Attwood notes:

> Oedipal trends figure strongly in the cinematic subtext. Female sexuality – indeed, sexual difference – represents a threat to men as individuals, since it confronts them with the possibility of their own castration. Similarly, sexually independent women represent a threat to patriarchy by subverting the traditional order of gender relations. Thus they have to be neutralized. (84)

Menshov's camera achieves this neutralization by allowing the Soviet gaze to control most of Sonia and Andre's encounters and intimate meetings and by inviting viewers to identify with the 'unseen'. The end of *Gods' Envy* reveals the tragic consequences of this relationship for Sonia. She is so devastated by Andre's deportation after writing a critical article about the Soviet destruction of a Korean civilian plane, that she attempts suicide on the rails at a train station. This ending undoubtedly reminds Russian viewers of Lev Tolstoy's Anna Karenina, who commits suicide by throwing herself in front of a train. Menshov, however, presents Sonia's tragedy with a twist. At the moment when Sonia lies on the ground waiting for the train, two trains approach her from opposite directions and pass by her, leaving her alive between the rails of the two trains. This ending is almost ironic: Sonia is able to control neither her life nor her death. It appears the Soviet system takes care of both. As noted above, the film situates people's intimate experiences in the context of the omnipresent and all-powerful Soviet gaze. In the impossible relationship between Sonia and Andre, the third party is actually not her husband nor Andre's wife, but Soviet power (Stishova 2000). Sonia is afraid that gods can become envious of people's happiness, and they do. In the film, gods blend with Soviet authorities.

Thus, the question of who and what caused Sonia's unhappiness and suicide attempt becomes more complicated. Is it Andre or the Soviet (patriarchal) system? It is well accepted in western scholarship to collude the male gaze with the imperial gaze, especially in western films exploring colonial travel from the 1930s to the present (Kaplan 1997). But in this film, the structure of the gaze appears to be linked to Soviet ideology, which, in turn, is anti-western.

"Dreams come true after all..."

French-Russian romances seem to fascinate Russian audiences, for many films that explore international romantic relationships involve French characters: *Window to Paris*, *East-West*, *Gods' Envy*, and most recently, *The Frenchman*. The stereotypical image of the French, being more passionate and romantic lovers than other western nationalities, entices the Russian imagination into watching on-screen love affairs with the French.

The Frenchman follows a paradigm of Russian films that present fairy-tale romances with happy endings occurring on New Year's Eve. The tradition was established by El'dar Riazanov's famous comedy *Irony of Fate* (1975), a comedy of social confusion with a hint of political satire, in which New Year's brings together two young people: Zhenia, after a drinking party in a bathhouse, is flown by his friends to Leningrad; without realizing that he is in a different city he finds what he believes is his apartment, only to realize that a woman lives there, and this woman turns out to be his destiny.[12]

Storozheva constructs a twenty-first-century New Year's fairy tale in *The Frenchman*. Paul, a rich and politically influential Frenchman, detests all women interested in him because he senses their mercantile motives. Nonetheless, he develops an epistolary relationship with a young Russian woman, Ira, who lives in a small town in Russia. Paul becomes infatuated by the sensitivity and the profound understanding of the meaning of life that the Russian woman expresses in her letters. He hides from her the fact that he is wealthy, just as she hides from him the fact that she is not the author of the letters; her friend, Ania, who graduated with a degree in French philology, writes them. As in the previously mentioned New Year's fairy tales, confusion brings Paul to Ania: while looking for Ira he meets Ania and realizes that he is actually in love with her. Ania shares his feelings and the film ends with a voice-over informing viewers that they happily left Russia and went to Paris.

The film plays with the already familiar stereotype that a foreigner is totally unable to comprehend Russian mentality or to survive in Russia, although the Frenchman Paul understands and loves Ania and asks her to marry him. Viewers see Paul travelling to the small town by train, similar to the way Jane in *The Barber* entered Russia. He also amuses himself at the New Year's town festival complete with fireworks and games, though the event is much more modest than Mikhalkov's presentation of Maslenitsa. Paul's gaze at all things Russian, however, is transformed into a looking relation vis-à-vis Ania. The love of two soul mates, despite their different nationalities, appears stronger than the differences their cultures present. Paul's gaze reveals more personal sentiments and desires than national anxieties.

Their love and mutual understanding for each other, which overpower national differences, is not a surprise considering Ania's education in French philology. She knows and appreciates French literary and cultural traditions. Moreover, her knowledge and apparent openness to western ideas make her character as much Russian as she is international. This perception is supported by the looking relationships, which do not objectify Ania. In most scenes focused on Paul and Ania, it is clear that she looks at him, as he is deprived of the dominant gaze.

Against the background of all other films that portray impossible international romantic relationships, *The Frenchman* emerges as a new beginning – a beginning which offers more chances for understanding and love between foreigners and Russians. This film, however, still follows the fairy-tale genre and presents so many difficulties and obstacles to Paul and Ania that only his wealth and political connections (*deus ex machina*) can save them and their happiness. In this way, the film is reminiscent of the early 1990s films (*On Deribasovskaia*, *Everything will be OK*, and *Moscow Vacation*), in which magical solutions determine the happy outcome of romantic relationships.

The Frenchman, however, differs from the enthusiastic films of the early 1990s in its construction of a mature relationship between Paul and Ania. The film does not perpetuate the possibility of accidental marriages between Russians and foreigners aided by marriage agencies: Storozheva clearly posits the impossibility of Ira and Paul ending up together. There are social and educational differences between Ira, a hairdresser with no apparent education, and Paul, a wealthy French aristocrat. It is Ania and Paul who fall in love, thanks to their prolonged epistolary exchange and their similar perception of life and the world. The letters here are important, for they provide the mental space (Rustin insists upon) for the thoughtful and healthy development of the relationship.[13] The event of the union ('marriage') functions as a symbolic representation of the emergence from late adolescence into the more mature world of adults (Waddell 1998a, 159). Thus, *The Frenchman*, still a fairy-tale love story, hints at the possibility for a more mature understanding of international romances than the films from the early 1990s by suppressing national and cultural differences and promoting happiness through universal (western) knowledge and values. At the same time, such a film challenges national sentiments of Russia's cultural uniqueness and yet

Storozheva's The Frenchman.

again poses the question, is the West the only path to happiness? Is there anything else but the West? It is significant to note that while Ania has a degree in French philology, she is also portrayed as a quiet and modest Russian intellectual who prefers the country to the vanity of the big city where she studied. A consequent vexed question arises, then, how much is the Russian intelligentsia separated and independent from the West in its ideas and educational foundation?[14] As a film directed by a woman (unlike the rest of the films), *The Frenchman* opens space for imagining how women directors deal with interwoven concepts such as gender and nation and how in so doing they question the objectification within stereotypical looking relationships.

All films discussed in this chapter show, in different ways and to different extents, the overall disbelief in the possibility of healthy and happy international relationships. Only *The Frenchman* fosters some hope but at the same time probes Russian cultural identity. The stability and confidence of national identity can be determined by the capacity to autonomously relate to others and to develop relationships based on equality and respect. Waddell argues that the transition from the unstable world of adolescence to the more stable and confident world of adulthood is marked by the capacity to seek intimate partnership and to establish a genuine and more permanent relationship (1998a, 157–59). The films' reluctance to embrace international relationships thus reveals the unpreparedness of the Russian political and social conditions for such relationships and the insecurity of the Russian national identity.

International relationships still challenge the formation of the Russian national identity. In most films, national anxieties are displaced into the dominance of the male gaze that refuses to look at the other but objectifies and gazes at all things non-Russian. In discussing the workings of the gaze, I contend that the male and the Russian/Soviet gazes collude often with one another, thus gendering and sexualizing Russian relationships with the West (usually portrayed as feminine). This chapter supports the understanding that most national fantasies are gendered. To a certain extent Russia resembles the West in its similar fantasies of encounters with the other, but Russian national and cultural specificities need to be always taken into account

Notes

1. Here Rustin draws on Klein and Wilfred Bion. Klein directed attention to the developmental issue of the capacity to think, which she connected to the emotional capacity of the child to recognize and seize in mind the mother as a whole person, not divided into bad and good objects, and the ability to remember her in her absence (1975b, 94–122). Klein believed that the capacity for thought in human beings was a sign for a certain kind of relatedness. Bion furthered this idea in his work with disordered psychotic patients studying the mental condition of patients who were not able to think in logical and consistent ways. Both Klein and Bion believed that parents have to be able to contain and tolerate their children's anxieties and pain in order to provide the necessary conditions for the children's capacities for emotions and thoughts to develop.
2. For more on the discussion around the use of the 'gaze' and especially the feminist approach to film and psychoanalysis, see Doane (46–64) and Kaplan (1990, 1–24).
3. Piotr Todorovskii's *Intergirl* (1989), a popular film of the perestroika period, focuses entirely on international marriage and hints at fatal outcomes to such enterprises, but since I set a goal to examine mainly post-communist film productions, this film remains outside the scope of my study.
4. For more on Danila's sexual conquest of the African American journalist in *Brother 2*, see chapter two.
5. For more on Mikhalkov's futile flirt with the West, see chapter three.
6. For more about the role of Duniasha in the film, see Beumers (2000).

7. Régis Wargnier's *East-West* (1999), exploring the troubled situation of a French woman in the Soviet Union, is worth mentioning here. Aleksei Golovin (Oleg Menshikov), a Russian émigré in France, believes in Stalin's appeal to the Russian community abroad to return and rebuild Russia after World War II. Golovin, together with his French wife Marie and their son Serezha, return to Russia only to be accused of spying for France and to be subjected to oppressive manipulation, surveillance, and the unbearable conditions of communal living. The film portrays Marie in the already-familiar fashion (resembling the portrayal of Nicole from *Window to Paris* and Jane from *The Barber*) as a stranger, a foreigner who is incapable of comprehending the complex manoeuvres of the Russian soul as well as the Russian political and social conditions. At the end of the film, Golovin finally reaches his goal of arranging for his wife and son to defect. What is interesting and different in this film compared to *The Barber of Siberia* is that both Golovin and Sasha (Sergei Bodrov, Jr), a young Russian in love with Marie, are alienated from Soviet conditions and aspire to universal (western) values of freedom and human rights. Although the gaze objectifies Marie, the controlling gaze in the film is actually the Soviet gaze and its agents are not Golovin or Sasha.

8. With the exception of the brief absence of sexual restraint immediately after the revolution of 1917, when Aleksandra Kollontai and Clara Zetkin dared to openly claim that the question of the relations between men and women was important for Soviet society, it is well known that the former Soviet Union and the even older Orthodox church had a decidedly prudish and puritanical attitude toward sex. Religious bigots condemned almost all sexual relations (even marital) for going against religious dogma, and communist ideologists saw sexual relations as disruptive. (Attwood 66) Abram Room's film *Bed and Sofa* (1927) is one of the rare cinematic attempts to honestly portray the emotional and physical entanglement of one woman and two men (Graffy 2001).

9. For more details on the changing dynamics of Russian attitudes towards sexuality and prostitution, see "*About That*: Deploying and Deploring Sex in Post-Soviet Russia" (Borenstein 2000) and "Pornography in Russia" (Goldschmidt). Goscilo records the increased interest in sexuality and especially the growing concern of men's emasculation and their purported sexual identity crisis in the 1990s as evident in media and popular magazines (2000).

10. Irina Levi, "Igra v kotoroi net pobeditelei," *Molodoi kommunist*, 1990, #4, p.96, quoted in "Sex and the Cinema" (Attwood 64).

11. Metz calls this cinematic technique 'extension of the fetish proper in the very text of the film' (77).

12. Mikhail Agranovich and Oleg Iankovskii's *Come Look at Me* (2000), which fashions itself after *Irony of Fate*, also presents a New Year's confusion ending in a happy union of two middle-aged people fated for each other.

13. Ira, who showed signs of acting out her impatience with Russia's conditions and who wanted at all costs to leave Russia, will live in Paris but with her Russian boyfriend, Tolik, thanks only to Ania and Paul's help.

14. As already pointed out, this is a centuries-long debate in Russian culture and it has no one-sided or easy answer. Again, it depends on the beliefs of the westernizers versus those of the Slavophiles. Pertinent here is Neumann's remark that even a vehemen neo-Slavophile like Solzhenitsyn, when arguing against the West, uses literary and public debate genres established in Europe.

5

WEST, EAST, AND RUSSIA: AMBIVALENCE, REFLECTION, AND TRAVERSING THE FANTASY

Continuing the discussion of the parallels between the transition from adolescence to adulthood and similar challenges presented to national identity formation during a political and social transition, this chapter explores symptoms of maturity as reflected in Balabanov's *Of Freaks and Men* and Rogozhkin's *Peculiarities of the National Hunt in Fall* and *Cuckoo*. Freud saw maturity in the ability to work and love. Klein equated maturity to the increased capacity to live in the depressive position and accept the world as one complex body both frustrating and gratifying. Lacan believed maturity to be in the ability to accept lack and symbolic castration which, if related to the national Thing, means an acceptance of the illusion, of the fundamental inconsistency that disturbs the protective/repressive screen of fantasies. Lacan calls this process 'traversing the fantasy'. The films discussed in this chapter all signal a more reflective perception of self and other, of nationhood and difference, and suggest traversing the fantasy. In addition, they indicate an understanding of the complexity of the world in which Russia plays an ambiguous role. This chapter also explicates some differences between Klein's depressive position (or mature state of mind) and Lacan's idea of traversing the fantasy.

Central to the adult state of mind is the capacity to integrate and accept problematic and unwanted aspects of the self rather than denying them by projecting them elsewhere. The integration process requires one to relinquish external figures of dependence and attachment and abandon superficial identification. Waddell remarks on these particular psychological mechanisms:

> For the task of being oneself, now and always, involves relinquishing the denigrated and idealized versions of the self, of other people and of relationships, in favor of the real. It involves (re)negotiating dreams, choices, and hopes, whether self-generated or imposed from without. It involves tolerating opportunities lost, and roads not taken. Such difficulties confront a person at every stage of life, but they are perhaps most demanding and intransigent at major points of transition. (1998a, 159)

In Lacan's terms, acceptance of 'opportunities lost' and 'roads not taken' relates to the traumatic dimensions of the real and marks the transition from desire to drive. 'In "traversing the fantasy,"' Žižek writes, 'we find *jouissance* in the vicious cycle of circulating around the void of the (missing) object, renouncing the myth that *jouissance* has to be amassed somewhere else' (1997, 33). In other words, traversing the fantasy constitutes a move from desire (constantly seeking the object of desire) to drive (circling around a void). In his work on the fantasy structure in the film *Dark City*, Todd McGowan contends: 'One resists this transition because it entails the loss of any hope for escape. Desire promises a transcendent future, a future beyond present constraints. But the drive makes no promises' (165).

This is precisely the space in which one can locate one of the main differences between Klein's and Lacan's theories: where Klein perceives hope connected to growth and maturity (even though traumatic and depressive), Lacan positions a hopeless realization that the fantasy structure (the representative of reality) is sustained by an empty signifier. At the same time, it is important to add that, according to Lacan, traversing the fantasy liberates the subject from the dominance of ideology, of symbolic authority. This is why Žižek insists that 'the crucial precondition for breaking the chains of servitude is thus to "traverse the fantasy" which structures our *jouissance* in a way which keeps us attached to the Master – makes us accept the framework of the social relationships of domination' (1997, 48). This radicality, however, this confrontation with the void, this absence of *jouissance* which 'makes the universe vain' is rarely sustained (Lacan 1977, 317).

Balabanov's *Of Freaks and Men* and Rogozhkin's *Peculiarities of the National Hunt in Fall* and *Cuckoo* reveal a perception of the Russian national identity stripped of idealized versions of itself and of others. These films suggest that with the withdrawal of projections the Russian collective imagination is capable of facing its own destructiveness, inner conflicts, and guilt, and of knowing its ambivalence toward the self and the other. Simultaneously, they allude to attempts at traversing the fantasy of the West with all its traumatic consequences.

It is important to stress here that, although these films disclose signs of complexity and maturity, this does not mean that the Russian collective imagination has overcome adolescent impulses. First, adolescent psychology shows that the process to maturity is not linear and irreversible and, second, the development of Russian national identity (as perceived in post-Soviet film and culture) is not a unified process.[1] Despite all this, these films open space for imagining the Russian cultural mind as more reflective and open to controversies.

(Re)cognition of Guilt

Rogozhkin's 1995 *Peculiarities of the National Hunt in Fall*, conceived as a 'people's comedy', became an instant success.[2] It features a group of friends from various social strata (including a general with the Dostoevskian surname of Ivolgin) united by their unusual enthusiasm for hunting. They value the sport not for the result, but for its chronotope – the opportunity to enjoy friendship at a specific time in a specific place. The film lacks a traditional storyline; the only development is an increase in the quantity of vodka consumed. The image and role of vodka in these films achieves hyperbolic dimensions reminiscent of François Rabelais' *Gargantua and Pantagruel* (1532–1564) and Venedikt Erofeev's novel *Moskva-Petushki* (1968) [*From Moscow to the End of the Line*]. If *Moskva-Petushki* is a tragic poem, however, this film is a slapstick comedy. The characters do nothing but drink and get in and out of ridiculous situations. They constitute a typical male mini-society, though the vodka they consume makes them dense and inept, rendering them impotent in a sense as they lose the vaunted male capacity to dominate. In her analysis of *Peculiarities of the National Hunt in Fall*, Larsen notes that the film deflates violence and disaster:

Rogozhkin's Peculiarities of the National Hunt in Fall.

the hunters are in pursuit, rather, of beauty, friendship, and brotherhood (1999). Encouraged by the success of the film, Rogozhkin serialized the characters and the situation and created two more films *Peculiarities of National Fishing* (1998), and *Peculiarities of the National Hunt in Winter* (2000). [3]

In the first film, a young Finn, Reyko (Ville Haapasalo), joins the company of Russian hunters in his desire to learn more about Russian hunting. He has read about imperial Russian hunting and now is anxious to see a real hunt. Reyko arrives at the retreat with images and fantasies he has constructed from reading books about Russia and the Russian hunt and is rather shocked to see that Russian reality does not meet the colourful and bright fantasmic images of snow, beautiful horses, borzoi greyhounds, and cognac.

Russian reality is exposed and naked with no idealization or denial. The film does not glorify the Russian spirit but presents it with neither shame nor pride in its most controversial manifestations. All Russian characters accept their life and enjoy it. And there is something comforting and mature in their content. The most absurd episode involves a cow being transported in an aircraft's bomb bay. The crew is bribed with a few bottles of vodka, but the military base commander realizes that there is an animal in the bomb bay and orders the plane's return to the base. The pilot opens the bomb bay hoping to rid the plane of the cow. Upon landing, much to everybody's surprise, they all see the cow holding onto the walls of the bomb bay. There is no dignity or honour in this presentation of Russian air forces, but viewers laugh with the film characters, not at them.

The presentation of the West in the image of Reyko is also more multi-sided and controversial than in many films discussed in previous chapters. Reyko is portrayed as ecology-conscious, a bit naïve, eager to learn more about Russia's way of life, but at the same time very human in his quick acceptance of the temptations that his Russian friends offer him. By the end of the film Reyko understands and talks to his Russian companion Kuzmich (Viktor Bychkov) as each speaks his own language. Moskvina writes that at this moment the national differences are washed away (1996). Reyko has begun to appreciate and enjoy Russian life and reality the way they are, although they substantially differ from his earlier fantasies. At the very end of the film he abandons his dreams of imperial Russian hunting and announces in good Russian: 'It was a good hunt', to which his Russian friend replies: 'Just normal'. This brief exchange hides Reyko's complete satisfaction and acceptance of a Russian reality filled with imperfections, conflicts, and enjoyment. The film became very popular in Russia in the mid-1990s but also triggered some unfavorable critiques. Sergei Dobrotvorskii, a film critic, expresses dissatisfaction with the way Rogozhkin uncovers Russian national characteristics inherited from socialism: self-destruction as disinterest and non-participation. Film critic Irina Liubarskaia finds the film pretentious in its construction of Russian national peculiarities as the Sphinx's riddle proffered to the young Finn and the whole of Europe. The film, however, won over regular viewers with its self-irony and the humorous realization of imperfections and problems in Russia's modern experience, a realization that does not make this experience unwanted and does not blame anyone for it.

The self-awareness of Russia's internal conflicts and problems runs even deeper in Rogozhkin's *Cuckoo*, which enriches this self-awareness with pronounced feelings of guilt for past and present mistakes, for refusing to recognize and accept the (cultural) other. The film's story unfolds at the very end of World War II somewhere in Finland. The war brings together the three characters in the film: Ivan (Viktor Bychkov), a Russian soldier; Veikko (Ville Haapasalo), a Finnish soldier; and Anni (Anni-Christina Juuso), a Laplander. Ivan was arrested for subversive activities, or more precisely for writing poetry, and is being transported while Russian bombs destroy the convoy. Anni, living isolated and alone, finds him wounded and barely alive. Veikko, in turn, is a pacifist who has been punished by being chained to a rock, dressed in a Nazi uniform and left with a gun. His option is to shoot at Russians before they shoot at him. In a way the three characters have distanced themselves from their respective communities. Their otherness makes possible their acceptance of each other, although it takes a long time especially for Ivan, to recognize Veikko as a human being and not a Nazi.

In their first meeting each speaks in his or her language and the others understand nothing. Once Ivan sees Veikko in a German uniform he refuses to communicate with him or attempt to understand him. The uniform, an embodiment of a pure spirit of otherness, makes him an immediate enemy, and Ivan is incapable of noticing the human being behind the uniform. Rogozhkin creates a sharply ironic situation by dressing Veikko, a pacifist, in a Nazi uniform, which, for Ivan, speaks louder than any explanations Veikko tries to offer. At first Ivan's behaviour resembles the paranoid splitting and the creation of hateful others as discussed in the case of Balabanov's *Brother* films. The horrific reality of war creates fantasies that sustain it, including an all too clear image of the enemy. Ivan, a military subject, identifies with the military machine in his hatred of the enemy (although he writes poetry to distance himself from it). The uniform functions for Ivan as a racial mark: it is as arbitrary and as superficial as variations of bodily appearance and shape. In the case of Veikko, the superficiality of such negative attitudes becomes even more exposed. The characteristics of the enemy are defined by the other, a definition which is almost always negative. In his illuminating essay *Anti-Semite and Jew*, Jean-Paul Sartre pinpointed the core of the problem when he wrote that anti-Semitism is a passion. Hatred of the other develops irrationally and provokes physical reactions.

First, the Finn attempts to introduce himself by stating his name and asking the others their names. Ivan answers with a Russian curse 'Poshel ty' (Go to hell), which Veikko takes for his name and begins to call him Pshelty. Veikko employs all of his knowledge of Russian and world literature to convince Ivan that he is a pacifist and for him the war is over. The Finn talks to the Russian soldier about Tolstoy's *War and Peace* and Ernest Hemingway's *Farewell to Arms*, but Ivan stubbornly sees only a Nazi in Veikko.

The lack of common language and Ivan's stubborn animosity toward the Finnish soldier are their first barriers. Through life-changing experiences of love and death, Ivan begins to understand and accept Veikko as a human being, not a soldier and an enemy. By the end of their mutual existence the three characters develop warm, friendly feelings for each other and live harmoniously together. In a 2002 interview, Rogozhkin said that he created an inverted model of the Tower of Babel: they all speak different languages but reach a mutual understanding of each other.

One of the early experiences, which make Ivan relate to Veikko as a friend and a man, is their bathing together. The montage of the scene incorporates a long shot capturing the magnificence of northern scenery with a bright blue lake, while Anni attends to her daily chores in the shallow waters of the lake. The camera cuts to a close-up of Veikko in the sauna he built. Contrasting the open and wide blue sky of the previous shot, this one is tight and darker, with light coming only from the little fire Veikko started for the sauna. The next medium shot presents both Veikko and Ivan looking straight ahead at the camera, positioned at the two sides of the frame with the small fire in the middle. The light is warm, the space is intimate, and they are naked. For the first time Ivan relates to Veikko, sharing with him his unfortunate love stories. The persistent camera's gaze, which follows them closely in the sauna, uncovers their similar human characteristics, their similar experiences, and rejects the differences between them.

Later, however, again displaying animosity, Ivan nearly kills Veikko, but driven by guilt and remorse, he helps Anni to resuscitate him. This experience marks his transformation and almost coincides with Anni's acceptance of the Russian soldier (not only Veikko) as her lover. Ivan abandons his hostile, emotional responses to Veikko and engages in a relationship with him, which if not entirely friendly, is at least more thoughtful and understanding. His ascent – beyond irrational hatred to a more rational reflective response – signals maturity and acceptance of the other, of a problematic and conflicting reality.

Ivan has recognized the empty signifier (of difference) supporting his fantasy of the enemy and attempts to traverse the fantasy. Although the film does not stress the trauma and pain experienced by the Russian man when he traverses the fantasy of the enemy (sustaining the ideology of war), it appears that he frees himself from the power of ideological control. It is important to note here that Ivan subverts his libidinal investment and transforms it or (re)directs it to his love for Anni. Thus, he avoids facing the void of the drive and does not maintain the radicality of it.

At the end of the film viewers see both Ivan and Veikko as mortals; both fall in love with the same woman and have sons with her. Their mutual experience and mutual understanding erases all animosities between nations. This does not lead, however, to the removal of all differences between people; the three characters are still different, even though they now understand each other. As Tatiana Iensen, a Russian journalist, writes: 'Here nobody converts the other in his ideology or religion. Veikko did not become a shaman, Ivan will hardy become a pacifist, and it is difficult to imagine Anni reading Dostoevsky. But each of them, despite language barriers, managed to listen to and hear the other.' Rogozhkin insists that this is not a film about war. The war is only a background. 'Perhaps, *Cuckoo* is my attempt to redeem my own guilt. We all need to just listen better to each other... Simply listen very carefully' (Rogozhkin).

The film, however, does more than simply present the advantages of listening to and hearing the other. Ivan becomes a free man literally, but also free in his understanding of the world, war, and the enemy (although still attached to an object of desire, Anni). He recognizes that the other is like him or in him (through the shared love for and of Anni).[4] Klein recognizes maturity and growth in this situation. Conversely, Lacan points to the difficulty of the subject to sustain traversing the fantasy. Where Klein suggests some hope, Lacan contends that the fundamental fantasy cannot be entirely eradicated, but that the subject can transform how s/he relates to it. At the end, Ivan leaves behind both his hostility to (and later acceptance of) Veikko and his love for Anni to eventually return home. In this off-screen and lonely journey the viewer can imagine that Ivan's relation to his fundamental fantasy will change. He will hardly anymore succumb to the power of ideology.

Of Russia and the West: (Sub)version of Blame[5]
Manifestations of ambivalence and guilt, as well as transformed relations to one's fantasy, are most pronounced in Balabanov's *Of Freaks and Men*, which at first glance stylistically and thematically stands in stark contrast to the adamant realism of Balabanov's thrillers, *Brother*, *Brother 2*, and *War*. Moreover, *Of Freaks and Men* contradicts the vehement aggression and anti-western sentiments portrayed in Balabanov's films, testifying to the splitting and projection state of mind rather than to the depressive position. This seeming contradiction only confirms the belief that the emotional and psychological states of individual development, used here to describe similar sentiments and shifts of the Russian collective identity, constantly modify and oscillate in relation to one another. Thus, the appearance of Balabanov's *Of Freaks and Men*, a more reflective and complex film, although not without its share of anti-western attitudes, does not actually contradict the one-sided and superficial perception of the world presented in his *Brother* films and *War*. Rather, it shows a shift in perception and a slightly different, more mature state of mind as well as a different stage of fantasy construction and deconstruction.

Balabanov's *Of Freaks and Men* is a rare cinematic oddity; like a disturbing dream it remains with viewers long after they have experienced it. Balabanov's film deliriously combines the perverse themes of pornography, sadomasochism, and the sex life of Siamese twins in a style that calls to mind both Russian literature and turn-of-the-century cinema and photography.

In the following pages, I will present both a synopsis of the film as well as alternatives for interpreting its individual subplots and its overall narrative. Although these separate readings may seem contradictory at times and interwoven at others, I will illustrate how they all come together to generate the film's meaning(s). In a rather complex manner, the film unveils links between dubious expressions of human nature and the expansion of western capital, both of which are driven by the unique properties of the most powerful artistic and commercial advancement of the twentieth century: the cinematograph. Human weaknesses – drives for domination and submission, sadism and masochism – fuel the global spread of western capital, a project paralleled by the discovery and development of the motion picture industry.

Of Freaks and Men borrows and subverts visual and stylistic elements from other genres (in this case pornography and silent film) to transform them into a modern psychological drama. In the film, characters superficially identified as freaks reveal human characteristics, while ostensibly 'normal' people attempt to hide freaky impulses. In addition, the film marks Balabanov's return to the thematic territory of his earlier film, *Trofim* (1995), in which a homicidal peasant accidentally stars in an early newsreel, and *Happy Days* in which a small group of people destined to meet encounter one another in cold and abstract St Petersburg.

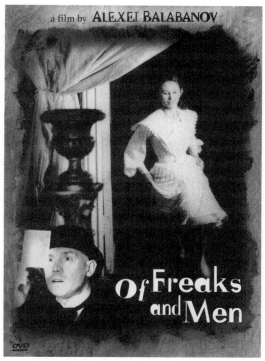

The film opens with a series of black-and-white erotic photographs that evoke the beginning of the pornographic card industry in turn-of-the-century St Petersburg. Through a masterful montage of vignettes, the viewer meets the two Chekhovian families at the center of Balabanov's drama: the Stasovs and the Radlovs. Dr Stasov and his blind wife, Ekaterina Kirillovna, are parents to adopted

Balabanov's Of Freaks and Men.

Siamese twin boys, Kolia and Tolia. Radlov, a wealthy widowed engineer, lives with his maid, Grunia, and his daughter Liza, who constantly yearns for the West.

The action begins when Grunia's brother Johann (Sergei Makovetskii) returns to St Petersburg from the West and starts up a pornography business that will disturb and eventually destroy the serene lives of the two families. Seamlessly, Balabanov weaves the film's disparate storylines together as the film shifts from the tranquil tones of Chekhov to a mode that resembles more Fedor Sologub's *The Petty Demon* (1905) or Andrei Bely's *St. Petersburg* (1913–14).

With the help of his henchman Viktor Ivanovich (Viktor Sukhorukov), Johann organizes nude spanking sessions, which are photographed by Putilov, a young man who is romantically attracted to Liza. Dr Stasov's maid, Daria, and Radlov's daughter Liza both secretly purchase these erotic photos from Viktor Ivanovich. Eventually Johann falls in love with Liza and proposes marriage to her, only to have his romantic overtures cruelly rejected by her father. Grunia then reveals Liza's secret hobby to Radlov, and the engineer dies of a heart attack. When Radlov's will names Grunia as temporary beneficiary of the engineer's estate, the pornographer moves into the family apartment, accompanied by his aged nanny. Kolia and Tolia are eventually relocated into the apartment, too, after being kidnapped and photographed in the nude by Viktor Ivanovich.

Things grow even more deviant as Ekaterina Kirillovna, Stasov's wife, willingly succumbs to Viktor Ivanovich's erotic propositions and becomes one of the players in Johann's pornographic cottage industry. Johann and Viktor Ivanovich launch the twins' singing career and begin shooting pictures of Liza and the old nanny in spanking scenarios and of Ekaterina Kirillovna being spanked by her maid.

Johann's lucrative pornography business expands as he embraces the innovation of moving pictures, after which his industry makes an evolutionary leap. The story of carnality and cruelty continues. One of the twins, Kolia, becomes Liza's lover; the other, Tolia, takes to drink. Johann suffers an epileptic seizure following the sudden death of his nanny, and, while he is unconscious, Kolia grabs Johann's gun and kills Viktor Ivanovich, who has attempted to assume a position of power in his master's moment of weakness. After this rather bleak *dénouement*, Putilov and Liza separately head for the West, while the twins travel to the East, where Tolia dies of alcohol poisoning.

In this grimly black comedy with its outrageous turns of events, Balabanov spares the viewer nothing. It becomes instantly clear that each of the men in the film in his own way uses his power to control and abuse the bodies of the women and the children, and to transform human relations into relations of things (to use Marx's description of commodity fetishism) (Marx 27).[6] Dark human nature and money come together to expose the mechanisms of capitalist relations driven by the human desire for both domination and submission.

The gaze that orchestrates the field of vision carries with it the power to subjugate subjects – in this case women and children – to the position of victimized objects whose bodies undergo brutality, a brutality captured by the camera and transformed into pornographic pictures. Johann, always calm and impassive, delights in his perverse industry. More than once, however, he murders people who object to his amoral activities. When the landlord of the building that Johann uses as his photographic studio discovers that his property is being used for indecent activities, he confronts Johann and threatens to expose him. Johann kills him instantly, with no hesitation or remorse. Later, after Viktor Ivanovich moves the twins into the Radlov's apartment, their father, Dr Stasov, storms in looking for them and is murdered by Johann.

Johann photographs people, perverts their souls, and kills those who interfere with his interests – with all of these acts taking on the shared significance of murder, of assassination. Susan Sontag insists that by taking pictures of other people, the photographer in fact takes possession of them, turns them into objects, and thus violates them. Balabanov's film goes beyond this metaphor and disturbingly asserts that there is no difference between actual murder and 'shooting' people with the camera, especially in the case of pornography. Of course, other films have suggested a similar connection between photography and murder. In the film *Before the Rain* (Manchevski, 1994), for example, the lead character, a war photographer and a Pulitzer Prize winner, causes the mass shooting of camp prisoners with the curiosity of his camera. However, whereas the prisoners of *Before the Rain* are constructed as completely innocent victims of the inquisitive gaze, a bit more complexity is at work in the situation of the victimized women in *Of Freaks and Men*.

The Gaze and Male-Female Affairs
Even if analyzing male-female relationships exposed through the intriguing work of the gaze sounds detached from the main preoccupation of this book's discussion of the Russian-western dialogue, at the end of the chapter it will become clear why such a digression is necessary.

In Johann's pornographic tableaux women beat other women while the male gaze remains strangely distant and detached. Indeed, one might even argue that while the film explores the exploitation of women and children, this exploitation is not based on heterosexual dynamics. Many scenes suggest homoerotic pleasures. Johann is portrayed eating carrot sticks dipped in sour cream, and the only time one sees some pleasure and satisfaction on his emotionless face is when he observes the (male) twins. Neither Johann nor any of the other male characters express any desire for physical contact with the naked women. All pleasure is derived and consumed voyeuristically.

At the same time the evil masters are fatally weak. Johann reveals an odd attachment to his half-senile nanny and has an epileptic fit at her death, while Viktor Ivanovich shows an ambivalent curiosity about the conjoined 'freaks'. Viktor Ivanovich's image – bold and clean-shaven with an unnerving smile – is no doubt a demonic reference to the vampiric lead character in F. W. Murnau's *Nosferatu* (1922). Despite his ominous appearance, Viktor is simultaneously insecure, hesitant, and fearful of Johann, who himself becomes a helpless body lying on the floor next to his dead nanny.

Taking it one step further, one can add the photographer, Putilov, to these odd dynamics. He amorously pursues Liza and declares his intentions to save her, but his detached affectation, gentle demeanor, long hair, and checkered suit suggest a femininity that may be linked to homosexual inclinations. Despite his repeated claims that he will rescue Liza from her victimization, he does nothing but continue to photograph her and to helplessly bear witness to her humiliation. Putilov, guilty and frustrated, silently watches and photographs the shame and the fall of his beloved.

On a technical level his gaze is aligned with the agency (or the immediate substitute) of the gaze of power, which organizes the field of vision. In this passage, however, the gaze of power, the agency that ideologically controls the vision, has been transformed into a gaze of impotence, which executes the ideological organization of sight. Žižek expertly defines the impotent gaze and the position of the impotent observer and finds them best explored in *film noir* scenes (1994, 73–75). Žižek illustrates his explanation with an example from Fritz Lang's *Scarlet Street* (1945).

> Robinson [the film's weak-willed protagonist] misperceives a simple 'lovers' tiff', which Joan Bennett is clearly *enjoying*, as the suffering she is to be *rescued* from. This scene provides the key to the constellation of the impotent gaze: the unbearable traumatic element witnessed by this gaze is ultimately *the feminine enjoyment* whose presence suspends the authority of the big Other, of the Name-of-the-Father, and fantasy (the fantasy of the 'threat' woman is to be 'rescued' from) is a scenario we construct in order to elude feminine enjoyment. (1994, 75)

Although Žižek's argument is appealing and persuasive for *film noir* scenes, it falls short of explaining the dynamics in *Of Freaks and Men*. Certainly, more complexity is at work in the Russian film. While the gaze executed through Putilov's character clearly reveals symptoms of impotence, in all other scenes the male gaze appears strangely distant, dispersed, and alien. These qualities challenge the understanding that the male gaze always bears power. In addition, in this film women willingly inflict pain on other women. Their interactions arouse male curiosity and excitement rather than evoking any desire in men to rescue them from a situation in which they participate readily. The fact that the women voluntarily participate in these tableaux is crucial here, but what is even more intriguing about the film's economy of erotic desire is that the viewer sees only female characters buying the pornographic pictures. It appears women are not only objects of the male gaze but of the female gaze as well. Or, perhaps, women can be seen as appropriating the male gaze.

To complicate matters further one may examine the function of the gaze in the scene of Johann's epileptic seizure. As he lies prostrate on the bedroom floor, Johann's power to orchestrate the gaze is usurped by Liza and Daria. Even then, however, the gaze remains distant, cruel, and alien, just as it was in earlier sequences. The scene is organized and presented as a 'viewer-view-viewer' sequence of shots in which Liza assumes the position of the viewer, and Johann (and later his body on the floor) that of the view. When the camera is once again aligned with Liza's point of view, it becomes apparent that the object reflected in the mirror near Liza's feet is, in fact, Johann's body. This *mise-en-scène* incorporates Johann's body in the same shot as Liza, and thus estranges the viewer's perception while simultaneously entrusting the gaze with more power; it collapses the field of the gaze by revealing both the subject and the object in the same plane. This shot necessitates both an estrangement of perception and a reinforcement of the power of the gaze, because the mirror mediates the perception and thus distances it; at the same time it presents an opportunity to show more than in an unmediated frame of view.

The women's willing participation in their own victimization adds yet another layer to the already complex position of the gaze and human relations. Ekaterina Kirillovna dislikes her husband, Dr Stasov, but meets Viktor Ivanovich's cruel sexual advances with quiet and quick compliance. She becomes just one of the characters in Johann's gallery of pornographic pictures. When Putilov confesses his love to Liza and tells her that he will save her, she firmly replies, 'It's already late.' Why is it late? What has happened to make it late? Oddly, women readily engage in this exploitive enterprise and willingly stay there. It appears that the seemingly Chekhovian family happiness reveals masochistic conditioning.[7]

Recently the idea that only women reveal masochistic tendencies has also been questioned. Kaja Silverman aptly argues that even Freud in his later writings turned to male patients in order to better understand masochism. Closely analyzing Freud's "The Economic Problem of Masochism" and Theodor Reik's *Masochism in Sex and Society*, Silverman concludes: 'Not only does it turn out that feminine masochism does not have very much to do with women, but that moral masochism does not have very much to do with virtue' (1993, 42). Considering all the work that has been done to explain masochism today, one can safely argue that masochism is not a trademark of female sexuality.

This conclusion, however, does not help in understanding the film *Of Freaks and Men*. If one cannot safely assume that women in this film are naturally/innately enjoying physical pain and humiliation, then what are women experiencing here? It is significant to note that women in the film inflict pain on themselves in front of the male gaze, which remains oddly distant and impotent. Are the women enjoying this situation and thus triggering the impotence of the male gaze and undermining its authority, or are they enjoying the pure homosexual, albeit abusive, relations that they form in the pictures? Or is their desire merely the desire of the Other, which in this instance is latently impotent?[8] And if so, does this not prompt the disintegration of social relationships and the symbolic structure?[9] In her article "I Burn for Him: Female Masochism and the Iconography of Melodrama in Stahl's *Back Street*" (1932), Susan White argues that masochism in film sometimes reveals transgressive functions and that 'this form of masochism is a means of female self-regulation more powerful than any external regulation' (66). In the context of the film *Of Freaks and Men* this argument certainly deserves further exploration, and I will return to it later.

Balabanov not only challenges the viewer's stereotypes of female masochism, but also masterfully destroys many other expectations of social and cultural constructions.[10] He ironically subverts social structures: servants take over the households and control the lives of their masters; the newly emerging profane proletariat takes over the production of culture and replaces the educated class; freaks reveal more human characteristics than people who express a freakish nature; high culture is transformed into low culture. Balabanov decisively reduces the high canon of Russian culture to the level of cinema, employing the music of Mussorgsky and Prokofiev, and showing sinister and ugly monstrosities under the veil of some of St Petersburg's most magnificent buildings. It is interesting to point out that the women who were marginalized in life, such as the old nanny and Dr Stasov's maid, take the position of dominance in the pornographic films, a kind of redemption or reclamation. This subversion presents the female discourse in the film, the discourse of the victims, as competing and controversial. The victimized position does not help in eliminating conflicting and aggressive drives.

Not surprisingly, the names and characters in *Of Freaks and Men* undoubtedly allude to Dostoevsky's dark and odd world. One senses the presence of the enigmatic and emotionally sterile Stavrogin in some of Johann's manifestations; of the gentle soul of Prince Myshkin entangled in the corrupt affairs of the world in the character of Putilov; of Svidrigailov, the violator of young girls in both Johann's and Viktor Ivanovich's abuse of female bodies; and of Grushenka from *The Brothers Karamazov*, who is at times soft and playful and at times malicious, in the character of Liza. Sergei Astakhov's sepia photography also helps to veil the world in a Dostoevskian mode of primitive drives.

Victim and/or Victimizer?
The storyline, which initially bounces from one thread to another, comes together with the help of narrative title cards, very much like those of silent films, and with scenes showing the persistent movement of a train. The image of the train is so relentless that the viewer is not merely invited, but forced to think of western industrial advancements and the Russian position toward western expansion. Not incidentally, the film begins with Johann's return from the West and passage through Russian immigration. As already discussed, since the time of Peter the Great, Russia has established an ambivalent relationship with the West of acceptance and approval, as well as simultaneous rejection and denial. This film, in its turn, makes a statement about the nature of 'Russianness' positioned between the West and the East. Again, it is no accident that Dr Stasov's adopted Siamese twins are Asian. It is significant to note that the Russian parents do everything possible to introduce their Asian children to Russian culture and to raise them as Russians. The film suggests an interesting process of cultural and even economic influence: from the West to Russia and from Russia to the East, in which Russia has a decisive presence.

With the train comes Johann to produce pornography, and, in so doing, to exploit and corrupt Russian women and the Asian twins. The dream of western might and freedom is problematized from the start. With Johann's arrival, relationships between people are immediately transformed into relationships between commodities, and this is true for all relationships in the film. The only people to escape this destiny are Liza's father who dies of a heart attack and the twins' father who is killed. An excessive production of commodities and surpluses ensues. Johann's business flourishes quickly following the basic formula of supply and demand. Marx illuminated the paradoxical mechanism according to which the more supply is offered, the more demand there will be for it, and thus Marx pointed toward the phenomenon of the global expansion of capital.[11] The moment Viktor Ivanovich begins to sell his pornographic cards, Grunia and Liza cannot get enough of them. It appears Russia becomes an object and arguably a victim of western economic expansion, but paradoxically Russia is also inviting and feeding on this invasion. The film presents a Russian attitude sensitive to western might and uncovers the freakish nature of both people and capitalism.

A third narrative of interpretation uncovers Russia's own perception of its position in today's globalization. In a time of global capitalism and cultural integration, when everything is for sale, women have more than ever become objects of desire and money. In the post-Soviet era, numerous Russian popular magazines attempt to boost men's perceived weakness or lacking self-esteem and to prepare them for the new global world. Money and desire are intrinsically connected in the pages of these magazines. Those men who can buy the advertised commodities, including women, are assured social status and sexual identity. Above all, these magazines promote the westernization of Russian men. At the same time, hundreds of Internet pages offer Russian women to western men for love, friendship, and marriage. These websites have categorized the 'objects' for sale according to appearance, hair colour, age group, and communicative skills. More interestingly, an analysis of these websites reveals that female characteristics are often linked to national characteristics. The site 'East Meets West', for example, presents links such as 'New Ladies', 'Price List', and 'Apartments' along with 'Mother Russia Photos'. Pictures of a female warrior statue (Mother Russia) rotate with photos of smiling Russian women. This seemingly unanticipated connection follows a long cultural tradition of the myth of Mother Russia. For centuries Russians have called the land Mother and given its physical features feminine/maternal epithets. 'If nature was mother, so too were the very monuments built to testify to a measure of human power–cities, roads, churches' (Hubbs xiii). The myth nourishes the idealization of womanhood in fiction, which, however, is very much abased in reality. What is for sale in today's Europe? It appears Russian women are turned into objects for sale not only by western men, but by Russian men as well.

Interestingly, *Of Freaks and Men* addresses similar undercurrents, portraying Russian women exposed to western capital and the perceived emasculation of Russia. The film, however, suggests a surprising perception of today's globalization and the Russian position in it. Russian women in the film (Liza and Grunia), and perhaps Mother Russia if one accepts the above cultural tradition (and the websites' allusions), are perceived as victims of western expansion. They are not, however, the only victims. The Asian twins are exploited too by the same economic westernization. It is important to recall here the earlier discussion of the male-female relationships, which concluded that women in this film are not simple victims, for matters are more complex than that. The film implies that they feed in and participate in their own victimization. In this context Russia perceives itself not as a unique victim of the West, but rather as part of a world crisis, which positions the West as the ultimate beholder of power and subjugates the rest of the world, and in which Russia holds an ambiguous position. Moreover, the twins are not positively affected by Russian culture. They seem well assimilated into Russian culture – they sing Russian songs, Kolia becomes Liza's lover, and Tolia takes to drink. But in the end, Tolia dies of alcoholism and Kolia is alone in the East, having lost much more than Tolia. In a way they become victims of Russianization.

Etkind argues that the roads of Russian and European colonization have been different. While Europe colonized outside its territories in Africa and Asia, Russia colonized within its own empire –

colonized its exotic other – which could be an ethnic or religious other, or even its own folk (*narod*) viewed as the other. 'Russia colonized itself; tamed its own *narod*. This was internal colonization, self-colonization, secondary colonization of its own territory' (Etkind 2001, 65–66). In addition to the internal colonization of which Etkind speaks, the film unveils the primary colonization of the ethnic eastern other, the Asian twins.[12] The exoticism of the Siamese Asian twins Tolia and Kolia, who sing and play Russian songs, fascinate and please the theatre audiences in St Petersburg.

The last few scenes of the film present still another twist. As Jonathan Romney states in a review article in *Sight & Sound*, 'Even Lynch and Greenaway have rarely left an audience with such a bitterly ironic punch line' (58). Liza's longing for the West and her journey there result in her walking along depressingly deserted autumn streets, and she cleanses her melancholy with a spanking session at the hands of a curiously androgynous creature. In the West, Putilov is a celebrity pursued by a crowd of enthusiastic young women. The viewer very soon realizes that he has gained this fame solely on the basis of his pornographic films. Putilov has learned and mastered the western skills of pornography and has brought them back to the West with a vengeance. The West in its wild and blind expansion is facing nothing but the return of its repressed. Or, as Lacan points out, the 'sender [always] receives his own message back from the receiver in an inverted form' (1977, 85).[13]

The scene of Liza's willing submission in the hands of an androgynous prostitute deserves a more detailed analysis. She enters the shop and leans over a chair with her back to the window and the street. The viewer sees a close-up of her face staring at the camera with indifference and even mastery as the prostitute beats her. In other words, the viewer can see both the prostitute and a close-up of Liza's face. For a while there are no other angles or camera moves in this shot. At this moment the spectator is identifying with the camera and directly perceiving Liza's image which is deposited on the viewer as if on a second screen, and it is at this moment and place when the 'perceived imaginary accedes to the symbolic by its inauguration as the signifier.'[14] Metz insists that at a moment like that the viewer identifies with him/herself as a pure act of perception. This scene, in which the viewer and Liza become one as the boundaries between subject and object seem to vanish, suggests a masquerade of submission revealed through Liza's expressionless and controlling face. One can argue that it is a liberating moment for her. She has overcome the objectified and victimized position she assumed earlier in the film. White's argument about masochism's transgressive role also supports the interpretation that Liza's position in this scene undermines male power and domination. Paradoxically and certainly controversially, Liza's involvement in Johann's pornographic industry has led to her independence. She is in the West, away from home, experiencing pleasure or pain on her own accord.

To take the analysis of this scene a step beyond the imaginary/symbolic identification, I also suggest that here Liza's relation to the West (with its perverse manifestations), or to her object cause of desire, is not only a function of imaginary identification but extends into the real. Beyond Liza's empty/content/mastering gaze, the viewer can locate the void resulting from traversing the fantasy. In this scene, the move from desire (continuous search for the object which promises a future) to drive (the circular movement around an objectless void) can easily be recognized. Chasing her desire, leaving the domestic space, Liza now wanders the streets of a western town, where she becomes the master of her pain and pleasure only to face the void of the drive's monotony. The scene does not end here. Liza slowly turns her head away from the camera, which follows her glance and shows a male passer-by in the street observing the whipping session. Liza's expression still does not change.

Nonetheless, the viewer can detect that this experience is not a single occurrence and will continue as the drive circles and turns in on itself. Immediately following this scene, Balabanov cuts to a shot of Johann entering a theatre where Putilov's film of Liza's session at the hands of Johann's nanny is being screened. Johann sits alone in an audience of silent men, crying.

In these sequences Liza's naked body is on a double display – first, at the prostitute's window and second, on the screen in the local theatre. What follows, one can imagine, is the history of twentieth-century cinema, or, as Jean Baudrillard puts it, 'whence the characteristic hysteria of our time: the hysteria of production and reproduction of the real. The other production, that of goods and commodities, that of *la belle époque* of political economy, no longer makes any sense on its own, and has not for some time. What society seeks through production and overproduction is the restoration of the real that escapes it' (199).

Of Freaks and Men certainly does not offer easy answers or a clear one-sided understanding of human nature, Russia, and the world. One can detect traces of the maturity of the Russian collective mind in this complexity and in the readiness to subvert preconceived ideas, to question established beliefs, and to point to Russia's conflicting and troubling history and its ambiguous role in today's world. Balabanov leads the viewer through a labyrinth of competing and contradictory human expressions – of domination and submission, of power and impotence, of bondage that leads to liberation and perhaps to a new dependence. At times he teasingly suggests hope and then snatches it abruptly away to challenge stereotypes and destroy expectations. Hence, a Kleinian reading of the more reflexive and mature vision of the world hints at hope, whereas Lacan's interpretation leads to a perpetual circular motion, which, even if liberating, offers no promises.

On a large scale the director unveils the twentieth-century obsessions with money and representation, with appearance and simulacrum, which posit for the real, whereas the real remains dangerous and hidden. The film with its series of doublings, questioned and subverted in their usual interaction, invites deliberation of the way other couplings are viewed: Russia and the East as a symptom of the West, for example.[15]

On the one hand, the three films discussed in this chapter signal a transformation of Russia's relation to its fundamental fantasy. On the other, the films reveal an attempt of the Russian collective imagination to acknowledge and integrate problematic aspects of Russia's past and present, rather than to seek to renounce them by projecting them elsewhere. To evoke once again Waddell's discussion of adulthood: 'A sense of mature adulthood may be achieved, at least some of the time, not by disclaiming, ignoring or enacting whatever infantile impulse may arise, but by recognizing such impulses for what they are and managing them appropriately' (1998a, 177). It is hard to say whether the Russian collective imagination is appropriately managing its infantile impulses (the idealization and glorification of the past, happy romances with the West achieved by *deus ex machina*, or the complete rejection and hatred of the West). One can argue with certainty, however, that these three films suggest an effort to see the world not as black and white but as grey and complex and to recognize Russia's responsibility and guilt for the darkness and the violence in the world.

Notes

1. Also, Rogozhkin's films, in particular, can be seen as a result of the director's consistent and long engagement with liberalism.

2. It won the *Kinotavr* Award (1995) and the Special Prize at the international festival *Karlovy Vary* in the Czech Republic (1995). The success was marked by controversy: some despised the film as kitsch and others called Rogozhkin a 'Russophobe', criticizing his portrayal of Russians as nothing but alcoholics. The film, however, became a hit.

3. *Peculiarities of a Russian Bathhouse* [*Osobennosti russkoi bani*, 1999] and *Peculiarities of a Russian Bathhouse 2* (2000) are erotic comedies directed by Aleksei Rudakov. Only the main protagonist from Rogozhkin's films is present. The setting and pacing likewise differ, as the characters drink beer and talk about (and have) sex for two hours.

4. The title 'cuckoo' also hints at this fusion of self and other or at acceptance of the other. Cuckoos are known for leaving their offspring to other birds to raise.

5. For the analysis of *Of Freaks and Men* I am indebted to all participants at the conference *Psychoanalytic Approaches to Ideology in Film* (University of Illinois at Urbana-Champaign, April 2002), but particularly to Nancy Blake, Slavoj Žižek, and Ann Kaplan for their observations and provocative comments.

6. Marx insists that commodity fetishism occurs when social relations between men assume the fantastic form of a relation between things.

7. For more on how the film challenges the stereotypical understanding of masochism as an innately female feature, see "The Gaze of Power, Impotence, and Subversion in Balabanov's *Of Freaks and Men*" (Hashamova 2003).

8. The Other in this sentence is used in the Lacanian sense as the big Other, the Law, the Symbolic, hence it is spelled with capital 'O'.

9. In *The Metastases of Enjoyment*, Žižek (1994) argues that the rape of Muslim women in the presence of their fathers was used as a 'weapon' by the Serbs in the recent war in Bosnia. '[T]he father – the representative of authority, of the big Other – is exposed in his utter impotence, which makes him guilty in his own eyes as well as in those of his daughter... The rape thus entails, beside the girl's physical and psychic suffering, the disintegration of the entire familial socio-symbolic network' (74). I use this argument to suggest that if women's desire is the desire of the big Other, and there is evidence in this film that it is latently impotent, then this poses a threat to the symbolic structure.

10. Beumers notes the subversion of social structures (1999b, 86).

11. Žižek connects this vicious circle of capitalism with Lacan's discourse of the hysteric: 'the apparent satisfaction only widens the gap of its dissatisfaction' (1993, 209).

12. On the subject of Russia's primary and secondary colonization, see also "V otsutstvie mediatora" (Lipovetskii 2003).

13. Žižek offers a similar argument about the post-communist relations between the West and the former socialist counties (1993, 208).

14. Metz develops the idea that film is like a mirror, but differing from it in one essential point: the viewer's own body is not reflected on the screen. The experience, however, of the mirror stage (in the Lacanian sense) helps the viewer to constitute a world of objects without the necessity to recognize himself/herself within it. 'In this respect, the cinema is already on the side of the symbolic' (Metz 46). Later he continues: '[I] also know that it is I who am perceiving all this, that this perceived-imaginary material is deposited on me as if on a second screen, that it is in me that it forms up into an organized sequence, that therefore I am myself the place where this really perceived imaginary accedes to the symbolic... In other words the spectator identifies with himself, with himself as a pure act of perception' (Metz 48–49).

15. Nancy Blake called my attention to this Lacanian view of the doublings in the film (Blake 271).

CONCLUSION – THE WEST AND BEYOND

This book examined Russia's imagination of the West as it developed at the turn of the millennium, an imagination which in its shifting sentiments, fantasies, fears, and anxieties resembles changes similar to those the adolescent undergoes in search of a more stable and permanent identity. Russian national identity had to adjust to staggering political, social, economic, and cultural transformations occurring in Russia and in the global world. In this adjustment, the Russian collective imagination reacts to the western presence in Russian society and culture as it exhibits disparate attitudes that take the form of superfluous and impatient relations with the (western) other, aggressive and paranoid urges, complete rejection of external (western) models, search for positive internal sources (past and culture) for identification, and a more mature and reflective perception of self (Russia) and other (West) with their constructive and destructive aspects.

Attempting to establish links between political ideology, psychoanalysis, and cinema, I have also traced the shifting dynamics of Russia's fantasy of the West as it appears in post-Soviet cinema. Thus, my cultural critique (literate in fantasy) of early 1990s films reveals the apparently illusionary nature of this fantasy as manifested in clichéd images and patriotic messages. The collapse of the Berlin Wall tempted Russian viewers with unimagined opportunities, but, as it becomes clear in the films, these opportunities were deceptive and the fantasy of the West remained potent. In the mid-1990s when the West became a part of Russian life, the distance between the (Russian) subject and his/her fantasy collapsed and new fantasies emerged, namely aggressive anti-western sentiments as well as admiration for Russia's moral superiority (evident in Balabanov's films).

Russia's openly aggressive anti-western, and especially anti-American, films are fewer, but they have become cult films and have reached large audiences, while the more considerate films though greater in number have not evoked the successful identification process of Balabanov's films. To speak only of the production side of films says little about the way they actually reproduce and sustain sentiments or political meaning. What is important is how viewers receive the messages of the films and how they act upon them at the level of the story, the characters, or the imagery. Balabanov's character, Danila, for instance, became 'the brother' of millions of Russian youth; he morphed into a cult figure, a rare achievement in post-Soviet culture. This, no doubt, is due in part to the blatant anti-Americanism that *Brother 2* promotes.

There are various reasons – political, economic, and cultural – for the recent eruption of vehement anti-Americanism in Russia. I insist, however, that the drive of these anti-American sentiments can be found as much in America's recent manifestation of megalomania as in Russia's identity crisis itself. Anti-Americanism is part of Russia's inferiority struggles and paranoia. America continues to be a focal point, attracting more aggression because of its position of unchallenged military, economic, and cultural power in today's world. Still, the root of Russia's anti-Americanism lies partly in Russia's wounded national pride, which aggressively expresses itself against everybody non-Russian, not only against America. I share Shiraev and Zubok's conclusion: 'The development of massive disappointment with the United States and the West coincided with the beginning of a search for a new national Russian identity' (145). I, however, believe that these two processes (western political expressions of triumphalism and Russia's search for national identity) do not simply coincide, but are actually entwined. Russia's disappointment with the West and America comes also from Russia's own failures. The West with its political behaviour of imposing capital, power, and values transforms Russia's pain into a traumatic experience. Shiraev and Zubok write: 'national humiliation...sparks explosions of xenophobia and fascism' (145). Again, I insist here that this humiliation is caused as much by the West's triumphs as by Russia's national disappointments.

At the same time, I cannot emphasize enough how I do not want in any way to underestimate destructive western behaviour. After the Iraq War began in the spring of 2003, much has been said and written about the United States's aggressive and unilateral politics. The United States government, together with other western governments, shares the responsibility of the increased anti-American and anti-western sentiments that have overwhelmed the rest of the world at the beginning of the twenty-first century. But my purpose in this study is to shed light on Russia's own responsibility for the position in which the country and its people find themselves today in the global world.

I do not believe that Russia's anti-western sentiments will escalate in violence and active aggression in the near future. There have been enough examples in the films discussed that reveal the opposite, more considerate and reflective attitudes. These films also testify to a more diverse discourse of anxieties and fantasies that not only produce aggression but also deflate it. *Peculiarities of the National Hunt in Fall* and *Cuckoo* encourage understanding and acceptance of difference. Rogozhkin advocates agreement and friendship and resists hatred and violence. *Of Freaks and Men* even suggests Russia's own destructive attitudes and the way it is capable of victimizing its own ethnic others. Russia's position and its role in the process of globalization is problematized in the film, for Russia is portrayed as a victim of the West but not as an innocent victim. In turn, Russia victimizes its Eastern other. Such films signal Russia's traversing its fantasy of the West or at least show a transformation of Russia's relation to its fundamental fantasy. This traversing can be liberating and at the same time traumatic, for the process offers no hope.

To compensate for such a traumatic experience, Russia's search for a new national identity finds expressions in films that glorify Russia's uniqueness in history, art, and religion. *The Barber of Siberia* and *Russian Ark* turn the Russian viewers' attention to Russia's rich history of honour, dignity, and loyalty to one's country, as well as world-class culture, and, thus, its potential for a glorious future. The need to believe in the ever-lasting continuity of the nation expresses itself in these films as they appropriate the imperial past, especially positive characteristics ascribed to the past such as decency, devotion to principles and moral standards, faith, love, and hope. In a country that at the beginning of the 1990s knew only fear and mistrust, these films generate optimism in Russia's future. The future promises to uphold and resurrect all the positive national characteristics that viewers see uncovered in Russia's imperial past. These films provide a historical and cultural alternative to the conflicts and problems of globalization. It is worth noting that Sokurov is more impartial than Mikhalkov in his quest for Russia's cultural uniqueness and in his interpretation of Russia's imperial past. Both attempt to symbolize the irreducible kernel of Russian national identity, but Mikhalkov offers a surrogate of this kernel (or Lacan's *object a*), whereas Sokurov at least acknowledges the impossibility to symbolize it and hints at a presence of displaced elements that orchestrate the field of vision and appearance. While Mikhalkov blatantly idealizes the past and constructs a monumental one-sided presentation of Russia's history, Sokurov attempts to show the complexities of this history by suggesting double historical temporality, one of identity and another of difference.

Russia's entanglement with the West also becomes apparent in films that portray romantic relationships between Russian and western characters. Russian viewers' desire to find happiness in a union that transgresses national borders is inscribed in films such as *On Deribasovskaia*, *Window to Paris*, *The Barber of Siberia*, *Gods' Envy*, and *The Frenchman*. Most of these films, however, deny the possibility of such happiness, which in turn speaks of political, social, and historical conditions hostile to international relationships. The desire to identify with one's country and its problems reigns over the desire to be cosmopolitan. *On Deribasovskaia* and *The Frenchman* are the only two films that offer happy endings and, while the former gives in to the euphoria of the first post-perestroika years, the latter attempts to transgress national differences and to advocate love between two similar souls regardless of their national differences. In most of these films, Russian male characters gaze at their western romantic partners, as the male gaze and the Russian/Soviet gaze collude with one another.

Having established the importance of the West for Russia's identity formation, I must emphasize again that Russia has played its own role in shaping the West's political and cultural identity. America's political demonology and Europe's attempt to construct Russia as its other were mentioned in the discussion of the interactions between Russia and the West. Driven by fears and anxieties projected onto Russia, America convinced itself of its superior morality by demonizing the evil communist empire. Europe, in turn, imagined itself a model of culture and civilization while perceiving Russia as a disciple of its high achievements. The collapse of the Soviet Union (re)confirmed the sense of moral superiority imbedded in America's collective imagination and triggered a series of new fantasized projections that have resulted in America's role as a world crusader for democracy and freedom in general, and in a conflicting relationship with Russia in particular. In an interview for *The New Yorker* (13 October 2003) Dmitrii Rogozin, the chairman of the Russian Parliament (Duma) foreign-affairs committee, jokingly said: 'There was the Soviet Union and the balance of pressures. Now, with this having disappeared, it's like in sumo wrestling. The United States simply fell forward for the lack of the opponent, and you became responsible for everything.'

I began this book with the thought that the West functions as a cultural screen for the Russian collective imagination, a cultural mirror that can provide both an idealized image and at the same time a disjunctive conjunction between the Russian collective identification and this idealized (western) model. Now, in the conclusion, after tracing in detail the intricate dynamics of Russia's imagination of the West at the turn of the millennium, I can imply that during the first years of the period of transition Russian attitudes to the West were more pronounced and focused outward, seeking to find answers for Russia's changing identity. But at the beginning of the twenty-first century they are becoming more introjected and focused inward towards Russia's own image. If during the 1990s Russians looked at the western cultural mirror and saw mainly the western idealized/demonized image, today they continue to look in the same mirror but more clearly see themselves.

The most recent films that I have discussed, such as *Russian Ark*, *Cuckoo*, and *The Frenchman*, all seek the West. In these films, however, the cultural gaze looks deeply into Russia's unique national and cultural identity, related to but different from the West. The tour through three hundred years of Russia's history and culture advocates for the power and exclusivity of Russian culture that at the same time is closely tied to western culture.

Cuckoo constructs Ivan, Veikko, and Anni as strangers to each other, but in the end of the film each of them has accepted something from the other and has carried it with him or herself. This film cinematically (re)produces Kristeva's idea of recognizing the uncanny strangeness within ourselves. *Cuckoo* does not advocate similarities or brotherhood but rather precisely what Kristeva calls 'a cosmopolitanism of a new sort that, cutting across governments, economies, and markets, might work for a mankind whose solidarity is founded on the consciousness of its unconscious – desiring, destructive, fearful, empty, impossible' (1991, 192). Is this not a very apt description of the parable of coexistence and acceptance of difference portrayed in the film through the meeting of Anni, Ivan, and Veikko and through the metaphor of the cuckoo, a bird that lays its eggs in other birds' nests to be raised by others?

Fathers and Sons: Screening Myth and Meaning beyond the West

In 2003, Russian cinema produced films that turned viewers' attention to their own collective experience. Many of the most recent Russian films pose questions about universal human values and attempt to avoid a direct portrayal of the present with its specific concerns. Discussing the films presented at the 2003 Kinotavr Film festival in Russia, Nancy Condee and Vladimir Padunov notice:

> [P]reoccupation with prehistory: a once promising photographer becomes a local bum (Galin's *Photo*); an ambitious poetess gradually resigns herself to being an ordinary Russian language teacher (Nikulin's *Do Not Make Biscuits in a Bad Mood*); Soviet physicist encounters political trouble and...ends up a provincial electrician (Konstantin Khudiakov's *Michel*); a policeman turns to crime and ends up a serial killer (Khvan's *Carmen*).

Elena Stishova similarly observes the departure from the construction of the male hero and a shift toward universal values experienced through a collective past (2003). Genadii Sidorov's *Little Old Ladies* (2003) received the Golden Rose (among other prizes) and became a favorite film of Russian audiences. It tells a story of a remote forgotten village of the Kostroma Region where old Russian women live together with a Down's syndrome boy, all of whom are forgotten by the world and civilization. Their life changes when a Tadzhik refugee family settles in one of the decrepit old houses of the village. The film expounds the enigma of human destinies situated in the neutral, almost timeless, land of Russia's vast provinces, far away from the vanity of big metropolises like St Petersburg and Moscow.

Among Russia's most prominent films of 2003–2004, interestingly, there is a group that portrays fathers and their relationship to their sons and society at large. The theme of father-son relationships dates backs to numerous ancient myths and biblical sources. In the modern world it still draws attention, but the focus has shifted to the authority of the father, as many perceive the function of the father figure in today's patriarchal societies as inadequate. This perception does not make these societies less patriarchal but changes the generational and gender dynamics and testifies to challenges of predetermined identifications.

In "The Collapse of the Function of the Father and its Effect on Gender Roles", Paul Verhaeghe argues that the successful feminist movement of the last quarter of the twentieth century weakened the function of the Father, and, precisely because of its success, simultaneously prompted a longing for the old authority. He writes: 'Nowadays popular opinion is asking, sometimes even begging, for a return of law and order, that is a return of the authoritarian father, again both at the individual and at the sociological level' (Verhaeghe 132). He believes that this striking reversal is due to the widespread distrust of Freud's myth of the primal father and, by extension, of the symbolic function of the father and of any authority. In other words, the destabilized father figure produced problems of identity hesitations and uncertainty, which in turn evoke law and order as a defense mechanism.[1]

Recent West European films, such as *The Full Monty* (Peter Cataneo, 1997), *TwentyFourSeven* (Shane Meadows, 1997), *Character* (Mike Van Diem, 1997), and *Gabriel and Me* (Udayan Prasad, 2001), explore the obsession with absent or failing father figures as well as perceived pressure on homosocial bonds and territories (Leggott). Generally these films tell stories about the efforts working-class fathers make to keep their roles of good fathers, but they also convey the children's confusion with the challenged patriarchal authority and their attempts either to restore it or break the paternal union. Although *Character* differs from the rest of the films in its emphasis on the tyrannical and destructive father, it nonetheless reveals the same concern with the role of the father figure and its effect on the son in his pursuit of power and authority.

The theme of father-son relationship is not new in Russian culture. Ivan Turgenev's *Fathers and Sons* (1862) portrayed generational conflict and brought it to the forefront of intellectual discussions. Dostoevsky's *Brothers Karamazov* (1879–80) raised ethical questions about the responsibilities of fathers for the sins of their sons. In the history of twentieth-century Russian totalitarianism, the father figure occupied a special place as 'the father of the nation'. The father image positioned the leader (Lenin and Stalin) as a paternal god who reigned above all. Later in the twentieth century, however, this paternal function of the leader weakened. 'Indeed, changes in the leader's authority after Stalin had turned the communist party first secretaries from heroes to government functionaries' (Schoeberlein 202). Thus, although the metaphorical function of the father figure in society is questioned in the modern world in general, the nostalgia for the return of the paternal figure in Russian culture results from the particular political tradition of upholding the leader as the father of the nation, a tradition that faded away in the last quarter of the twentieth century. Most recent Russian films exploring father-son relationships address some of the universal aspects of this relationship as well as some of its Russian manifestations.

An emphasis on the father-son bond is exhibited in Sokurov's *Father and Son* (2003) shown at Cannes (2003) where it received the International Federation of Film Critics (FIPRESCI) award. The director focuses on the tender and deep love between father and son and attempts to elevate it to an ideal bond, which appears forced and unreal. Although the son's girlfriend abandons him for an older man (perhaps the father), the cinematic narrative excludes woman who does not have a place in this relationship of male mutual respect and infatuation. And even if Sokurov vehemently rejects the notions of homoerotic overtones, they resurface in this idyllic homosocial bond. A lot has been written about the film, and I will not expand on it any further. I mention the film here only as an example of an indomitable homosocial union which marginalizes and/or excludes women, concurring with Tashiian's assertion: 'Nothing is clear and all is evident: this is a triumph of a man's view of the world. Reflections on the patriarchal society, in which women's presence is rather unnecessary.'[2]

The big Russian film surprise of 2003 came from the international acclaim of Zviagintsev's debut film *The Return*, a film intensely preoccupied with the father-son relationship and the paternal metaphor. It won two Golden Lion Awards at the Venice International Film Festival, and the director was quickly recognized as an heir of Andrei Tarkovsky. The most one can say about *The Return*'s chronotope is that the story unfolds in modern times somewhere in Russia. The film, positioning conflicts and emotions beyond time and place, reinforces their universal value. After years of absence, a father returns home to visit his boys (ages twelve and fifteen). The father's history is unclear; viewers do not learn where he has been or what he does, and even the sons need to look at a photograph hidden in the attic to reassure themselves that he is their father. The film presents a journey of a father and his sons seeking understanding and trying to unravel the meaning of fatherhood. While the older boy, Andrei, instantly likes his father and obeys all of his (often odd) requests, the younger son, Ivan, is in doubt and resists accepting a man whom he sees for the first time in his life. Ivan often confronts his father and questions his authority. Interestingly, the image of the father is a dual fantasy of the two sons: for Andrei the father is a trustworthy and protective figure, while for Ivan he is an imposter and an abuser.

The film opens with Ivan on a high diving tower. He is afraid to jump in the water, but if he climbs down, his friends will laugh at him. The tower invites association with phallic symbols and one of the last scenes, in which the father falls off the tower and dies, also implies emasculation. It is the same tower which empowers Ivan. At the end of the film, he has overcome his fear of heights, perhaps due to his experience with his father, but one can question the course of this empowerment. Ivan is emotionally and verbally abused by his father and somehow miraculously at the end of the film finds strength and love. The execution of the father-son bond (and Ivan's maturity) falls short of being emotionally credible. Or as Aleksandr Sekatskii argues, the problem emerges from the impatient and hasty attempts of the 'prodigal father' to correct in a few days his long absence from his sons' lives (203).

At first glance, the film offers a modern (re)vision of Freud's myth about the primal father, especially his murder by the sons, as well as an echo of Oedipus, all of which is familiar to Russian culture as much from Freud or Sophocles as from Dostoevsky's complex execution of the theme. Yet, questions about authority, leadership, and guidance posed in the film come across as ambiguous. If Zviagintsev's goal was to (re)enforce the need for a bond between father and sons, the films fails at the level of warm emotions and love.

Unlike *The Full Monty*, for instance, in which the father feels guilty and inadequate because he cannot afford to take his son to an expensive football game and therefore cannot secure a place for his son in a traditional homosocial ritual, the father in *The Return* feels no guilt and has no doubts about his position and power despite the fact that he was absent during his sons' childhood. He unquestionably believes that he can omnipotently assert his paternal status through a few days' retreat in the country and through the traditional homosocial ritual of fishing. Despite the father's death, the film ends with the alternation of black-and-white photographs that convey the boys' happiness and enjoyment during the trip. The last photograph, from an early period, again shows the father with one of his sons as a baby. Despite possible interpretations (one pointing to the 'murder' of the father and the other to Ivan's maturation through his relationship with his father), *The Return* divulges a certain nostalgia for the return of the father and the reconstruction of homosocial experience. Analyzing the film, Stishova contends that Zviagintsev accumulates the new existential experience of the deconstruction of the patriarchal world in which Russia still lives (Stishova 2004). While sustaining her findings, I want to stress that Zviagintsev's film also surmounts fears and confusion about the weakened paternal function and unveils a latent melancholy born out of this (imaginary) change.

The film proffers several layers of meaning (even though questionable), infusing it with a mystery and sophistication that set it apart from mainstream Russian films. One thing can be said with certainty about this film: it captivates viewers emotionally and visually, its camerawork and cinematography are unusual and stunning, and the pace and the rhythm are unmistakably Tarkovskian.

The father-son relationship is a topic also featured in Popogrebskii and Khlebnikov's *Koktebel*. The film visually narrates a father-son trip from Moscow to Koktebel, Crimea. The director presents a string of episodes and encounters with strangers that they experience on their way. The father quietly shares his story with a woman who saves his life: after his wife died he was led astray, and his son grew up on his own.

Zviagintzev's The Return.

Soon after the opening of the film, the directors offer a long take of the son sitting in an enclosed space of a cargo train. From a full shot of the sitting boy, the camera zooms in to a close-up of his profile and remains there for a while. The film concludes with a similar profile shot of the boy, but this time he is sitting on the edge of a quay and looking at the vast open space. This image suggests the son's maturation and independence, which becomes more pronounced in the following scene. A seagull lands next to the boy and pulls his sleeve with its beak. The boy grabs the bird by the throat and, after squeezing it, throws it in the air. Like Ivan, who overcomes his fear and climbs the tower, the son at the end of *Koktebel* manifests strength (even cruelty) and independence. The camera then cuts to an aerial shot of the lonely (and somewhat sad) boy at the end of the quay who is shortly joined by his missing father. The last shot incorporates both father and son in a frontal medium frame.

Although the film shows a comfortable bond between father and son through their mutual survival adventures and suggests the lead of the father who teaches his son about birds and planes, in the middle of the narrative the son appears to appropriate the leading and more decisive position in the relationship. Several episodes (locating a doctor who can treat his injured father, his escape from the father, and his handling of the seagull) reaffirm the boy's independence and decisiveness. The father's mysterious appearance and their reunion, resulting from *deus ex machina*, testify to a collective desire for the return of the father despite his problematic role in the life of his son.

Aleksei Popogrebskii and Boris Khlebnikov's *Koktebel*.

Unlike the West European films mentioned earlier, which at the end reveal the fathers' failures to assert their parental status, *The Return* and *Koktebel* insist on the resurrected father even if it contradicts the logic of the narratives and the characters. The Russian father-son films also eliminate the mother figure and unquestionably proffer homosocial bonds and relationships. At the same time, however, through narrative and characters' inconsistencies the films divulge cracks in the desire for the return of the omnipotent father.

Significantly, these films, among others such as Valerii Todorovskii's *My Stepbrother Frankenstein* (2004) and Vladimir Mashkov's *Father* (2004), advance particular Russian sentiments about the father-son relationship and the weakened father function (different from the overall western distrust in the father figure). As Sekatskii argues, all these films (*Father and Son*, *The Return*, *Koktebel*, *My Stepbrother Frankenstein*, and *Father*) in an apparent or more latent way reverse the roles of fathers and sons and portray the sons as more adequate, reliable, and ready to forgive their fathers. Hence, Sekatskii looks at these films as portrayals of 'prodigal fathers' (199–205). These films open space for imagining the future of society with strong sons in the absence of mighty fathers.

The Russian film scene today is becoming more diverse and appealing, testifying to the ongoing development of Russian national identification. It is difficult to predict the new wave of fantasies, fears, and desires that will accompany this identification process. It is also difficult to say whether the West will continue to function as a cultural screen for Russia's cultural identity in the future, especially with the same intensity as it has been in the past fifteen years. It is significant, however, to know and understand how Russia imagines itself in the global world. This study attempts to describe Russia's concerns and hesitations vis-à-vis the globalization process and also attempts to elucidate shifting sentiments that often appear irrational and difficult to fathom.

At the beginning of the twenty-first century the global world is experiencing a crisis: political, economic, and cultural. There is no political consensus in the world and world politics has been dictated unilaterally by the United States and other Western European countries much to the objection of the rest of the world. The world economy can easily slide into a depression. The invasion of western culture is both revered and hated in most non-western countries. This crisis is challenging the only solution that the world appears to have today – global capital. Liberal minds seek alternatives and the only hope (if any) is focused on Russia or China to offer such alternatives. Russia certainly has to solve many political, economic, and cultural problems of its own before it can put forward an alternative to the current situation in the world. Still, it is encouraging to remember that the western cultural screen provides a disjunctive conjunction for the Russian collective imagination, which in turn suggests a possibility (even if bleak today) for developing such an alternative to the West.

Over the last two centuries, Russia has continually shocked the world. It implemented Marxist theories – the first in the world to do so – much to Marx's own disbelief in that country's readiness for revolution. Ready or not, the October Revolution shook the world with its attempt to liberate people from their idols (money, property, and religion) and in its own way prepared the postmodern rearrangement of knowledge by questioning all traditions. This book uncovers Russia's latent desires and fantasies in her relations with the West, but in spite (or because) of them, Russia has always been a fascinating place, with its mixture of globe-shaking politics and world-class culture. The future – whatever it holds – promises nothing less.

Notes

1. Freud's *Moses and Monotheism* constructs the myth of the primal father as follows: Once there was a primal father in total possession of all females, who was murdered by rebellious sons. His death, surprisingly, resulted in the establishment of matriarchy. With time, the fraternal clan reintroduced the father figure and created the cult of the father, and thus of patriarchal power. For more on the myth, see Freud (1953, 23: 80–84, 130–32). Here, however, I follow Lacan's interpretation of Freud's myth as a metaphor for paternal power and an organizational principle (Lacan 1977, 179–225).

2. For more on the film, see Plakhov.

BIBLIOGRAPHY

Anderson, Benedict (1983), *Imagined Communities: Reflections on the Origin and Spread of Nationalism*, London: Verso.

Appadurai, Arjun (1996), *Modernity at Large: Cultural Dimensions of Globalization*, Minneapolis: University of Minnesota Press.

Arendt, Hannah (1951), *The Origins of Totalitarianism*, New York: Harcourt Brace.

Attwood, Lynne (1993), "Sex and the Cinema", *Sex and Russian Society*, eds Igor Kon and James Riordan, Bloomington: Indiana University Press, pp. 64–88.

Azhgikhina, Nadezhda and Helena Goscilo (1996), "Getting Under Their Skin: The Beauty Salon in Russian Women's Lives", *Russia. Women. Culture*, eds Helena Goscilo and Beth Holmgren, Bloomington: Indiana University Press, pp. 94–125.

Bakhtin, Mikhail (1981), *The Dialogic Imagination*, ed. Michael Holquist, trans. Caryl Emerson and Michael Holquist, Austin: University of Texas Press.

—— (1986), *Speech Genres and Other Late Essays*, eds C. Emerson and M. Holquist, trans. V. W. McGee, Austin: University of Texas Press.

—— (1990), "Author and Hero in Aesthetic Activity", *Art and Answerability: Early Philosophical Essays*, eds M. Holquist and V. Liaunov, Austin: University of Texas Press, pp. 4–256.

Balabanov, Aleksei (2002), "Voina urodov i liudei [War of Freaks and Men]", interview conducted by Nina Nechaeva, *Itogi*, (26 March): 45–47.

Barker, Adele Marie (1999), ed., *Consuming Russia: Popular Culture, Sex, and Society since Gorbachev*, Durham: Duke University Press.

Baudrillard, Jean (1993), "The Evil Demon of Images and the Precession of Simulacra", *Postmodernism: A Reader*, ed. Thomas Docherty, New York: Columbia University Press, pp. 194–200.

Beaumarchais, Pierre Augustin Caron de (2003), *The Figaro Trilogy*, trans. David Coward, Oxford: Oxford University Press.

Bell, David (1999), ed., *Psychoanalysis and Culture: A Kleinian Perspective*, London: Duckworth.

Bely, Andrei (1959), *St. Petersburg*, trans. John Cournos, New York: Grove Press.

Berdiaev, Nikolai (1962), *The Origin of Russian Communism*, trans. R. M. French, Ann Arbor: University of Michigan Press.

Berry, Ellen E., and Anesa Miller-Pogacar (1995), eds, *Re-Entering the Sign: Perspectives on New Russian Culture*, Ann Arbor: University of Michigan Press.

Beumers, Birgit (1999a), ed., *Russia on Reels: The Russian Idea and Post-Soviet Cinema*, London: I. B. Tauris.

— (1999b), "To Moscow! To Moscow? The Russian Hero and the Loss of the Centre", *Russia on Reels: The Russian Idea and Post-Soviet Cinema*, ed. Birgit Beumers, London: I. B. Tauris, pp. 76–91.

— (1999c), "Cinemarket, or the Russian Film Industry in 'Mission Impossible'", *Europe-Asia Studies*, 51.5: 871–96.

— (2000), "The Barber of Siberia", *European Cinema*, eds Jill Forbes and Sarah Street, London: Palgrave, pp. 195–206.

— (2003a), "Soviet and Russian Blockbusters: A Question of Genre?" *Slavic Review*, 62.3, (fall): 441–54.

— (2003b), "'And the Ship sails on...': Sokurov's Ghostly Ark of Russia's Past", *Rossica*, 9: 56–59.

Bhabha, Homi (1999), "DissemiNation: Time Narrative, and the Margins of the Modern Nation", *Contemporary Social Theory*, ed. Anthony Elliott. Oxford: Blackwell Publishers, pp. 211–19.

Bion, W. R. (1967), *Second Thoughts: Selected Papers on Psychoanalysis*, London: William Heinemann Medical Books Limited.

Blake, Nancy (2003), "Beyond Postmodernism: An Introduction", *The Communication Review*, 6.4: 269–75.

Bloom, Solomon (1967), *The World of Nations*, New York: AMS Press.

Bogomilov, Iurii (1999), "Skazanie o zemle Sibirskoi – 2 [A Tale of the Siberian Land – 2]", *Iskusstvo kino*, 7: 60–65.

Borenstein, Eliot (1999), "Suspending Disbelief: 'Cults' and Postmodernism in Post-Soviet Russia", *Consuming Russia*, ed. Adele Marie Barker, Durham: Duke University Press.

— (2000), "*About That*: Deploying and Deploring Sex in Post-Soviet Russia", *Studies in Twentieth Century Literature*, (spring): 51–83.

Bovt, Georgii (1999), "Rossiia, kotoruiu postroit president Mikhalkov [Russia, which President Mikhalkov will Build]", *Segodnia*, 38 (February 20).

Bykov, Dmitrii (1999), "V Rossii nichego ne byvaet slegka [In Russia Nothing Happens Easily]", *Iskusstvo kino*, 7: 49–51.

Condee, Nancy (1995), ed., *Soviet Hieroglyphics: Visual Culture in Late Twentieth Century Russia*, Bloomington: Indiana University Press.

Condee, Nancy, and Vladimir Padunov (2003), "Subtropical Cinema: Kinotavr, Collective Heroes, and Small Screens", *Kinokultura*, (July). <www.kinokultura.com/articles/july03.html>.

Custine, Astolphe de (1989), *Empire of the Czar: A Journey through Eternal Russia*, anonymous trans. of *Russie en 1839*, New York: Doubleday.

Diawara, Manthia (1998), "Toward a Regional Imaginary in Africa", *The Cultures of Globalization*, eds Fr. Jameson and M. Miyoshi, Durham: Duke University Press, pp. 103–25.

Doane, May Ann (1990), "Remembering Women: Psychical and Historical Constructions in Film Theory", *Psychoanalysis and Cinema*, ed. E. Ann Kaplan, London: Routledge, pp. 46–64.

Dobrotvorskaia, Karina (1994), "Uvidet' Parizh i vyzhit [To See Paris and Survive]", *Seans*, 9: 85.

Dobrotvorskii, Sergei (1995), "I nemedlenno vypil... [And Drank Immediately...]", *Iskusstvo kino*, 12: 77–79.

Dondurei, Daniil (1992), "Cinema, Cinema! Turn Your Face to Film-goers", *Cine-Eye*, 1: 27.

— (1998), "Ne brat ia tebe, gnida... [I'm Not Your Brother, Worm...]", *Iskusstvo kino*, 2: 64–67.

— (1999), "The State of the National Cinema", *Russia on Reels: The Russian Idea in Post-Soviet Cinema*, ed. Birgit Beumers, London: I. B. Tauris, pp. 46–50.

— (2000), "Vy ganstery?" – "Net, my russkie [Are You Gangsters?" – "No, We are Russians]", *Iskusstvo kino*, 11: 68–71.

Dostoevsky, Fedor (1965), *Prestuplenie i nakazanie [Crime and Punishment]*, Chicago: Russian Language Specialties.

— (1880), *Bratia Karamazovy [Brothers Karamazov]*, Russia: Znanie Bookstore.

Dubinsky, Helene (1998), "The Fear of Becoming a Man", *Facing It Out: Clinical Perspectives on Adolescent Disturbance*, eds Robin Anderson and Anna Dartington, New York: Routledge, pp. 99–113.

Epstein, Mikhail (1995), *After the Future: The Paradoxes of Postmodernism and Contemporary Russian Culture*, Amherst: University of Massachusetts Press.

Erofeev, Venedikt (1994), *From Moscow to the End of the Line*, trans. H. Williams Tjalsma, Evanston: Northwestern University Press.

Erofeev, Viktor (1994), *Russian Beauty*, USA: Penguin.

Etkind, Aleksandr (1996), "Psychological Culture", *Russian Culture at the Crossroads*, ed. Dmitri Shalin, Boulder: Westview Press, pp. 99–127.

— (2001), "Fuko i tezis vnutrennei kolonizatsii [Foucault and a Thesis of Internal Colonization]", *NLO*, 49: 50–74.

Faraday, George (2000), *The Revolt of the Filmmakers*, University Park: Pennsylvania State University.

Freidin, Gregory (1993), *Russian Culture in Transition*, Stanford: Stanford University Press.

Freud, Sigmund (1953), *The Standard Edition of the Complete Psychological Works*, ed. J. Strachey, London: Hogarth Press.

— (1961), *Civilization and Its Discontents*, London: W. W. Norton & Company.

Friedberg, Anne (1990), "A Denial of Difference: Theories of Cinematic Identification", *Psychoanalysis and Cinema*, ed. E. Ann Kaplan, New York: Routledge, pp. 36–46.

Gillespie, David (2002), "Reconfiguring the Past: The Return of History in Recent Russian Film", *New Cinemas: Journal of Contemporary Film*, 1.1: 14–23.

Gladil'shchikov, Iurii (2004), "Ernst izvestnyi [Ernst the Known]", *Ogonek*, 29 (19–25 July): 26.

Goldschmidt, Paul (1999), "Pornography in Russia", *Consuming Russia*, ed. Adele M. Barker, Durham: Duke University Press, pp. 318–39.

Goncharov, V. (1963), "Parizhskaia zima [Parisian Winter]", *Novoe vremia*, 3: 25.

Goscilo, Helena (1996), *Dehexing Sex: Russian Womanhood during and after Glasnost*, Ann Arbor: University of Michigan Press.

— (2000), "Style and S(t)imulation: Popular Magazines or the Aestheticization of Postsoviet Russia", *Studies in Twentieth Century Literature*, (spring): 15–51.

Graffy, Julian (2000), "Brother", *Sight & Sound*, 10.5: 44.

— (2001), *Bed and Sofa: The Film Companion*, London: I. B. Tauris.

Grant, Bruce (1999), "The Return of the Repressed: Conversation with Three Russian Entrepreneurs", *Paranoia within Reason*, ed. George E. Marcus, Chicago: University of Chicago Press, pp. 241–69.

Graubard, Stephan R. (1993), ed., *Exit from Communism*, New Brunswick: Transaction Publishers.

Gusiatinskii, Evgenii (2001), "Brat zhil, brat zhiv, brat budet zhiv [Brother Lived, Lives, and will Live]", *Iskusstvo kino*, 3. <kinoart.ru/2001/3/7.html)>.

Harte, Tim (2005), "A Visit to the Museum: Aleksandr Sokurov's *Russian Ark* and the Framing of the Eternal", *Slavic Review*, 64.1: 43–58.

Hashamova, Yana (2001), "Winnie: The Woman Who is Not-All? (Beckett's *Happy Days*)", *Proceedings of the 16th International Conference on Literature and Psychoanalysis*, ed. Frederico Pereira, Lisbon: Instituto Superior de Psicologia Aplicada, pp.167–172.

— (2003), "The Gaze of Power, Impotence, and Subversion in Balabanov's *Of Freaks and Men*", *The Communication Review*, 6.4: 289–301.

Hemingway, Ernest (1929), *Farewell to Arms*, New York: Charles Scribner's Sons.

Hoberman, J. (2002), "And the Ship Sails On", *Film Comment*, (Sept/Oct): 54.

Horton, Andrew (2001), "Oh Brother!" *Central European Review*, 3.5 (5 February). <ce-review.org/01/5/kinoeye5_horton.html>.

— (2002), "War, what is it good for?" *Kinoeye*, 18. <kinoeye.org/02/18/horton18_no3.html>.

Horton, Andrew, and Michael Brashinsky (1992), *The Zero Hour: Glasnost and Soviet Cinema in Transition*, Princeton: Princeton University Press.

Hubbs, Joanna (1993), *Mother Russia*, Bloomington: Indiana University Press.

Ilf, Il'ia, and Evgenii Petrov (1937), *Odnoetazhnaia Amerika [One-Storey America]*, Moscow: Sovetskii pisatel'.

Iensen, Tatiana (2002), "Kukushka [Cuckoo]", *Iskusstvo kino*, 11. <kinoart.ru/magazine/11-2002/repertoire/Cookoo/>.

Iordanova, Dina (1999), "Political Resentment Versus Cultural Submission: The Duality of U.S. Representations in Bulgarian Media", *Images of the U.S. Around the World*, ed. Yahya R. Kamalipour, Albany: SUNY Press, pp. 71–87.

— (2000), *Cinema of Flames*, London: BFI.

— (2003), *Cinema of the Other Europe*, London: Wallflower Press.

Jameson, Fredric (1981), *The Political Unconscious: Narrative as a Socially Symbolic Act*, Ithaca: Cornell University Press.

— (1991), *Postmodernism or the Cultural Logic of Late Capitalism*, Durham: Duke University Press.

Jameson, Fredric, and Masao Miyoshi (1998), eds, *The Cultures of Globalization*, Durham: Duke University Press.

Johnson, Vida (2002), "Rossiiskie rezhisery boiatsia amerikanskikh mifov [Russian Directors are Afraid of American Myths]", *Iskusstvo kino*, 9: 18–22.

Kachurin, Pamela and Ernest A. Zitser (2003), "'After the Deluge': *Russian Ark* and the (Ab)uses of History", *AAASS Newsnet*, (August): 17–22.

Kang, Liu (1998), "Is There an Alternative to (Capitalist) Globalization? The Debate about Modernity in China", *The Cultures of Globalization*, eds Fredric Jameson and Masao Miyoshi, Durham: Duke University Press, pp. 164–91.

Kaplan, E. Ann (1983), *Women and Film: Both Sides of the Camera*, New York: Methuen.

— (1990), "Introduction: From Plato's Cave to Freud's Screen", *Psychoanalysis and Cinema*, ed. E. Ann Kaplan, London: Routledge, pp. 1–24.

— (1997), *Looking for the Other: Feminism, Film, and the Imperial Gaze*, New York: Routledge.

Kapur, Geeta (1998), "Globalization and Culture: Navigating the Void", *The Cultures of Globalization*, eds Fredric Jameson and Masao Miyoshi, Durham: Duke University Press, pp. 191–218.

Kennedy, Michael D. (1994a), ed., *Envisioning Eastern Europe: Postcommunist Cultural Studies*, Ann Arbor: University of Michigan Press.

— (1994b), "An Introduction to East European Ideology and Identity in Transition", *Envisioning Eastern Europe: Postcommunist Cultural Studies*, ed. Michael D. Kennedy, Ann Arbor: University of Michigan Press, pp. 1–46.

Klein, Melanie (1975a), *The Writings of Melanie Klein*, 4 vols, London: Hogarth.
— (1975b), *Envy and Gratitude and Other Works 1946–1963*, New York: Free Press.
Komm, Dmitrii (2002), "Uzh ne protokol [Not a Protocol at all]", *Iskusstvo kino*, 12: 19–23.
Kon, Igor (1993), "Sexuality and Culture", *Sex and Russian Society*, eds Igor Kon and James Riordan, Bloomington: Indiana University Press.
Kristeva, Julia (1986a), "Word, Discourse, and Novel", *The Kristeva Reader*, ed. Toril Moi, Oxford: Blackwell Publishers, pp. 34–61.
— (1986b), "Women's Time", *The Kristeva Reader*, ed. Toril Moi, New York: Columbia University Press, pp. 187–214.
— (1991), *Strangers to Ourselves*, New York: Columbia University Press.
Kujundzic, Dragan (2004), "After 'After': The *Arki*ve Fever of Alexander Sokurov", *Quarterly Review of Film and Video*, 21:3: 219–39.
Lacan, Jacques (1977), *Ecrits: A Selection*, trans. Alan Sheridan, New York: W. W. Norton & Company.
— (1981), *The Four Fundamental Concepts of Psycho-Analysis*, trans. Alan Sheridan, New York: W. W. Norton & Company.
Lapitskii, I. (1963), "V bedstvennykh raionakh SSHA [In the Disastrous Regions of the United States]", *Novoe vremia*, 7: 20.
Larsen, Susan (1999), "In Search of an Audience: The New Russian Cinema of Reconciliation", *Consuming Russia*, ed. Adele Marie Barker, Durham: Duke University Press, pp. 192–216.
— (2003), "National Identity, Cultural Authority, and the Post-Soviet Blockbuster: Nikita Mikhalkov and Aleksei Balabanov", *Slavic Review*, 63.3: 491–512.
Lawton, Anna (1992), *Kinoglasnost: Soviet Cinema in Our Time*, Cambridge: Cambridge University Press.
— (2002), "The Russian Cinema in Troubled Times", *New Cinemas: Journal of Contemporary Film*, 1.2: 98–112.
— (2005), *Imaging Russia 2000: Film and Facts*, Washington, DC: New Academia Publishing.
Leggott, James (2004), "Like Father?: Failing Parents and Angelic Children in
Contemporary British Social Realist Cinema", *The Trouble with Men: Masculinities in European and Hollywood Cinema*, eds Phil Powrie, Ann Davies, Bruce Babington, London: Wallflower Press, pp. 163–176.
Lenin, V. I. (1960–70), *Collected Works*, vol. 28, Moscow: Progress Publishers.
Lipovetskii, Mark (2000), "Vsekh liubliu na svete ia! [I Love Everybody in the World!]", *Iskusstvo kino*, 11: 55–59.
— (2003), "V otsutstvie mediatora [In the Absence of a Mediator]", *Iskusstvo kino*, 8. <kinoart.ru/magazine/08-2003/review/lipovetski/>.
Liubarskaia, Irina (1996), "Utinye okhotniki na plenere [Duck Hunters at a Plenary Session]", *Seans*, 12: 26.
Lorde, Audre (1997), "The Erotic as Power", *Writing on the Body*, eds Katie Conboy, Nadia Medina, and Sarah Stanbury, New York: Columbia University Press, pp. 277–82.
Lotman, Yuri M. (1990), *Universe of the Mind: A Semiotic Theory of Culture*, London: I. B. Tauris.
Lupinin, Nickolas (2004), "Conjecture as Criticism: Revising the *Russian Ark*", *AAASS Newsnet*, (January): 21–22.
Macnab, Geoffrey (2002), "Palace in Wonderland", *Sight & Sound*, 12.8: 20–22.
Margolit, Evgenii (1998), "Plach po pioneru, ili nemetskoe slovo 'Iablokitai [Cry for the Pioneer, or, The German Word 'Yablokitai']", *Iskusstvo kino*, 2: 57–61.

Marx, Karl (1886), *Capital*, New York: Humboldt.

Mayakovsky, Vladimir (1960), *The Bedbug and Other Poems*, New York: Meridian Books.

Mayne, Judith (1990), "*The Woman at the Keyhole: Feminism and Women's Cinema*, Bloomington: Indiana University Press.

— (1993), *Cinema and Spectatorship*, London: Routledge.

McGowan, Todd (2004), "Fighting Our Fantasies: *Dark City* and the Politics of Psychoanalysis", *Lacan and Contemporary Film*, eds Todd McGowan and Sheila Kunkle, New York: Other Press, pp. 145–73.

Metz, Christian (1977), *The Imaginary Signifier: Psychoanalysis and the Cinema*, Bloomington: Indiana University Press.

Mikhalkov, Nikita (1999), "The Function of National Cinema", *Russia on Reels*, ed. Birgit Beumers, London: I. B. Tauris, pp. 50–57.

— (2000), "Obraz very. Diskussii [Image of Faith: Discussion]", interview conducted by Lev Karakhan, *Iskusstvo kino*, 12: 4–68.

Mochizuki, Tetsuo (2001), "Igraia so slovami klassiki: Dostoevskii v sovremennoi literature [A Game with the Words of Classics: Dostoevsky in Contemporary Literature]", *Russian Culture on the Threshold of a New Century*, ed. Tetsuo Mochizuki, Sapporo, Japan: Hokkaido University, pp. 159–81.

Moskvina, Tatiana (1996), "Istochniki zhizni eshche ne issiakli [Life Sources Haven't Dried up Yet]", *Seans*, 12: 26.

— (1999), "Ne govori, chto molodost' sgubila [Don't Say That You Wasted Your Youth]", *Iskusstvo kino*, 6: 30–35.

Mulvey, Laura (1989) [1975], "Visual Pleasure and Narrative Cinema", in *Visual and Other Pleasures*, Bloomington: Indiana University Press, pp. 14–26.

Neumann, Iver (1996), *Russia and the Idea of Europe*, London: Routledge.

— (1999), *Uses of the Other*, Minneapolis: University of Minnesota Press.

Norton, Anne (1988), *Reflections on Political Identity*, Baltimore: Johns Hopkins University Press.

O'Conner, John E., and Martin A. Jackson (1979), "Introduction", *American History/American Film: Interpreting the Hollywood Image*, eds John E. O'Conner and Martin A. Jackson, New York: Frederick Ungar Publishing, pp. xv–1.

Ong, Aihwa (1999), *Flexible Citizenship: The Cultural Logics of Transnationality*, Durham: Duke University Press.

Pavlova, Irina (1994), "Salade russe [Russian Salad]", *Seans*, 9: 84.

Plakhov, Andrei (2003), "Muki interpretatsii [Interpretation Pains]", *Iskusstvo kino*, 9. <kinoart.ru/magazine/09-2003/repertoire/fatherson>.

Pratt, Ray (2001), *Projecting Paranoia: Conspiratorial Visions in American Film*, Lawrence: University Press of Kansas.

Prince, Stephen (1992), *Visions of Empire: Political Imagery in Contemporary American Film*, New York: Praeger.

Prokhorov, Aleksandr (2003), "Cinema of Attractions versus Narrative Cinema: Leonid Gaidai's Comedies and El'dar Riazanov's Satires of the 1960s", *Slavic Review*, 63.3: 455–73.

Prokhorova, Elena (2003), "Can the Meeting Place be Changed? Crime and Identity Discourse in Russian Television Series of the 1990s", *Slavic Review*, 63. 3: 512–25.

Pushkin, Aleksandr (1987), *The Captain's Daughter* [*Kapitanskaia Dochka*], USA: Hiperion Books.

Rabelais, François (1934), *Gargantua and Pantagruel*, trans. Sir Thomas Urquhart and Peter Le Motteux, London: Oxford University Press.

Rancour-Laferriere, Daniel (2000), *Russian Nationalism from an Interdisciplinary Perspective: Imagining Russia*, Lewiston: The Edwin Mellen Press.

Read, Christopher (2002), "In Search of Liberal Tsarism: The Historiography of Autocratic Decline", *The Historical Journal*, 43.1: 195–210.

Reik, Theodor (1962), *Masochism in Sex and Society*, New York: Grove Press.

"Reiting Otechestvennogo prokata [Ratings of National Film]" (2003), *Novyi ekran*, 1/2: 85; 3/4: 77.

Ries, Nancy (1997), *Russian Talk: Culture and Conversation during Perestroika*, Ithaca: Cornell University Press.

Rogin, Michael (1987), *Ronald Reagan: The Movie and Other Episodes in Political Demonology*, Berkeley: University of California Press.

Rogozhkin, Aleksandr (2002), "Chelovek – eto zvuchit... [A Person – It Sounds...]", (interview), *Iskusstvo kino*, 11. < kinoart.ru/magazine/11 2002/repertoire/Cookoo2/>.

Romney, Jonathan (2000), "*Of Freaks and Men:* Review", *Sight & Sound*, 5: 57–58.

Rustin, Michael (1991), *The Good Society and the Inner World: Psychoanalysis, Politics and Culture*, London: Verso.

Salecl, Renata (1994), *Spoils of Freedom*, London: Routledge.

— (2000), *(Per)versions of Love and Hate*, London: Verso.

Sartre, Jean-Paul (1948), *Anti-Semite and Jew*, Paris: Schocken.

Schoeberlein. John S. (2004),"Doubtful Dead Fathers and Musical Corpses: What to do with the Dead Stalin, Lenin, and Tsar Nicholas?" *Death of the Father: An Anthropology of the End in Political Authority*, ed. John Borneman, New York: Berghahn Books, pp. 201–220.

Segal, Hanna (1974), *Introduction to the Work of Melanie Klein*, New York: Basic Books.

— (1997), *Psychoanalysis, Literature and War*, London: Routledge.

Sekatskii, Aleksandr (2005), "Otsepriimstvo [Acceptance of the Father]", *Seans*, 21/22: 198–206.

Shalin, Dmitri (1996), ed., *Russian Culture at the Crossroads*, Boulder: Westview Press.

Shiraev, Eric, and Vladislav Zubok (2000), *Anti-Americanism in Russia: From Stalin to Putin*, New York: Palgrave.

Silverman, Kaja (1993), "Masochism and Male Subjectivity", *Male Trouble*, eds C. Penley and S. Willis, Minneapolis: University of Minnesota Press, pp. 67–87.

— (1996), *The Threshold of the Visible World*, New York: Routledge.

Sirivlia, Natalia (2000), "Bratva [Brotherhood]", *Iskusstvo kino*, 8: 23–29.

Sokolov, Nikita (1999), "Slav'sia great Russia [Be Proud Great Russia]", *Itogi*, (9 March): 48–49.

Sokurov, Aleksandr (2001), "Interview", *Kinovedcheskie zapiski*, 51: 21–25.

Sologub, Fedor (1983), *The Petty Demon*, trans. S. D. Cioran, Ann Arbor: Ardis.

Sontag, Susan (1977), *On Photography*, New York: Farrar, Straus and Gioux.

Stiglitz, Joseph E. (2002), *Globalization and Its Discontents*, New York: W.W. Norton & Company.

Stishova, Elena (2000), "Pro eto [About That]", *Iskusstvo kino*, 9: 27–31.

— (2003), "Krizis srednego vozrasta: Sochi-2003 [Middle-age Crisis: Sochi-2003]", *Iskusstvo kino*, 10. <kinoart.ru/magazine/10-2003/review/stishova0310>.

— (2004), "Na glubine [On the Bottom]", *Iskusstvo kino*, 1. <kinoart.ru/magazine/01-2004/repertoire/homewardbound0104/>.

Stishova, Elena, and Natalia Sirivlia (2003), "Solov'i na 17-i ulitse [Nightingales on 17th Street]", *Iskusstvo kino*, 10. <kinoart.ru/magazine/10-2003/mow/antiamer/>.

Stishova, Elena, Irina Liubarskaia, and Natalia Sirivlia (2000), "Zhanr nachinaet i vyigryvaet [A Genre Begins and Wins]", *Iskusstvo kino*, 11: 97–110.

Stojanova, Christina (1998), "New Russian Cinema", *Kinema*, (fall). <http://kinema.uwaterloo.ca/sto982.htm>.

Tashiian, Alin (2003), "Novoe ozarenie Sokurova [Sokurov's New Revelation]", *Iskusstvo kino*, 9. <kinoart.ru/magazine/09-2003/repertoire/fatherson/Tashiyan>.

Tasker, Yvonne (1993), *Spectacular Bodies: Gender, Genre, and the Action Cinema*, London: Routledge.

Todorov, Tzvetan (1984), *The Conquest of America: The Question of the Other*, trans. Richard Howard, New York: Harper & Row.

Tolstoy, Lev (2003), *Anna Karenina*, trans. Richard Pevear and Larissa Volokhonsky, London: Penguin Classics.

— (1982), *War and Peace*, trans. Rosemary Edmonds, New York: Penguin Books.

Turgenev, Ivan (1998), *Fathers and Sons [Otsy i deti]*, Oxford: Oxford World's Classics.

Upson, Paul (1998), "Play, Work and Identity: Taking Up One's Place in the Adult World", *Facing It Out: Clinical Perspectives on Adolescent Disturbance*, eds Robin Anderson and Anna Dartington, New York: Routledge, pp. 159–73.

Verhaeghe, Paul (2000), "The Collapse of the Function of the Father and its Effect on Gender Roles", *Sexuation*, ed. Renata Salecl, Durham: Duke University Press, pp. 131–157.

Vighi, Fabio (2006), *Traumatic Encounters in Italian Film: Locating the Cinematic Unconscious*, Bristol, UK: Intellect.

Waddell, Margot (1998a), *Inside Lives: Psychoanalysis and the Growth of the Personality*, New York: Routledge.

— (1998b), "Scapegoat", *Facing It Out: Clinical Perspectives on Adolescent Disturbance*, eds Robin Anderson and Anna Dartington, New York: Routledge, pp. 127–43.

Walters, Margaret (1978), *The Nude Male*, London: Paddington Press.

White, Susan (1994, 1995), "I Burn for Him: Female Masochism and the Iconography of Melodrama in Stahl's *Back Street* (1932)", *Post Script: Essays in Film and the Humanities*, 14.1–2 (fall, winter-spring): 59–80.

Wohl, Victoria (2002), *Love Among the Ruins: The Erotics of Democracy in Classical Athens*, Princeton: Princeton University Press.

Wolff, Larry (1994), *Inventing Eastern Europe*, Stanford: Stanford University Press.

Wood, Robin (1986), *Hollywood from Vietnam to Reagan*, New York: Columbia University Press.

Zassoursky, Yassen (1991), "Changing Images of the Soviet Union and the United States", *Beyond the Cold War: Soviet and American Media Images*, eds Everette Dennis, George Gerbner, and Yassen Zassoursky, Newbury Park: Sage Publications, pp. 11–20.

Žižek, Slavoj (1992), *Looking Awry: An Introduction to Jacques Lacan through Popular Culture*, Cambridge, MA: Massachusetts Institute of Technology Press.

— (1993), *Terrying with the Negative*, Durham: Duke University Press.

— (1994), *The Metastases of Enjoyment*, London: Verso.

— (1997), *The Plague of Fantasies*, London: Verso.

— (2000), *The Ticklish Subject: The Absent Centre of Political Ontology*, London: Verso.

— (2001), *The Fright of Real Tears: Krzysztof Kieslowski between Theory and Post-Theory*, London: British Film Institute.

FILMOGRAPHY[1]

Air Up There, The (USA; Paul Glaser, 1994).

Alaska, Sir!/Aliaska, ser! (Russia; Viacheslav Rebrov, 1992).

All of Which We've Dreamed so Long/Vse to o tom my tak dolgo mechtali (Russia; Rudol'f Fruntov, 1997).

American Boy (Ukraine; Boris Kvashnev, 1992).

American Daughter/Amerikanskaia doch' (Russia, Kazakhstan; Karen Shakhnazarov, 1995).

Anna from Six to Eighteen/Anna: Ot shesti do vosemnadtsati (Russia, France; Nikita Mikhalkov, 1993).

Antikiller/Antikiller (Russia; Egor Mikhalkov-Konchalovsky, 2002).

Antikiller 2: Antiterror (Russia; Egor Konchalovsky, 2003).

Assassin of the Tsar, The/Tsareubiitsa (Russia; Karen Shakhnazarov, 1991).

Back Street (USA; John M. Stahl, 1932).

Barber of Siberia, The/Sibirskii tsiriul'nik (Russia, France, Italy, Czech Republic; Nikita Mikhalkov, 1999).

Bed and Sofa/Liubov' v troem (USSR; Abram Room, 1927).

Before the Rain/Pred dozhdom (UK, France, Republic of Macedonia; Milcho Manchevski, 1994).

Blindman's Buff/Zhmurki (Russia; Aleksei Balabanov, 2005).

Brigade/Brigada (Russia (TV miniseries); Aleksei Sidorov, 2002).

Brother/Brat (Russia; Aleksei Balabanov, 1997).

Brother 2/Brat 2 (Russia; Aleksei Balabanov, 2000).

Burnt by the Sun/Utomlennye solntsem (Russia, France; Nikita Mikhalkov, 1994).

Carmen/Karmen (Russia; Aleksandr Khvan, 2003).

Castle, The/Zamok (Russia, France, Germany; Aleksei Balabanov, 1994).

Chapaev/Chapaev (USSR; 'Brothers' Vasiliev, 1936).

Character/Karakter (Netherlands, Belgium; Mike Van Diem, 1997).

Circus/Tsyrk (USSR; Grigorii Aleksandrov, 1936).

Close to Eden/Urga (Russia, France; Nikita Mikhalkov, 1991).

Come Look at Me/Prikhodi na menia posmotret' (Russia; Mikhail Agranovich and Oleg Iankovskii, 2000).

Cranes are Flying/Letiat zhuravli (USSR; Mikhail Kolotozov, 1957).

Cuckoo/Kukushka (Russia; Aleksandr Rogozhkin, 2002).

Dark City (Australia, USA; Alex Proyas, 1998).

Delta Force, The (USA; Menahem Golan, 1986).

Do Not Make Biscuits in a Bad Mood/Ne delaite biskviti v plokhom nastroenii (Russia; Grigorii Nikulin, 2003).

Drum Roll/Barabaniada (Russia, France; Sergei Ovcharov, 1993).

Diuba-diuba (Russia; Aleksandr Khvan, 1993).

East-West/Est-Ouest/Vostok-zapad (Bulgaria, France, Russia, Spain, Ukraine; Régis Wargnier, 1999).

Encore, Once More, Encore!/Encore eshche encore! (Russia; Piotr Todorovskii, 1992).

Everything will be OK/Vse budet khorosho (Russia; Dmitrii Astrakhan, 1995).

Extraordinary Adventures of Mr. West in the Land of the Bolsheviks/Neobychainye prikliucheniia mistera Vesta v strane bol'shevikov (USSR; Lev Kuleshov, 1924).

Farewell, America!/Proshchai, Amerika! (USSR; Aleksandr Dovzhenko, unfinished).

Father/Papa (Russia; Vladimir Mashkov, 2004).

Father and Son/Otets i Syn (Russia, Germany, Italy, Netherlands; Aleksandr Sokurov, 2003).

Foretelling, The/Predskazanie (Russia; El'dar Riazanov, 1994).

Frenchman, The/Frantsuz (Russia; Vera Storozheva, 2003).

Full Monty, The (UK; Peter Cataneo, 1997).

Gabriel and Me (UK; Udayan Prasad, 2001).

Game with No Rules/Igra bez pravil (USSR; Iaropolk Lapshin, 1965).

Gods' Envy/Zavist' bogov (Russia; Vladimir Menshov, 2000).

Happy Days/Schastlivye dni (USSR; Aleksei Balabanov, 1991).

Harry Potter and the Chamber of Secrets (USA; Chris Columbus, 2003).

Heartbreak Ridge (USA; Clint Eastwood, 1986).

House under the Starry Sky, The/Dom pod zvezdnym nebom (Soviet Union; Sergei Solovev, 1991).

Idiot/Idiot (Russia, TV Drama Channel 1; Vladimir Bortko, 2003).

Inspector General/Revizor (Russia; Sergei Gazarov, 1996).

Intergirl/Interdevochka (Soviet Union; Piotr Todorovskii, 1989).

Invasion USA (USA; Joseph Zito, 1985).

Iron Eagle (USA, Canada; Sidney J. Furie, 1986).

Irony of Fate/Ironiia sud'by ili s legkim parom (USSR; El'dar Riazanov, 1975).

It Doesn't Hurt/Mne ne bol'no (Russia; Aleksei Balabanov, 2006).

Katia Izmailova/Podmoskovnye vechera (Russia, France; Valerii Todorovskii, 1994).

Khrustalev, my car!/Khrustalev, mashinu! (Russia; Aleksei German, 1998).

Koktebel/Koktebel (Russia; Aleksei Popogrebskii and Boris Khlebnikov, 2003).

Last Days of Petersburg, The/Konets Sankt-Peterburga (Soviet Union; Vsevolod Pudovkin, 1927).

Last Tango in Paris, The/Ultimo Tango a Parigi (Italy, France; Bernando Bertolucci, 1972).

Little Demon, The/Melkii bes (Russia; Nikolai Dostal', 1995).

Little Giant with a Big Sex Drive/Malen'kii gigant bol'shogo seksa (Russia; Nikolai Dostal', 1992).

Little Old Ladies/Starukhi (Russia; Genadii Sidorov, 2003).

Little Vera/Malen'kaia Vera (USSR; Vasilii Pichul, 1988).

Lord of the Rings: The Two Towers, The (USA, New Zealand; Peter Jackson, 2003).

Luna Park/Luna park (Russia, France; Pavel Lungin, 1992).

Makarov/Makarov (Russia; Vladimir Khotinenko, 1993).

Michel/Mishel' (Russia; Konstantin Khudiakov, 2003).

Mission to Moscow (USA; Michael Curtiz, 1943).

Moloch/Molokh (Russia, Germany, Japan, Italy, France; Aleksandr Sokurov, 2000).

Moscow Does Not Believe in Tears/ Moskva slezam ne verit (USSR; Vladimir Menshov, 1979).

Moscow Parade/ Prorva (Russia, France, Germany; Ivan Dykhovichnyi, 1992).

Moscow Vacation/ Moskovskie kanikuly (Russia; Alla Surikova, 1995).

Moslem/ Musul'manin (Russia; Vladimir Khotinenko, 1995).

My Stepbrother Frankenstein/ Moi svodnyi brat Frankenshtein (Russia; Valerii Todorovskii, 2004).

Neutral Waters/ Neitral'nye vody (USSR; Vladimir Berenstein, 1969).

Night Watch/ Nochnoi dozor (Russia; Timur Bekmambetov, 2004).

Non-Love/ Neliubov' (Russia; Valerii Rubinchuk, 1992).

Nosferatu (USA; F. W. Murnau, 1922).

October/ Oktiabr' (Soviet Union; Sergei Eisenstein, 1927).

Of Freaks and Men/ Pro urodov i liudei (Russia; Aleksei Balabanov, 1998).

Oligarch/ Oligarkh (Russia, France, Germany; Pavel Lungin, 2002).

On Deribasovskaia the Weather is Fine, or, On Brighton Beach It's Raining Again/ Na Deribasovskoi khoroshaia pogoda ili na Braiton Biich opiat' idut dozhdi (Russia, USA; Leonid Gaidai, 1992).

Out of Africa (USA; Sydney Pollack, 1985).

Passport/ Passport (USSR; Georgii Daneliia, 1990).

Patriotic Comedy, A/ Patrioticheskaia komediia (Russia; Vladimir Khotinenko, 1992).

Peculiarities of the Russian Bathhouse/ Osobennosti russkoi bani (Russia; Aleksei Rudakov, 1999).

Peculiarities of the Bathhouse Politics or Bathhouse 2/ Osobennosti bannoi politiki (Russia; Aleksei Rudakov, 2000).

Peculiarities of National Fishing/ Osobennosti natsional'noi rybalki (Russia; Aleksandr Rogozhkin, 1998).

Peculiarities of the National Hunt in Fall/ Osobennosti natsional'noi okhoty (Russia; Aleksandr Rogozhkin, 1995).

Peculiarities of the National Hunt in Winter/ Osobennosti natsional'noi okhoty zimoi (Russia; Aleksandr Rogozhkin, 2000).

Photo/ Foto (Russia, Italy; Aleksandr Galin, 2002).

Prisoner of the Mountains, The/ Kavkazkii plennik (Russia, Kazakhstan; Sergei Bodrov, 1996).

Promised Skies, The/ Obetovannye nebesa (Soviet Union; El'dar Riazanov, 1991).

Quickie/ Davai sdelaem eto po-bystromu (UK, France, Germany; Sergei Bodrov, 2001).

Rambo III (USA; Peter MacDonald, 1988).

Red Dawn (USA; *John Milius,* 1984).

Return, The/ Vozvrashchenie (Russia; Andrei Zviagintsev, 2003).

River/ Reka (Russia; Aleksei Balabanov, 2002).

Rocky IV (USA; *Sylvester Stallone,* 1985).

Romanovs: An Imperial Family, The/ Romanovy Ventsenosnaia Semia (Russia; Gleb Panfilov, 2000).

Russia We Have Lost, The/ Rossiia, kotoruiu my poteriali (Russia; Stanislav Govorukhin,1992).

Russian Ark/ Russkii kovcheg (Russia, Germany, Japan, Canada, Finland, Denmark; Aleksandr Sokurov, 2002).

Russian Rebellion, The/ Russkii bunt (Russia; Aleksandr Proshkin, 1999).

Russian Souvenir/ Russkii suvenir (USSR; Grigorii Aleksandrov, 1960).

Scarlet Street (USA; Fritz Lang, 1945).

Scorpio Rising (USA; Kenneth Anger, 1963).

Second Circle, The/ Krug vtoroi (Russia; Aleksandr Sokurov, 1990).

Silence of Dr. Ivens, The/Molchanie Doktora Ivensa (USSR; Budimir Matel'nikov, 1974).

Silver Dust/Serebristaia pyl' (USSR; Abram Room, 1953).

Solo Voyage/Odinochnoe plavanie (USSR; Mikhail Tumanishvili, 1985).

Something Wild (USA; Jack Garfein, 1961).

Strike/Stachka (USSR; Sergei Eisenstein, 1925).

Taxi Blues/Taksi Bliuz (USSR; Pavel Lungin, 1990).

Telets (Russia; Aleksandr Sokurov, 2001).

Thief/Vor (Russia; Pavel Chukhrai, 1997).

Time for Sadness Has Not Come Yet, The/Vremia pechali eshche ne prishlo (Russia; Sergei Sel'ianov, 1995).

Top Gun (USA; Tony Scott, 1986).

Trofim/Trofim (Russia; Aleksei Balabanov, 1995).

TwentyFourSeven (UK; Shane Meadows, 1997).

War/Voina (Russia; Aleksei Balabanov, 2002).

Window to Paris/Okno v Parizh (Russia, France; Iurii Mamin, 1993).

You are My Only One/Ty u menia odna (Russia; Dmitrii Astrakhan, 1993).

Note

1. To compile this filmography, I have used various sources, such as scholarship for the Soviet/Russian films as well as the International Movie Data Base (www.imdb.com). Occasionally, the release dates (of a limited number of films) differ from one source to another. In such cases, I have followed the printed material as more reliable.

INDEX